W9-ARB-783

MORMON
COUNTRY

by

WALLACE STEGNER

Bonanza Books · New York

Acknowledgments

I am especially grateful for help and suggestions to Dale L. Morgan of the Utah Writers' Project; to Mrs. Leah Frisbie of the University of Utah Library; to Dean Brimhall of Washington, D. C.; to Jonreed Lauritzen of Short Creek, Arizona; to Hector Lee of the University of Utah; to Charles Kelly of Fruita, Utah; and to Joël Dorius of Harvard University, who did much of the dirty work. Also to John G. Neihardt and The Macmillan Company for permission to quote from "The Song of Jed Smith," and to the SOUTHWEST REVIEW *for permission to reprint "A Pioneer Record . . . Earl Douglass and His Work" which appears in this volume as "Notes on a Life Spent Picking at a Sandstone Cliff."*

Contents

Contents

PART II

THE MIGHT OF THE GENTILE

PART I

THE ROCK OUR FATHERS PLANTED

Meet Me at the Ward House . . .

JUST as the sun slipped down over the Pavant—Sigurd Mountain to her—the girl came out and sat down on the porch steps. It was May. The lilacs, though almost over, filled the air under the great cottonwoods with scent, and the snowballs were out at the corner of the house. As she looked up through the leaves at the high, suspended sunset, she saw the cottonwood balls hanging like clusters of grapes, and beyond them, on the flat profile of the mountain, the pines and piñons furry with light.

It was very quiet in the street, in the whole town. She heard only the rattle of the cottonwood leaves and the grassy guggle of water in the irrigation ditch. She watched the cliffs of Sigurd Mountain, the terraced red ledges with black junipers toenailed into their sides, stepping backward to the plateau's rim, and as she watched she felt the dusk come on, the earth darkening before the sky, as if a smoke came up out of the valley and blotted out the shadowed ledges, merged black juniper and red rock, laid a quieting hand over the mouth of the town. She sat listening, because tonight was Mutual night, and the M-Men were throwing a dance for Heber Christianson's farewell, and Milton was coming down from the herd to go with her. Milton always got out of school a month early, as soon as the lower slopes of the mountain cleared of snow, to help with the shearing and then run the sheep up from the desert to graze them in the forest reserve. She wished she could get off school for something as good as that. All she ever got was a week in the spring, so she could break her back thinning beets. The only good thing about beet-thinning was that everyone did it at the same time, and it was a kind of picnic sometimes, in spite of the cricks it put in you.

The coating of red dust on leaves and trunks of the cottonwoods was invisible now. A cricket under the stoop chirped. From down the street, down by the Ward House, she heard laughter and the calling of a girl's voice. A cornet brayed, laughing like a jackass. That would be Henry Dahl. He was always horsing around with his horn. But he could play it. Sometimes he and his Koosharem Koyotes got a call to play for dances as far up the valley as Salina or Gunnison. She smoothed her dress over her knees, thinking that it was about time Milton showed up.

A puff of wind rattled the leaves and blew away the clinging smell of lilacs and was gone. Far up the road toward the canyon the girl heard the clop of a trotting horse. She rose and leaned on the fence, and a frog plumped into the ditch at her feet. The shoes of the approaching horse rang loud on the ledge of bare stone at the edge of her father's pasture, and then the sound died to low puffs in the dust of the trail worn deep by the hay wagons. She looked and listened until the rider came in sight in the lane, turned very deliberately to break a branch from the lilac bush. When she turned again he was sitting his horse on the other side of the fence—all dolled up, she noticed, with high-heeled boots, clean levis, a belt three inches wide, a red silk handkerchief tight around his throat, his hat on the back of his head. His horse had a spray of chokecherry blossom stuck in the cheekstrap of the bridle.

"Hi," she said.

"Hi," said Milton. "They telegraphed up the creek that there was a struggle down to the Ward."

"Never heard about it," she said, and laughed. "Imagine my surprise!"

"Thought I might be able to stir up a date."

They grinned at each other over the pole fence. The girl leaned her head on one side, sniffing at the spray of lilac and using her eyes on him. "I haven't got a thing to wear," she said.

"That's all right with me."

"Don't get fresh," she said, and came out through the gate. "What'll you do with the horse?"

"Thought maybe he could mow your lawn."

"All right. Pa won't mind, I guess. Only Ma'll shoot him for glue if he gets in her flowers."

"I'll tie him short." He led the horse inside, gave him ten feet of rope, and tied him to the fence bar. The cornet hee-hawed again from down the street. "Come on!" he said, and grabbed her arm. "We're wasting time."

They went hand in hand, sixteen and eighteen, up the grassy ditch bank. People were coming in twos and threes and clusters into the glow of the Ward House lights. Cars were parked solid along the side street. Because of Hebe's farewell there were more people than usual, more older people, even some strangers, friends or relatives from neighboring towns. They saw John Christianson and his wife and all the little Christiansons, seven of them.

"Hi, Mr. Christianson," said the girl. "Hi, Mrs. Christianson. How's Hebe feel to be starting out on his mission?"

"Scared," Mrs. Christianson said. "I can't say I blame him. Two and a half years is a long time, with the war on and everything. He'll be all grown up when he gets back." She sighed comfortably. "They say the mission experience is the finest time of a man's life," she said. "I'm sure he'll do the Lord's work well, but he'll miss all his old friends back home."

"Shucks," Milton said. "He'll be back jabbering Spiggoty before you know he's gone."

"He's lucky," the girl said. "Think how lucky he is to get called to Brazil."

"There's not much of any place he could have gone to, now," Mr. Christianson said. "So many of the missions are inactive now on account of the war."

"Yeah," said Milton. He hitched up his levis. "If they give me a break like that," he said, "and the army don't call me before the Church does, you won't hear any complaints from my Pa's boy. I'll be whipping up and down that old Amazon shaking congas and rhumbas from sundown to sunup."

Mr. Christianson looked at Milton rather hard and led his family into the Ward House. The girl kicked Milton briskly in the shins. "You shouldn't go saying things like that. Mrs. Christianson'll get scared Hebe might do just what you'd do."

He rolled his eyes and chortled. "He hasn't got the imagination. Those señoritas, oh!"

She kicked at him again. "You and your big talk!"

"I just wish they'd give me a call," he said. "I'd like to get out in that old world and see what she's like."

The girl giggled. "I can imagine you standing on street corners preaching, and passing out tracts from door to

door. What would you do if you had to baptize somebody?"

"I'd baptize him," Milton said. "I'd baptize him so all-
fired deep he'd think he was drownding."

The hall was already jammed for "Mutual," the weekly
recreational and faith-promoting meeting that fills Tuesday night in every Ward of Zion. Elders and children were
down front, the young people paired off in the back rows.
An M-Man passed them a couple of Hebe's programs as
they entered. Hebe's startled-looking face was on the outside, white eyebrows and all. Elder Heber Christianson, it
said underneath. Inside there was a sketch of his life. Born
November 18, 1923, son of Brother John F. and Sister
Mary D., etc. Called to the South American Mission at São
Paulo, Brazil, the eighth member of his family to serve a
mission for the Church.

At the bottom of the aisle Bishop Newton was talking
with Hebe's parents, and Hebe, his hair plastered down
and his face earnest and a little pale, his motion of recognition a little too quick when people smiled or waved at
him, stood on one foot, leaning against a pew.

Milton and his girl sat close together, holding hands.
Other couples were doing the same. Even in the grave and
decorous atmosphere of the Ward House, even in Sunday
Meeting, the back rows were converted into a preserve for
courting couples.

The Bishop, Hebe, the Bishop's counselor Vincent Allred, and a man strange to the Ward climbed up on the platform. The Bishop prayed, quite a long time. Then he
called for a song from the *M.I.A. Songbook,* page 13. The
audience looked at the book only long enough to see what

the song was, and then sang lustily, to the tune of "The
Battle Hymn of the Republic":

The call to willing service is the nation's call today,
And Zion's youth have answered in the cause of M.I.A.
One hundred thousand strong they come, a joyous band
*   are they,*
With service leading on.

". . . vuss leading on!" bawled the Boy Scouts, a little
behind the rest.

"They gonna run all through Mutual?" Milton whispered. The girl shook her head. "I think they'll cut it
short, account of Hebe's farewell and the dance." She
looked around, snuggled a little closer, and laid her head
on his shoulder.

Bishop Newton was reading off announcements. It was
almost time for the M.I.A. to close for the year, but he
wanted to remind all presidents, secretaries, activities leaders, and teachers to consult their handbooks on The Summer Way for M.I.A. There would be a general meeting to
organize the summer program next Thursday, seven-thirty.
Next week at Mutual the adult class would be addressed by
Elder James Robinson, recently returned from the Eastern
States Mission. On Saturday afternoon, two o'clock sharp,
the M-Men would play a baseball game with the M-Men
of Richfield First Ward. Everyone should turn out and
support the baseball team, which was a new wrinkle but a
good one. There was no reason the M-Men should have to
confine their athletics to basketball. Tomorrow night at
the usual time the Relief Society would meet, and Sister
Allred would report on what was being done for the Indians on the Koosharem Reservation. As the last activity
of the regular year for the Gleaner Girls, the annual out-

ing would be held one week from Saturday if the road to Fish Lake were open. Brother MacLean and Brother Howard were donating their cottages as usual. Arrangements should be made with Sister MacLean or Sister Christianson. Cars would leave the Ward House at eight in the morning, charges for gasoline and food would be a dollar a head.

It was also, the Bishop said, his pleasure to announce that two members of the Boy Scout troop had recently been awarded Eagle Scout badges. He made the boys stand up, and embarrassed them witless.

Next on the program was a musical selection by the Bee-Hive Girls. At the Bishop's nod they trooped up on the stage. They stood in a ragged line, their hands tight at their sides, while Mrs. MacLean, down below, raised her baton. They sang, throats straining and voices shrill, never taking their eyes off the hypnotic waving point of the stick.

In our lovely Deseret, where the Saints of God have met,
There's a multitude of children all around;
They are generous and brave, they have precious souls to
*   save,*
They must listen and obey the gospel's sound.

*   Hark! hark! hark! 'tis children's music—*
*   Children's voices, O how sweet,*
*   When in innocence and love*
*   Like the angels up above*
*   They with happy hearts and cheerful faces meet.*

That the children may live long, and be beautiful and
*   strong,*
Tea and coffee and tobacco they despise,
Drink no liquor, and they eat but a very little meat;
They are seeking to be great and good and wise.

They should be instructed young how to watch and guard
    the tongue,
And their tempers train and evil passions bind;
They should always be polite and treat ev'rybody right,
And in ev'ry place be affable and kind.

The Bee-Hive Girls were applauded, and trooped back flushed and self-conscious to their seats. Then it was Hebe's turn. The Bishop's dignity settled and deepened. The audience composed itself for more serious business. Bishop Newton talked for almost ten minutes, one hand on Hebe's shoulder, speaking half to him and half to the audience. They had all watched Elder Christianson grow up, and they knew that he was fit to be one of the great company spreading the gospel to all the nations and peoples of the earth. It was a solemn undertaking to go into the world without purse or script and carry the gospel of Jesus Christ abroad. It was doubly solemn at a time when the world was torn by war, when it was even more the duty of the missionary to affirm Christ's teachings and prepare for the time when the nations of the earth would again be at peace. He prayed that Elder Christianson would persevere, that he might grow in strength and wisdom, and he urged him, whenever he felt discouraged, to pray to our Heavenly Father. He recalled his own missionary experiences in the South German Mission, when in spite of the friendliness of the people he had sometimes felt that he was useless, helpless, and worse. He had prayed, and that very afternoon, at a meeting in the home of a local Saint, he had been given an eloquence and an assurance of the truth of what he taught that he had never felt before. He had seen the reflection of God's Word shining in the faces of his hearers, and never since that time had he been weak enough to doubt. Finally, he prayed that the spirit of the Lord would be with Elder Christianson, and he bore witness to the truth of the gospel: "Faith, repentance, baptism, and the laying on of hands for the Gift of the Holy Ghost."

He introduced the strange man on the platform, who turned out to be Hebe's uncle from Gunnison and who recalled Hebe's childhood in half-humorous anecdotes. The hand of the Lord, he said, had been with him that day when he pulled Heber half drowned from the irrigation ditch. Something had spoken to him, making him rise and go to the window and look out, and there was the child being swept down toward the culvert. He recalled a similar experience when the Lord had bestowed upon him the gifts of the spirit in Austria, on his mission. Finally he too bore his testimony and sat down.

And now Hebe, Elder Christianson:

"Look at him," the girl whispered to Milton. "He's petrified."

"So would you be," Milton grunted. They snuggled their elbows together and watched Heber shoot out his jaw to loosen the constricting collar. His voice cracked a little, and he cleared his throat savagely. His face was very earnest and very red. He would try his best to be a good missionary and to bear in mind the good counsel that Bishop Newton and other friends had given him. He knew he had undertaken a solemn trust, and he hoped they would all give him their prayers. Also, he wanted to bear his testimony. He knew that the gospel of Jesus Christ was true, and he knew that Jesus was the Christ, that God lived and that Joseph Smith had had a divine vision, and was ordered to establish upon the earth in these latter days the true gospel of Christ.

That little set speech about finished him. He shot his
collar again, paused. He thanked them all for their friend-
ship, shown in this farewell. He would think of them
often, and he knew that Bishop Newton spoke the truth
when he said that the Ward was solidly behind him.
Finally, he wanted to thank them for this farewell dance
in his benefit. He hoped—getting his wind a little now, and
grinning—that they had a good crowd.

The audience tittered. Hebe would get the proceeds
from the dance as well as the money deposited in the collection box at the door by non-dancers. At twenty-five
cents a head, he might collect as much as forty or fifty dollars during the evening.

The Bishop rose again. Classes would be cut short, he
said, but would meet briefly for the transaction of any
business the groups had. At nine o'clock they would adjourn to the amusement hall. They had good music, Henry
Dahl's band. (He did not refer to them as the Koosharem
Koyotes; that would have been a little below his dignity
as Bishop.)

They broke up into groups. M-Men and Gleaner Girls,
Explorers, Boy Scouts and Bee-Hive Girls, Special Interest
Groups, Junior Girls, every age group from twelve to
twenty or more. Still holding hands, Milton and his girl
strolled down the aisle, hung around a moment shame-
lessly lollygagging under the nose of the Bishop, who was,
outside of meeting, too genial to mind much of anything.
(His children called him Bish.)

"Every dance," Milton said as they parted. "If you trade
any off I'll start a riot."

At the dance Brother Vincent Allred was everywhere.
He was the official "mixer" for all Ward sociables. He

oversaw the two M-Men who took in the cash, he transplanted wallflowers from sterile corners to more salubrious
soil, he broke up couples who were growing too thick, he
grafted young sprouts on old stock, he urged sedate old-
sters to get out in there and get young again. He carried
messages and suggested tunes to the Koosharem Koyotes,
who in cow-puncher duds and orange handkerchiefs sat on
a portable stage at the end of the amusement hall and punished cornet, drums, piano, and guitar. He carried a box
of soap chips under his arm, dribbling treacherous slick-
ness in his wake. He chucked babies, held them while their
mothers danced. He perspired and smiled and radiated
heat and good humor, and once or twice he took a casual
look outside to make sure that Marv Brandon and one or
two other boys suspected of surreptitious smoking were
not breaking the Word of Wisdom around the dark corners of the Ward. When the older dancers called for a
contra or square dance, Brother Allred grinned and lined
up a Mormon Quadrille, in which each man leads out two
partners. Henry Dahl blew himself purple on "Old Dan
Tucker," and hands clapped and feet thumped around
the hall.

Milton and his girl stood out the quadrille. They had
been ducking Brother Allred's attempts to break up couples, and the girl said that if Milton wouldn't trade any
dances she wasn't going to share him with anybody in a
square dance. When they got music to their liking again
they went back to their oblivious narrow circling in an un-
crowded corner. They went egg-eyed and dreamy on the
waltzes, minced with quick turns and half-clogging feet on
the foxtrots, burst into a sudden spasm of energy on the
"Beer Barrel Polka" and wheeled around the room like a
pair of fighting elk, endangering everybody in the hall and

not even aware of it. At the end of the polka Milton tore off his coat and leaped high to swing it over the basketball standard at the end of the room.

"Whooeeee!" he said. "Some struggle!"

At eleven o'clock Henry Dahl lifted his cornet and hee-hawed with it. Intermission. Immediately there was a scramble. The hall cleared itself of young people, the married couples moved down together on the benches and talked. Out almost with the first, Milton guided the girl through the crowd and out to the road. Most of the couples were hitting for the lovers' lane out back of the Ward House.

"Cold?" he said.

She shivered her shoulders to see, and said she was. He put his coat around her and then put his arm around the coat, and they walked up the slope toward Monroe Mountain, behind the town. They walked clear out from under the cottonwoods, clear out of town, up the sagebrush slope, up to a smooth, grassless knob of half-formed rock. There they sat while the long rampart of Monroe Mountain began to smoke with moonrise; they watched the Lombardy poplars by the foothill springs catch silver fire till they looked like light-tipped foxtails; they watched the light come down the ledges of Sigurd Mountain, across the valley, and the junipers emerge again from their dark background; they watched the valley open tree by tree and field by field into the moonlight, and the sagebrush slope below them go liquid silver. For a long time, much longer than the intermission, they sat above the town with its dark buildings and its silver-touched trees and roofs and its shadows like pools of oil.

Finally they started back, cutting across an alfalfa field whose tight fabric glimmered like water.

"It's like walking on lamé cloth," the girl said.

"What's lamé cloth?"

She didn't answer. She was holding her breath and walking almost on tiptoe, because it was all so beautiful, and soon Milton would get a call like Hebe Christianson, and then she would have almost three years of waiting—maybe more if the war went on and Milton went into the army after his mission—and on nights like these she would just have to go into her room and cry.

Their shadows loomed monstrously ahead of them, dipped into the sunken road at the gate, ran like spilled ink down the ruts, climbed the heavy foliage of the first cottonwood. It was past midnight. As they walked they heard the last departing bray of Henry Dahl's cornet, and then after a few minutes they heard singing and a guitar. A handful of boys and girls remained in front of the darkened Ward House, grouped around the guitar player and singing "My Gal Sal."

The two joined them, twined arms in the circle and with complete and dedicated abandonment sang into the town's quiet the sentimental songs, the cozy songs, the barbershop favorites, until after almost an hour a window went up somewhere down the street and a voice said, "Ain't that about enough for one night?" Then they broke up, going home under the deep shadows of the cottonwoods by two and two, and there was kissing at gates, and mothers waked from their first sleep to rise on an elbow and inquire of the silent house, "Is that you, Verda?" And a horse which had exhausted its circle of grass stood dejectedly until the weight came on the stirrup, and then turned back up the canyon road it had come down in the evening, up to where the snow still lay in the aspens and the sheep-smell polluted the air even over the smell of pines.

In any Mormon town or village, on any Tuesday night from September to June, something like this goes on. The social life of Mormondom is centered in the Ward House as surely as the religious life is, and every Mormon child from the age of twelve upward is a member of either the Young Men's or the Young Ladies' Mutual Improvement Association—the M.I.A., or Mutual. That Association, like everything else in the Church, is completely and efficiently organized. In the local Wards, which are the Mormon equivalent of parishes, everybody from children to adults is organized. The Wards are grouped into Stakes, roughly equivalent to the dioceses of the Catholic Church, and in every Stake is a group of officers charged with maintaining the M.I.A. program in their area. Over all the Stakes is a general M.I.A. Board, whose members are constantly stumping the state and the outlying centers of Mormonism, making suggestions and reports, jacking up slovenly practices, inspiring scoutmasters and athletic coaches and presidents and secretaries and activities counselors to greater effort. The organizational pyramid broadens down from the leaders to the subleaders to the followers, and in that descending series of hierarchies virtually every good Mormon has a job, an office, a responsibility, from his childhood up.

Designed as a faith-promoting scheme among the young people, the M.I.A. is in practice a highly-developed youth movement. In origin, if not in name, it goes back to the very early years of Salt Lake City, when the Church formed a group of junior riflemen under eighteen years of age to supply recruits for the official militia, the Nauvoo Legion. By 1857 the organization had spread downward until it took in boys of twelve, who under adult leaders learned woodcraft, camping, and military maneuvers. That outfit, known as the "Hope of Israel," antedated the Boy Scout movement by fifty years. Twelve years after the Hope of Israel came into being, Brigham Young talked the girls of Zion into forming a "Retrenchment Society," designed to promote modesty of dress and deportment. In 1875, out of these several groups, grew the Mutual Improvement Association, which included and replaced them all. Since about 1878 all the activities have been administered under one department, and one magazine, the *Improvement Era,* serves as the official publication.

Especially in the smaller and more isolated towns, but to some extent in the cities as well, the M.I.A. focuses the social life of the Wards. Beyond that, it has been an instrument of good will between Mormon and Gentile, since Gentile children, who like to belong to things as much as Mormon children do, are welcomed into M.I.A. activities. At twelve they can become Bee-Hive Girls and learn to adore their Bee-Keeper, or Boy Scouts and emulate their scoutmaster. At fifteen they are graduated into the Junior Girls or the Explorers. After sixteen they become Gleaner Girls or M-Men. It is by no means uncommon for Gentile children to wind up as members of the Mormon Church. In the long pull, the M.I.A. has been a potent proselytizing device.

Every group in the ladder of youth activities has its own peculiar function and direction. Every president, teacher, secretary, or coach has his own little handbook of official Church suggestions. If a member of the basketball team sneaks out for a cigarette after a game, the Stake authorities or a board member is likely to hear of it, and the boy may find himself ineligible to participate in M.I.A. affairs. If there are boys and girls in town who seem to be indifferent to Mutual, someone will want to know why. If the fun of social gatherings seems to be taking precedence over the religious purposes, there will be an increase in prayer and singing and classwork all through that corner of Zion.

Despite that rigid supervision, Mutual is fun, and the directors walk a tight wire between austerity and latitudinarianism. The Church has never objected to social activities like music and dancing and the theater. Brigham Young guessed publicly that there was a lot more singing and dancing in Heaven than in Hell, and he saw no reason why the Saints should try to imitate the hot place. Mormons have always been a singing and dancing and sociable people. So long as fun is socially acceptable and decorous, the Church approves, and the establishment in every Ward House that can afford it of an amusement hall used variously as theater, basketball court, dance hall, and game room is a deliberate part of the Mormon plan to promote and preserve solidarity among its members. Young people will dance and play no matter what the Church does. The Church therefore gives them the opportunity—in fact by social pressures almost forces them—to dance and play in the place where the priesthood can keep an eye on them.

Occasionally the program gets out of hand. I have attended Ward dances in the tougher districts of Salt Lake and Ogden where I encountered all the characteristics of public dance halls, with pick-ups, around the corner drinking, and the rest. But generally the young people are more amenable, and in the country towns they most certainly are, because if the Ward House is closed to them there is often nowhere else to go and nothing to do.

All the way from hikes, outings, picnics, swimming parties, and hayrides to movies, dances, community singing, amateur theatricals, and athletic contests, the M.I.A. is the orbit within which the young Saint's life moves. The organized basketball leagues in every Stake put hundreds of teams in action every winter, and the playoffs for the Church championship produce a frenzy of partisanship like the grudge games of ancient college rivals.

Out of the Wards, in better times than these, went young missionaries to every corner of the globe, paying their own expenses, donating thirty months of their lives to the Church. As a matter of record, the missionary rolls as this is written have not fallen off too much, even with most of the world closed to the missionary effort. The proselytizers have turned south, or toward the regions of their own country. United States and South American missions have grown as European and South Sea Island missions have shrunk or closed down, and even yet almost every Ward in Zion has two or three young men in the field.

Hence the curious anomaly of the Mormon village: isolated, stuck off in the lost corners of plateaus and deserts, sometimes a hundred miles or more from a railroad, Mormon towns often contain their quota of world travelers. Their culture is a curious mixture of provincialism, parochialism, and cosmopolitanism. A few years ago, traveling through south-central Utah, I ran across a German doctor, exiled and in flight, who had wound up in that least-likely spot in all America. Reason—he had known Mormon missionaries in Germany before he fled. There were two other men in town who spoke German, so that the doctor was probably less lonely and out of place than he would have been in any village of comparable size anywhere else in western America. And if he was a good German, if he liked efficiency and regimentation of social and domestic life, he might hardly have felt his uprooting at all. The Mormons were very successful in Germany for years, and part of the reason for their success is that their discipline is a discipline related to that which Germans know from childhood.

The M.I.A. is by no means all of Mormonism, and by no means all the strength of the Mormon system. But put it partly down to the M.I.A. that the Mormons are an extremely law-abiding people. Put it partly down to the M.I.A. that there is as little apostasy, as little inclination to break with the parental system, as there is. Missionaries sometimes come home agnostics or jack-Mormons. Boys and girls in the larger towns, where the Gentile population is strong and the opportunities for wandering are greater, sometimes stray. But the boys and girls who stay at home in the small towns don't often get far from the Ward House. Radio and movie houses may have cut down Mutual attendance somewhat, and the hold of the Church over its youth may be weaker than it was a generation ago. But it is still strong. You can't play basketball over the radio; you can't dance as well to the radio, in a crowded living room, as you can on a large amusement hall floor to a stomp band of Koosharem Koyotes. You can't *participate* in movies or the radio, and it is participation, shrewdly calculated and carefully nurtured, that maintains the group spirit and the Mormon belief in the small towns of Zion long after one would have expected the American system to dilute and destroy it.

Mormon Trees . . .

WHEREVER you go in the Mormon country, whether through the irrigated Snake River Plains of eastern and southern Idaho, the infrequent oases among the Great Basin ranges of Nevada, the desert springs and flash-flood river bottoms of northern and central Arizona, or the mountain valleys of Utah, western Wyoming and western Colorado, you see the characteristic marks of Mormon settlement: the typical, intensively-cultivated fields of alfalfa and sugar beets and Bermuda onions and celery, the orchards of cherry and apple and peach and apricot (and it is not local pride which says that there is no better fruit grown anywhere), the irrigation ditches, the solid houses, the wide-streeted, sleepy green towns. Especially you see the characteristic trees, long lines of them along ditches, along streets, as boundaries between fields and farms. They are as typical as English hedgerows; perhaps, to the predominantly English converts of the early days, they had some force as a substitute, copying in the desert, under conditions vastly different from those of the old country, the angled and bisected and neatly-blocked landscape of their first home.

These are the "Mormon trees," Lombardy poplars. Wherever they went the Mormons planted them. They grew boldly and fast, without much tending, and they make the landscape of the long valleys of the Mormon Country something special and distinctive. The view across one of those valleys from the alluvial aprons of the mountains, when the wind is bending the tall poplars and the whole land leans a little tipsily and even the shadows yaw on tight alfalfa fields and brown pasture land, is a view one does not immediately forget. There are Lombardy poplars elsewhere in the world; there are few places where there are so many, and there is no place where the peculiar combination of desert valley and dark lines of trees exists as it does in this country.

They give a quality to the land so definite that it is almost possible to mark the limits of the Mormon Country by the trees. They do not grow in the mountains, but neither do the Mormons, except for scattered sheepherders and cowpunchers who by their very profession are cut off from the typical Mormon way of life. Mormons and Mormon trees are both valley races. And once in a while the presence of Lombardy poplars reveals surviving centers of Mormon population where one would never have suspected them. I was driving with a friend through Nevada some years ago and came through Sparks, just a short way down the Truckee from Reno—almost a suburb of that "biggest little city on earth." My companion looked at the roadside lined with poplars and said, "For God's sake, is this a Mormon town?" He had forgotten, if he ever knew, that Nevada was part of the old State of Deseret, that its first farmers were Mormons, that the Carson Valley towns under the lee of the Sierra were founded by Mormon colonists. He had forgotten that the Mormons once reached much farther than they do now, that Mormons participated in the gold strike at Sutter's Mill, that even Eilley Bowers, that fantastic wife of Sandy Bowers, himself one of the most fantastic figures in the history of western mining camps, was a twice-divorced Mormon wife when she married Sandy, and that she came to Nevada with her second husband as one of a colonizing group. The Carson Valley towns were abandoned early, for political reasons, but the stamp of the early settlers remains here and there far outside the reaches of the present Mormon Country. The trees in Sparks are a dead give-away that Nevada is not merely the home of sin and shame and cheap divorces and open gambling and Basque sheepherders and the Wingfield banks. It was and to some extent still is a part of the Mormon Country, and even in the biggest little city on earth there is a sizable Mormon population. That may, as a matter of fact, have something to do with the quiet and sobriety of Reno's residential section.

There are not as many Mormon trees as there used to be; it seems a pity. Trees of other varieties, wherever there has been developed a dependable water-supply, break up the clear patterns that existed in many parts of the Mormon Country only a generation ago. Some of the rows of poplars have been cut down in Salt Lake City streets and along the edges of fields east of the city, because their age and possible heart-rot made them a hazard. They are not a particularly long-lived tree. Increasingly, too, people have wanted wider-crowned trees that would throw more shade. But still in the rural districts, in the places where unreconstructed Mormonism maintains itself comparatively untouched, the Lombardy poplars line the ditch banks and the fields.

Perhaps it is fanciful to judge a people by its trees. Probably the predominance of poplars is the result of nothing more interesting than climatic conditions or the lack of other kinds of seeds and seedlings. Probably it is pure nonsense to see a reflection of Mormon group life in the fact that the poplars were practically never planted singly, but always in groups, and that the groups took the form of straight lines and ranks. Perhaps it is even more nonsensical to speculate that the straight, tall verticality of the Mormon trees appealed obscurely to the rigid sense of order of the settlers, and that a marching row of plumed poplars was symbolic, somehow, of the planter's walking with God and his solidarity with his neighbors.

Nonsensical or not, it is not an unpleasant thought. Institutions must have their art forms, their symbolic representations, and if the Heavenward aspirations of medieval Christianity found their expression in cathedrals and spires, the more mundane aspirations of the Latter-day Saints may just as readily be discovered in the widespread plantings of Mormon trees. They look Heavenward, but their roots are in earth. The Mormon looked toward Heaven, but his Heaven was a Heaven on earth and he would inherit bliss in the flesh.

That Lieth Four-Square . . .

JUST as clear a representation in its way, just as definite
an illustration of how ideas can harden into institutions, is the Mormon village. Behind it was an idea—the
idea of the Heavenly City, the New Jerusalem whose
golden towers dazzled the eyes of thousands of Americans
through a whole century, and in some quarters still dazzle.
The Mormons, being a practical people, a building people, a planning and organizing people, put it into adobe
and wood and stone.

This is the way the City of Zion is laid out:

The plat is a mile square. The blocks contain ten acres,
cut into twenty half-acre lots, and are separated by streets
eight rods wide (which is enough, just in case there are
traffic problems in Heaven, to allow for ten lanes of automobiles plus parallel parking on both sides). The blocks
and the houses and the streets sit four-square with the directions, and the houses are set back from the streets a uniform distance of twenty-five feet. No lots are allowed to
contain more than one house, but the tier of blocks down
the middle of the plat is half again as wide as the normal
ones, to allow for the greater size of public buildings,
schools, churches, and the like. Barns and stables are outside the town limits, as are the farming lands, each owner
of a town lot being also the owner of a plot of land, any-

where from five to sixty acres, but generally ten or twenty, from which he gets his sustenance.

In the beginning this city will be built on earth, of such materials as the Saints can lay hands to, but at the gathering-up of Zion it will be taken up to Heaven like the City of Enoch, and renewed. The Lord has promised: "I will lay thy stones with fair colors, and lay thy foundations with sapphires. And I will make thy windows agates, and thy gates of carbuncles, and all thy borders of pleasant stones."

In point of history, that gathering-up, those last days which the Mormons expected within a few years, have been delayed. Good Mormons still look forward to the restoration of Zion and the building of the miraculous City on the site of the former Garden of Eden near Independence, Missouri, but they have had to push the future back, postpone the Millennium. Even though in the Mormon Branch in Cambridge, Massachusetts, in 1941, there was a serious discussion of the problems of moving the Saints back to Joseph Smith's divinely-appointed Zion in the event of the last days, there was not in that discussion, or in any other which I have heard, any feeling that the move with all its sociological disruption was immediate. Still, the millennial belief which produced that vision of the final gathering-up of the faithful is important, because it was that belief that helped produce the Plat of the City of Zion forwarded from Ohio on to Missouri by Joseph Smith, Sidney Rigdon, and Frederick G. Williams in 1833. That plat became the model for Mormon villages, towns, cities. It existed as an idea long before the exodus to the Great Basin, and during the settlement of Utah and the surrounding territory it was used, with local modifications, as the plan for scores of Mormon settlements, from Salt Lake

City to the scrubbiest little hamlets on the Little Colorado or the Muddy.

Joseph and his counselors were undoubtedly influenced in their mile-square plan by the new rectangular surveys of the United States government, as well as by hints from Isaiah, Ezekiel, Revelations, and the Book of Ether (*Book of Mormon*), where the city "lieth four-square, and the length is as great as the breadth." Whatever the origin of the idea, most Mormon towns lie four-square, and except for the modifications forced upon the plan by frontier conditions or the exigencies of topography or the changes that came with time, their length is as great as their breadth. Their plan is that of the ten-acre block divided into half-acre lots, their houses are set back evenly from the street, their streets are so wide you can barely shout across them.

Occasionally, one suspects, the Saints may have looked forward to the gathering-up of Zion for other than spiritual reasons. The citizens of Mesa, Arizona, for example, have been known to complain loudly about their eight-rod streets. Walking that distance in the open sun is an invitation to sun stroke. And the problem of paving streets that wide from a limited budget has been a headache to more than one city council. They must have wished more than once that the Lord would keep His promise and lay their stones with fair colors. But time brings its compensations. Mesa, and in fact most Mormon towns, can sit back and chuckle when other places complain about the parking problem.

The social vision and the shrewdness which planned the Mormon towns represents, like many things in the Mormon Country, a collaboration between Joseph Smith and Brigham Young with the active co-operation of an obedient and strenuous people. Joseph furnished the vision,

Brigham the practical organization, and the people the man-years of labor necessary to bring the idea into practical operation. Grant if you want that here is an early example of town-planning, a right-angled and rather stiff-elbowed version of the garden city, created well ahead of its time and demonstrating the advantages of orderly town-building over the hit-and-miss squatting that characterized the usual western settlement. It was the people, still, who built those towns and villages as they were told to do, and it was the people who went further. Because Mormon colonization was group colonization, and because the family was and is of tremendous importance in the social structure of the Saints, and because the women of those families insisted (and would have insisted even if Brigham Young had not actively promoted the practice) on carrying rose cuttings and geranium slips and flower seeds and seedling trees across more than a thousand miles of wilderness, the Mormon village is a green village. The Gentiles who had driven the Saints from Ohio and Missouri and Illinois were contemptuous both of the Mormons and the arid desert they had settled upon. It was necessary to love these valleys of the mountains as the fairest land on earth, because they were sanctuary. And it was unthinkable that the gathering-place of the Saints should be a barren desert. It should be made to blossom, and it was.

There are in Mormondom very few of the typical western shack-towns with derailed dining cars and false-fronted stores and rubbish-strewn vacant lots and desolate, treeless, grassless yards. The Gentiles often built that kind of town, in the Mormon Country and elsewhere; the Mormons practically never did. Even in the outposts on the edge of the desert, which are sometimes forlorn enough and during the early days were very forlorn indeed, there are plantings, there is a quality of order and permanence. If poplars and cottonwoods won't grow, there are probably tamarisks and cacti in the front yards. As a people, Mormons have a great deal of civic pride.

In one sense, the Mormon village is not a village at all. The Plat for the City of Zion is not a plan for a city of the ordinary kind. Though the cities of the Mormon Country have drifted away from that original plan and become almost indistinguishable from other American cities, the Plat is closely followed in the farming communities, and that Plat calls for homes in the midst of the farm land. The Mormon village is like a medieval village, a collection of farm houses in the midst of the cultivable land. Like the Lombardy poplars, it is a symbol of the group consciousness and the group planning that enabled the Saints to settle and break a country so barren to look at that Jim Bridger said he would give a thousand dollars if he knew a bushel of corn could be grown there. There is no evidence that Brigham Young ever went back to make Jim Bridger eat crow, but Jim would have had to eat it. Valley land in Utah and the whole arid belt is, with irrigation, exceptionally fertile and rich in plant foods. But in the period of settlement, and to a large extent still, farmers did not live on their land. In the beginning of every settlement there was a survey, first of town lots and then of farming land. Every colonist drew his numbered properties from the hat. If he didn't like what he got he could swap or bargain with someone else, but whatever he got, he lived in the village with the rest.

Writers on the Mormons, taking the Mormon village as a typically frontier development, have speculated on the causes for its growth. There have been guesses: fear of Indian attack, the greater ease of irrigating land which was

farmed in solid blocks, the loneliness of frontier life and
the desire of people to be close together, the insistence of
Brigham Young that his people retain and increase their
group consciousness by common labor and common living.
Actually the Plat for the City of Zion is as important as
any of them, though all probably contributed to the final
institution. The peculiar conditions of the mountain frontier happened to strengthen rather than weaken the faith
that every village was a prototype of the divinely-ordered
city. The medieval town surrounded by its fields was a
practical and sound pattern of settlement, almost the only
possible pattern of settlement. A man could not by himself
build and keep in repair a dam, miles of ditch, and all the
laborious extras of irrigation farming. This was a country
that could be broken only by the united efforts of all.
They worked together or they starved out separately, because the supplies of both land and water were extremely
limited.

The Church itself, which initiated the group-settlement
plan and the farm-village, supported those institutions
long after the first frontier period was over. A letter from
John Taylor, President of the Church, to Stake President
William B. Preston of Logan, makes it very clear that to
the priesthood the village was much more than a protective
device against Indians. The letter was written in 1882,
when some families near Logan wanted to move out and
build houses on their farm land, and asked Preston's permission.

In all cases in making new settlements [Taylor wrote],
the Saints should be advised to gather together in villages,
as has been our custom from the time of our earliest settlement in these mountain valleys. The advantages of this
plan, instead of carelessly scattering out over a wide extent

of country, are many and obvious to those who have a desire to serve the Lord.

By this means the people can retain their ecclesiastical organizations, have regular meetings of the quorums of the priesthood, and establish and maintain day and Sunday schools, Improvement Associations, and Relief Societies. They can also co-operate for the good of all in financial and secular matters, in making ditches, fencing fields, building bridges, and other necessary improvements.

Further than this they are a mutual protection and a source of strength against horse and cattle thieves, land jumpers, etc., and against hostile Indians, should there be any; while their compact organization gives them many advantages of a social and civic character which might be lost, misapplied or frittered away by spreading out so thinly that inter-communication is difficult, dangerous, inconvenient, and expensive.

That puts it fairly succinctly. The village is a social, economic, educational, and religious unit, the sort of unit that best met conditions on the frontier and after the frontier had almost passed. A Japanese town is the result of approximately the same practical conditions. So is an Indian pueblo or cliff dwelling. By revelation and accident and adaptation the Mormons discovered what the cliff-dwellers had discovered centuries before: that the only way to be a farmer in the Great Basin and on the desert plateaus of the Colorado watershed was to be a group farmer. In more ways than one the Mormon village is a cousin to the towns of the Pueblo and the Zuñi.

These are the things a traveler notices even in a brief visit to the Mormon Country. Trees and villages and Ward Houses, intensive irrigation farming, the constant evidences of co-operative effort. The pattern is not the usual American pattern; in many ways the life and the institutions it has produced are unique. And it is endlessly repetitive—everywhere in the Mormon Country, some-times hundreds of miles from the center at Salt Lake City, you can see the same things going on in the same kinds of Ward Houses in the same kinds of villages on the same nights of the week. You can see the same lush fields and the same characteristic trees, and the same villages perched in the midst of the scrap of cultivable land that supports them, hives in the middle of the clover field.

The Land Nobody Wanted . . .

WHEN Brigham Young led his people westward in search of a country where they could live without interference from politicians, mobocrats, and all that the United States stood for in the Mormon mind, he was headed rather vaguely for the Great Basin, then Mexican territory. His destination, selected tentatively from John C. Frémont's report of his exploration of the route to California and from conversations with Father De Smet, was a "valley in the Rocky Mountains," secluded from the world, a wilderness that would be overlooked and by-passed by the emigrant trains moving to Oregon and California. He was looking, in other words, for a country no one else wanted, and when, sick with fever, he was hauled in his carriage through the mouth of Emigration Canyon and looked upon the valley of Great Salt Lake with the Jordan River winding across the far flats and the late sun glittering on the waters of the Dead Sea, he knew that he had arrived. "This is the place," he said. He had refused to listen to the importunities of Samuel Brannan, who had taken a boatload of Saints around the Horn from Brooklyn to San Francisco via Hawaii, and who was enthusiastic about the northern California valleys. Brannan came hurrying all the way to the Green River to entice the main party of emigrants on to California, but Brigham wouldn't

listen. Too many people would want California. The
Saints would be drowned under a flood of Gentiles, their
unity destroyed, their institutions undermined. This was
the place. He called the San Francisco colonists to gather
to the mountains, and most of them came.

By the time they got well settled in it, the Mormons
found their wilderness not Mexican but American, because of the Treaty of Guadalupe Hidalgo, signed in 1848.
Still, it was wide open. The floods of emigrants were
headed for Oregon, and after 1848 for the California gold
fields. They had no intention of stopping any longer than
they could help in the barren lands between the Rockies
and the Sierra. The Saints for a few years had a free hand.
They staked their claim on an immense area, and they
staked it with more than papers in a tobacco can hidden
under a cairn of stones. They staked it with farms and
villages, outposts that worked outward from Salt Lake City
and in the course of little more than a generation occupied
virtually every acre of arable ground for hundreds of
miles.

They bit off more than they could chew, and some of
the farthest-flung colonies had to be abandoned, but most
of what they bit off they chewed, and most of what they
chewed they swallowed and digested. Politically the Mormon Country has been whittled down to the State of Utah;
actually it is very much larger than that, almost as large
as the empire Brigham Young once dreamed of and labored to settle and hold.

Make a dot on a map of the western United States just
off the southwestern corner of Yellowstone Park, at St. Anthony, Idaho. Make another at Grand Junction, Colorado,
and another at Safford, Arizona, on the Gila River, and

draw a long segment of an oval connecting the three. The segment will mark approximately the north, east, and south extensions of the Mormon Country. The western boundary is harder to fix, because although the Mormons once claimed, and once dominated, the entire Great Basin, and although a scattered Mormon population still extends as far as the east slope of the Sierra, most of western Nevada now belongs outside the empire and looks to Reno or San Francisco rather than to Salt Lake. The towns along the two transcontinental trails—the old Mormon Road through Las Vegas to Los Angeles, and the California Trail across the salt desert to Emigrant Pass, are partly Mormon yet. The agricultural areas of Nevada are fairly heavily Mormon, the mining regions scarcely at all. It is more difficult, moreover, to tell a Mormon from a Gentile than it used to be. The western line is therefore tentative and fluid. But a compromise boundary might run from the Gila towns of Arizona northwestward to the junction of the Muddy and the Virgin (now under Lake Mead, behind the Boulder Dam), then curve northward to take in the eastern third of Nevada, and finally swing northeastward to enclose most of southern Idaho up to the Panhandle. All the boundaries are subject to question, and there is a twilight zone all around, as well as a large section of Arizona where the Mormons never got a foothold. Still, that rough oval will at least indicate the extent of Mormon culture.

It circumscribes a territory stretching from the thirty-third parallel to the forty-fourth, and from the western slope of the Rockies to an indeterminate line far out in the Great Basin. It includes all of Utah, most of southern Idaho, the southwestern corner of Wyoming, a strip of western Colorado, the northwestern corner of New Mexico, much of northern and central Arizona, and the eastern third of Nevada. Salt Lake City is somewhat north of the center, like a yolk in a hen's egg.

This is what is today called the Intermountain Empire. It is more an entity than most states, in spite of heterogeneous cultures and varied topography. Though there are thousands of Gentiles in the territory, some of them clinging to the historic animosities against the Mormons, they are guerrillas operating behind the lines. The dominant pattern is the Mormon pattern, and state lines mean little to a Latter-day Saint. He may pay taxes in Arizona or Nevada or Colorado or Idaho or Wyoming, but his economic, religious, and cultural life is probably centered in Utah. He is likely to save his city purchases until the spring or autumn conference of the Church, in April or October, and make them when he goes to Salt Lake on his semi-annual pilgrimage. The influx of Saints from all over the region can put a mighty hole in stocks of merchandise, as any Salt Lake merchant can tell you, and a great many stores in the capital depend considerably on that seasonal boom.

The provincial Mormon's town is modeled on the City of Zion, his history has been tied up with the history of Mormon dynamism, his fathers were perhaps polygamous pioneers, his loyalty even yet is given to a religious rather than to a political idea. An instance is the political alignment of Utah after the Mormon-Gentile split had been partially healed and the national parties began operating in state politics. The Mormon people had been traditional Democrats because Joseph Smith once aspired to run for President of the United States as a Jeffersonian Democrat, and if they had been allowed to vote as they wished the state would have been overwhelmingly against the Republicans. But the Church was by the 1890's deeply involved in capitalist enterprises which threw its own weight on the Republican side. The result was "counsel" (which the Gentiles spelled "coercion"), and mass meetings in which Apostles rose and asked for a show of hands of those who were willing to volunteer as Republicans. Most of the hands went up. No one who could "volunteer to become a Republican" could have very much interest in political affairs one way or the other. It is the social patterns of men like that which have been stamped upon the country; the Gentiles, in spite of almost a hundred years of assiduous and often violent opposition, have been able to deface them only here and there.

Topographically the Mormon Country has no natural boundary lines except on the east, where the Colorado Rockies form a barrier, and the north, where the southern end of the Bitter Root Range and the spurs of the Tetons and the Antelope Hills mark the transition to alpine and uncultivable wilderness. The arbitrary western line of Mormondom cuts through the middle of the Great Basin, and the southern fades out in the river valleys below the Painted Desert in Arizona. There is not even a unity of watershed, since the area includes a large part of the Colorado River system, flowing into the Gulf of California; the eastern half of the Great Basin, whose waters reach no ocean; and the Snake River in Idaho, part of the Columbia River system. Each of those watersheds has its own distinct and different topography, but that does not make the Mormon Country less a unit. Mormondom is a social and religious, not a topographical entity. The Latter-day Saints imposed their peculiar institutions indiscriminately on the fertile Snake River Plains and on the arid and forbidding sandrock country along the San Juan and the Colorado.

One element in Mormon settlement is invariable: water. Mormonism flowed down the rivers and the irrigable valleys. The whole region lies in the arid belt, which means that only in scattered localities is there normally rainfall enough to support agriculture. Because the Mormons were and are an agricultural people, they developed irrigation; because the supply of irrigable land in any one valley was likely to be small, and because the water supply was likely to be even smaller, and because Brigham Young insisted all his life that no man should own more land than he could personally cultivate, Mormon farming is small-scale, intensive farming. The original plots doled out to settlers were seldom over twenty acres, and although there has been some tendency to combine small plots into larger, machine-worked farms, there has also been a certain amount of sub-dividing among descendants of the families, so that the average farm in the Mormon Country is still relatively tiny. And although in the last thirty years dry farming has appeared, the bulk of Mormon agriculture is still carried on in the valleys where mountain water is available for irrigation.

If you start at the northern tip of the Mormon Country and come down the Snake, you come through a string of Mormon towns—St. Anthony, Sugar City, Rexburg, Rigby, Idaho Falls, Blackfoot—all of them green and lush, grown prosperous on potatoes and sugar beets and garden truck. South of the Snake are other rivers, the Malad, the Bear, and the towns they support. Then Cache Valley, probably the richest farming valley in Utah, watered by several mountain streams, and you are at the north end of the Wasatch Mountains, which form the east wall of the Great Basin. All down the length of that range the towns are thick, crowded between mountains and lake—Bear River

Valley, Salt Lake Valley, Utah Valley. That long north-south series of valleys is like an arm. At Mount Nebo, the southern end of the Wasatch, the solid strip of good land breaks up into a three-fingered hand, slightly spread, with three ranges of high plateaus separating the sunken strips. The outermost line of plateaus forms, like the Wasatch Mountains of which it is an extension, the boundary of the Great Basin, a region of jagged and crazy ranges rising from irreclaimable desert. Only along the immediate front of that wall is agriculture possible. But over the plateau is another long string of valleys, and over the next plateau is another. From those valleys—the valley of the Sevier, Grass Valley, Rabbit Valley, Potato Valley, Round Valley, Long Valley—the timbered steppes go up on both sides to heights of nine, ten, or eleven thousand feet. They are good for summer grazing and for wood and fence poles and fishing and hunting, but there are no towns on them. Practically all are forest reserves, and all of them are water reserves, holding the snow from which the irrigation streams come. On many of them are lovely mountain lakes, some of which have become summer resorts for the Mormons from down below. The climate in summer is cool, approximately like that of northern Vermont, though the valleys below scorch in desert heat. In winter the plateaus are smothered under yards of snow.

From the southern edge of the High Plateaus below the Vermilion Cliffs the country spreads away in broad, colored plains broken by buttes and mesas and split by canyons and washes. It rises gently from the Vermilion Cliffs to the mighty platforms of the Marble and Kaibab and Kanab Plateaus, through which the Colorado River has cut the Marble and Grand Canyons. Southward beyond the river the lower Colorado Plateau sweeps out into the

Painted Desert and breaks up into the mesa country of central Arizona and New Mexico.

On both sides of that long series of valleys is wilderness. The Great Basin on the west is an effectual bar to settlement, and on the east, going from north to south along the edge of the Mormon Country, is one major mountain range, the Uintahs, and a long, hot, arid plateau, the Tavaputs, split into two sections by the canyons of the Green River. Except for short stretches, the valleys of the Green and Grand and most of their tributaries are impossible for settlement, though the Mormons sometimes settled them and in places even hung on to the towns they planted in the sand and rock.

In the central part of the region, which was the first settled, the Saints made it plain that sagebrush land was fertile if it got water. They even used a good stand of sagebrush as an index of fertility. But water was always a problem, and it is not surprising that the northern end of the region, which has more abundant streams, is the fat land of Mormondom. The Wasatch, which goes up to altitudes above twelve thousand feet, is a perfect rain-and-snow-catcher, trapping the high moisture-bearing winds that blow over the trans-Sierran desert.

West of Salt Lake City lies the wilderness beyond Jordan. Fifteen miles of useless alkali flats bring you to the lake. Beyond the flats and the lake, which is not quite fifty miles wide, and extending on south of the lake for mile after flat, dead mile, is the Great Salt Lake Desert, once the graveyard of western wagons. Its waterholes are seventy-five miles apart and its heat is blistering. Its white wastes are as hard on the eyes as a snowfield. The present highway lies like a stretched black ribbon across it. It is a funereal ribbon binding a coffin; oxen, horses, and men left their bones in that desert after struggling twelve hundred miles westward on the way to California. It was that desert which almost killed the redoubtable Jed Smith when he made the first crossing in 1827; it was that same desert which betrayed the Donner party, killed off their cattle, weakened them, slowed them down so that when they hit the Sierra they were too late to make it across.

The Great Salt Desert is somewhat tamed by now. The railroad runs across it; little way stations like Wendover sprawl nakedly on the glaring flats and haul their water for miles. British racing drivers and the Mayor of Salt Lake City vie with each other in setting world's speed records for automobiles on the packed salt, and over the white wilderness humped with worn brown knobs of hills roar United States Army bombers. There is a kind of satisfaction in the thought that the desert is being put to use as a bombing range, as a race-track, as a highway. It is well to know that anything, even that, can be used for something. In fast cars and in planes we thumb our noses at the old monster that for years lay across the path of empire.

Still, it will not do to thumb our noses too vigorously. That desert is as dry, as hot, as endless as it ever was, and just as dangerous for a man afoot or on horseback. Ride across it about noon and watch the little brown hills across the baking flats. Watch those hills lift completely off the ground, watch them float on the lifting heat waves. Look at the blue sky visible under their uprooted bases, and be thankful for high-compression engines. It is incredible that men should ever have tried to cross that stretch on foot or with wagons. The mind refuses to accept it—but they did. All I have to do to acquire anew my respect for the forces that drove Americans westward in the forties and fifties is to remember the time I threw a wheel between Grantsville and Wendover and had to chase it a quarter of a mile across the flats at midday. I remember what the ground was like through my shirt as I lay down to get the jack under the axle. I remember the way the sun pounded my head as if someone were beating me with a plank, and the way the heat waves crawled inside my skull and my eyes saw bright red with the lids closed. It was one hundred and nineteen in the shade that day, and that was not a record.

On just such days as that men in the forties and fifties walked all day, or huddled all day in the pitiful shade of a wagon and then walked all night. They went without water for twelve, eighteen, twenty-four hours in a climate where water leaves the skin almost faster than a man with a hose could pour it into the mouth. They patched up wagon wheels whose hubs and spokes and felloes were shrunken and falling apart. They cut dying oxen out of the harness and went on. They shut their eyes to the curious ghostly dance of the little brown hills which heaved up off the ground and showed the sky under their lifted skirts. With their tongues like cracking leather in their mouths they staggered toward the nearest water, and some of them never made it.

That is not a part of the western adventure one would like to live over. But it is still possible to live it over. Just go out in the Salduro Desert and break your car down off the road.

Not all of the Great Basin is as uninhabitable as the Salt Desert, but all of it is dry and all of it is hot. The mountains are treeless and sometimes waterless; the land is an endless succession of swinging sagebrush valleys hammocked between the ranges; the natives are jackrabbits, rattlesnakes, tarantulas, and horned toads.

The Great Basin was formed by what geologists call the "Cascade Disturbance," which was something of a disturbance, since it created also the Rocky Mountains, including the Wasatch range which walls the Basin on the east. Earlier than that the Great Basin was an island continent pouring silt and gravel down upon the sea bottom where now the plateau country of Utah and Arizona lifts thousands of feet above sea level. That access to the sea was completely cut off by the Cascade Disturbance.

The enclosing of the Basin and the limitation of its drainage has done a number of things during geological history. For one thing, it caused the formation of a mighty fresh-water lake three hundred and forty-six miles long, one hundred and forty-five miles wide, and in places over a thousand feet deep. That was not so long ago as geologists measure time—twenty-five to fifty thousand years—but the country was considerably different then, and the climate was a great deal wetter. Because the lake had no outlet, it eventually overflowed, and while it was overflowing the Great Basin was no longer the Great Basin, because it had access to the sea through Red Rock Pass in Cache Valley and out to the Snake and the Columbia. When the water reached hard limestone in Red Rock Pass it stopped cutting its channel (the first overflow had dropped the lake three hundred and seventy-five feet), and gradually, as the climate dried up, the lake fell lower. The glaciers no longer emptied into the water, the water courses gave up being fjords and became canyons, islands grew to be mountain ranges connected with the mainland. All that is left of Lake Bonneville now is a series of terraces cut in the mountain sides at various levels, and two or three surviving puddles. One of those puddles is Great Salt Lake, which like its parent has no outlet, but which unlike its parent has not enough inflow to dilute the mineral salts. It can only evaporate, and evaporation leaves in its already-supersaturated water all the minerals washed down from the mountains. Another fossil remnant of Lake Bonneville is Utah Lake, forty miles south, which is fresh because it has an outlet, the Jordan River, emptying into Great Salt Lake. Still another remnant is Little Salt Lake, near Parowan in southwestern Utah. Still another is Sevier Lake, an enclosed sink which accepts and quietly spoils the water of the Sevier River.

Three or four little puddles, an interminable string of crazy, warped, arid mountains with broad valleys swung between them; a few waterholes, a few springs, a few oasis towns and a few dry towns dependent for water on barrels and horsepower; a few little valleys where irrigation is possible and where the alfalfa looks incredibly green as you break down out of the pass; a desert more vegetationless, more indubitably hot and dry, and more terrible than any desert in North America except possibly Death Valley; an uncounted wealth of minerals—gold, silver, lead, zinc, copper, mercury, antimony—that about sums up the Great Basin. Its rivers run nowhere but into the ground; its lakes are probably salty or brackish; its rainfall is negligible and its scenery depressing to all but the few who have lived in it long enough to acquire a new set of values about scenery. Its snake population is large and its human population small. Its climate shows extremes of temperature that would tire out anything but a very strong thermometer. It is a dead land, though a very rich one. Even the Mormons could do little with it. They settled its few watered valleys and let the rest of it alone. The Gentiles swarmed into its mining camps and when the leads petered out they swarmed out again. Even in terms of towns, the dead in the Great Basin outnumber the living.

A more interesting part of the Mormon Country, topographically and socially, is that part which lies within, or rather virtually includes, what geologists call the Plateau Province. There the settlements are literally hewn out of the rock, founded with incredible labor and sustained against conditions that would have driven out a less persistent people after one year. Everywhere in the Mormon Country the proportion of tillable land to wasteland is extremely small. Three and three-tenths per cent, the average for Utah, is a high estimate for the Mormon Country as a whole. In the Plateau Province it can hardly be more than one per cent. The tiny oases huddle in their pockets in the rock, surrounded on all sides by as terrible and beautiful wasteland as the world can show, colored every color of the spectrum even to blue and green, sculptured by sandblast winds, fretted by meandering lines of cliffs hundreds of miles long and often several thousand feet high, carved and broken and split by canyons so deep and narrow that the rivers run in sunless depths and cannot be approached for miles. Man is an interloper in that country, not merely because he maintains a toehold only on sufferance, depending on the precarious and sometimes disastrous flow of desert rivers, but because everything he sees is a prophecy of his inconsequent destiny.

It is not merely the immensity and the loneliness and the emptiness of the land that bothers a man caught alone in it. The feeling is not the same that one gets on the great plains, where the sky is a bowl and the earth a disc and the eye is invited to notice the small things because the large ones are so characterless. In the Plateau Country the eye is not merely invited but compelled to notice the large things. From any point of vantage the view is likely to be open not with the twelve- or fifteen-mile radius of the plains, but with a radius that is often fifty and sometimes even seventy-five miles—and that is a long way to look, especially if there is nothing human in sight. The villages are hidden in the canyons and under the cliffs; there is nothing visible but the torn and slashed and windworn beauty of absolute wasteland. And the beauty is death. Where the grass and trees and bushes are stripped off and the world laid naked you can see the globe being torn down and rebuilt. You can see the death and prognosticate the birth of epochs. You can see the tiny clinging bits of débris that historical time has left. If you are a Mormon waiting for the trump of the Last Days while you labor in building the Kingdom, you can be excused for expecting that those Last Days will come any time now. The world is dead and disintegrating before your eyes.

Nowhere in the world, probably, is the transitoriness of human habitation shown so outrageously. Nowhere is historical time pitted so helplessly and so obviously against the endless minutes of geological time. Almost anywhere in the Plateau Province, which stretches from southern Wyoming down across eastern Utah and western Colorado, and then fans out eastward and westward in Arizona and New Mexico, a man can walk into a canyon a block from his house and be face to face with two or three petrified minutes of eternity. That is worse, in some ways, than facing eternity itself, because eternity is a shadow without substance. Here is the residue of a few moments, geologically speaking. Here are thousands of feet of rock patiently deposited over millions of years, buckled up into the air with the slow finality of an express engine backing into an orange crate, and as patiently being worn away over other millions. In the Plateau Country you can read the rocks from Archaean to Quaternary, and see your own place in the ladder of an inhuman immortality. The Age of Man is there, a few hundreds or a few thousands of years old: Pueblo ruins in an arched cliff, tiny granaries cached in the worn rock, Basket-maker burial cysts among the crevices. That is the Age of Man—the relics of the Ho-ho-kim, the Old People Who Left, about whom even the Indians know nothing but a name. You can read it on down: the Age of Mammals in the Tertiary, the Age of Reptiles in the Jurassic, the Age of Fish, the Age of Molluscs, the Age of Nothing at All. It is all there from Basket-Maker to Trilobite in a few thousand feet of rock that the wind even now is gnawing.

Here is your true Ozymandias. Look on my works, Ye Mighty, and despair! Your destiny, as man, is to be a fossiliferous stratum in the crust of earth; the land where Time is everything and nothing makes it plain. It even makes plain how precarious is that petrified immortality of the fossil. Let the land rise, as it has been doing, for a few more millions of years. Let the wind blow against the faces of the cliffs, let cloudbursts roll mud and boulders down the washes, and the Ho-ho-kim dwellings are gone, wiped off like a mark sponged off a blackboard. Let stones break from the faces of the cliffs through the centuries, let the cliffs retreat and retreat and retreat, and the Age of Mammals is gone, stripped off, reduced to the dust from which a new cycle can begin. Away go the Age of Reptiles and the Age of Fish, away go Brontosaurus and Pteraspis and the shelled sea-worms. Many of those layers of history are already gone from much of the Plateau Country. In places more than a vertical mile of them are gone. They survive clear to the Eocene in the High Plateaus, fortuitously and temporarily, because lava capped those tablelands and retarded the eraser. Shellac over a mark on a blackboard and you can preserve it for a while, but not forever. Geology knows no such word as forever.

When the Great Basin was an island continent, the Plateau Province was part of the ocean. The silt of rivers came down and was dropped evenly over the depths. The sea filled in, the new deposits were lifted up and eroded, sank again and had more sand and gravel and lime laid over the eroded surface. There were several risings and fallings before the movement ceased. The water became brackish, and for a long time remained shallow, filling in constantly with sediment and sinking as fast as it filled in. By the beginning of the Eocene period the sea had gone for good and the whole region was one vast fresh-water lake, its bottom still sinking evenly to accommodate sediment coming down from the Wasatch and Uintah Mountains. At the end of the Eocene the lake dried up gradually from the south, and the land began to lift. But it lifted not in great folds, as it had lifted to form the Cascades and the ancestral Rockies. The Plateau Province is an even-tempered country. It had no need of catastrophe, it felt no call to buckle the rock like soft leather. Evenly, slowly, the whole block of country rose, shearing here and there to drop down another block between two uplifts. The beds, for the most part, remained as horizontal as when they were laid down. As the land rose, the surface water drained off down the estuary that had formerly connected the lake with the sea. That drainage channel drew tributaries to itself, forming a system of rivers, and started at once to cart thousands of tons of soft Eocene sandstone into the Gulf of California.

The rivers are still there, and in substantially the same places. The rivers are older than any of the local topographical features of the region—are actually the prime movers in the carving of that topography. When the climate began to dry up, the rivers cut down into their channels faster than incidental erosion could break down the walls. The river valleys became canyons with steep clifflike sides. Floodwaters charged with sand and gravel scoured the channels, ate at the cliff sides and undermined them. The cliffs fell slowly back and the wind got at them. Sand-bearing winds chewed at their bases, undermined them again, chewed at the fallen talus slopes and bore them away and went again after the solid rock.

Give that double process of corrasion and erosion millions of years, and the topography of the country becomes credible and understandable, and the cumulative effect becomes tremendous. The cliffs backed up, inch by inch, from every main or tributary canyon. The level strata on their roofs, still soft and easily eroded, were scoured by winds, swept by flash floods. As steadily and inexorably as the land was formed it was destroyed again, stripped clean, sent in red mud down the Little Colorado, the San Juan, the Green, the Grand, the Escalante, the Paria, the Dirty Devil, the Virgin, into the Colorado and down to the sea for the making of another country. In its history the Colorado has built Imperial Valley on top of the sea bottom, cut off the Salton Sea from its parent gulf, and until the Boulder Dam forced it to drop its load higher up, was engaged in filling in the Gulf of California like a child digging with a paddle on the beach.

If you looked for the Eocene Lake deposits around the

Grand Canyon now you wouldn't find them. You wouldn't
find the Trias or Jura. You wouldn't find the Cretaceous.
You wouldn't find the Permian except in isolated buttes
in the Kanab Desert miles back from the river—cameos of
circumeroded stone, reliefs on a tomb, already beginning
to be undecipherable. Thousands of feet of strata that
once lay flat and solid over the whole Grand Canyon region both north and south are there no longer. They're at
the bottom of the Gulf of California; your winter tomatoes
from Imperial Valley have explored that lime with their
roots.

But pretend for a moment that you are a bird (you'd
have to be to do this) and are flying backward from the
Grand Canyon, from the Kaibab Plateau, whose strata, like
all the strata in this country, slope gently northward.
You'll fly over solid Carboniferous limestone until you
pass the Permian buttes in the Kanab Desert near Fredonia
or Moccasin Springs. You'll come face to face with the retreating edges of the Jura-Trias at Kanab, fifty or sixty
miles by airline from the canyon. That retreating edge
forms the Vermilion Cliffs, the southern edge of the High
Plateaus. Start multiplying (forget you're a bird for a moment). Limit yourself to the area north of the canyon and
multiply a mile of depth by sixty miles of width by the
more-than-hundred miles east and west that this denuda-
tion covered, and you have a limited idea of how many
cubic miles of solid rock such mild things as wind and rain
can remove if you give them geological time to work in.
Now you're a bird again. Fly ten miles up Kanab Canyon
and you come to another tier of cliffs, the White Cliffs.
Those are your Cretaceous shales. Rise above those and go
fifteen miles more and the Pink Cliffs of the Eocene,
capped with basalt, tell you that you are at the top of the

ladder. These are the most recent and the least eroded rocks in the region. Then perch and look back.

Step by step, cliff-line by cliff-line, the terraces break off to the Colorado. Layers of rock thousands of feet thick have come off as neatly as layers of paint before a scraper. The further you get back from the Grand Canyon the more recent the layer, until you meet the top in the Bryce Canyon formations of the Paunságunt Plateau. You stand and contemplate that vast wreckage, and the wind blows sand against your ankles and you yell and step back as if the wind were a mower blade.

Put it in terms of geological time, it is.

This was the country the Mormons settled, the country which, as Brigham Young with some reason hoped, no one else wanted. Its destiny was plain on its face, its contempt of man and his history and his theological immortality, his Millennium, his Heaven on Earth, was monumentally obvious. Its distances were terrifying, its cloudbursts catastrophic, its beauty flamboyant and bizarre and allied with death. Its droughts and its heat were withering. Almost more than the Great Basin deserts, it was a dead land. The ages lay dead in its brilliant strata, and the mud houses of the Ho-ho-kim rotted dryly in caves and gulches. In the teeth of that—perhaps because of that—it may have seemed close to God. It was Sanctuary, it was Refuge. Nobody else wanted it, nobody but a determined and God-supported people could live in it. Settle it then, in God's name, and build the Kingdom under the very eaves of that geological charnel-house.

Mud over Lyonesse . . .

WHEN archaeologists from the Museum of the American Indian began, in the middle twenties, to dig into the sprawling ruins which they called the Pueblo Grande de Nevada, and which the natives and the tourist folders called the Lost City, they unearthed remains and artifacts indicating a continuous occupation lasting over five hundred years. For five or six miles along the valley of the Muddy River, which flows (or did flow) into the Virgin a little above the Virgin's own confluence with the Colorado, the diggers uncovered dwelling houses, granaries, kivas, pit dwellings, prehistoric apartment houses of adobe and stone. The refuse mounds and the foundations of the houses indicated one cultural level on top of another, Early Pueblo sitting on Post-Basket-maker. The salt mines nearby gave up stone hammers, axes, *atlatls* or throwing sticks, cotton cloth and dyed cotton strings. Burial cysts contained, along with the flexed skeletons of the ancient town dwellers, pottery, baskets, cloth breechclouts, and remnants of rabbit-fur robes.

I remember being obscurely shocked, when I first visited that straggling line of eroded walls and circular pits, all carefully cleaned out and looking like the forts that children build in vacant lots, to think that sometime a few hundred or a few thousand or a few million years hence our civilization might be carefully and painfully pieced together and guessed at and reconstructed with the help of just such household trivia. Sometime a broken fragment of a plastic umbrella handle might overthrow scholarly reputations. One of the innumerable cast-off dice from a Nevada gambling joint might arouse learned argument about whether it was an instrument for teaching numbers to the young or whether it had some ritualistic or cabalistic significance. A chipped Mickey Mouse cup, now prized by the daughter of some Moapa Valley farmer, might go carefully into the museum case along with the duck-effigy water bottles of the Pueblo or the cheap conical ware of the Paiutes. A rusted zipper might baffle a scholarly digger as completely as zippers have always baffled me.

The things archaeologists find in their erudite picking-over of the garbage dumps of vanished civilizations are pretty disappointing, really. They give us only the most tantalizing glimpses; they make us judge of a culture by the contents of a small boy's overalls pocket. Time sucks the meaning from many things, and the future finds the rind.

Still, the rind will be there a long time from now, and not by any accident of nature. The Lost City will be there, and the broken rubble of that interesting people smothered under the name of Post-Basket-makers. And to them will be added another collection of trivia contributed by the Mormon pioneers of the Muddy. The Boulder Dam fixed that.

At the point where the Boulder Basin of Lake Mead narrows into Boulder Canyon, just below the watery cleft named somewhat loftily the Cathedral of the Rainbow God, the old Mormon river port of Callville lies under five hundred feet of blue water. The old stone fort (minus its doors, which were used as a raft by three escaping horse thieves years ago) is being silted up for what among human beings is called Eternity, and sometime, if the lake bottom goes through its geological growing pains of uplift and erosion and destruction by weathering, some representative of a future culture (maybe a large black ant) will poke his feelers into the crumbling rock that was once Colorado River mud and dust off particle by particle the rubble covering the precious find. A hundred yards from the buried and enigmatic masonry he may uncover the elk-horn handle of somebody's pocket knife, or a Pop Gear spinner snagged on the bottom and covered over, and polish them carefully with his front legs and stow them away.

Farther up Lake Mead, in the great man-made sea known as the Virgin Basin, where the Virgin and the Muddy come in on two sides of a rocky cape, our ant-man may make another find. He may find the houses of the Ho-ho-kim, minus most of their artifacts, which were removed before the water rose, and a mile or so away he may find the remains of the Mormon village of St. Thomas. On the basis of those three finds he will have grounds for a lifetime of speculation.

The pickings will be lean at all three places. The Pueblos, or Pre-Pueblos, undoubtedly took everything they thought worth taking when they left the Lost City. The museum at Overton now contains most of what they left. Callville, abandoned since 1869, has been an empty ruin for over seventy years. And St. Thomas residents, when the diversion tunnels of the dam were closed and the water began to back up the canyon, salvaged everything they wanted and left their village—all but two or three families. Those two or three were the kind of people archaeologists love. They wouldn't believe that the water would rise clear up the valley of the Muddy. They listened to the explanations of the engineers and their neighbors with solemn stubbornness, and they stuck. If they had been intelligent people St. Thomas would have been as clean as a picked bone before the waters of Lake Mead engulfed it. But they were not intelligent, or they didn't have any other place to go. The lake was a long time filling, because two hundred and twenty-nine square miles are not inundated in a day or a month, even by the Colorado River, and when those miles are covered with water sometimes hundreds of feet deep they are not inundated in a year, either. The sturdy conservatives of St. Thomas had three years to think the engineers silly. Then one morning they woke and found the water at their doorsteps, and the learning process was complete. They cleared out, leaving a few houses, a shed or two, a litter of odds and ends and rubbish.

Over that village, as over the Lost City and the old port of Callville, the Colorado is spreading the load of silt that it used to carry on to the Gulf. Engineers estimate that it will take a hundred years to fill the dam's basin and render the dam useless, and in the meantime pumping or dredging processes may be devised to clear the lake. But it will take millions of years for those buried ruins to come to light again through the endless cycle of geological change, and if you think in long-range terms it is by the leavings of the Mormon farmers of St. Thomas or some other similarly preserved town that the Mormon culture of the desert valleys will be judged.

There is not even a bell in a church tower to be tolled by the melancholy waves. There is nothing preserved in those ruins of the fervid hope of Heaven the Mormon farmer lived by; there is none of the human frailty, none of the fatigue or bad temper or the sweetness of the good hours, none of the laughter or the obedience or the loyalty or the stubbornness. The archaeologists, ant or human, can have St. Thomas and Callville and the Pueblo Grande de Nevada. Their submersion and their later possible emergence may be the only long-range immortality they will have, or Mormon civilization will have, but that immortality is a distortion as well as a death. There is more life in a legend than in petrifaction. Let that Lyonesse lie under its river mud. People are more interesting than their relics, and more interesting than the country they live in. Let us look at some people.

Forty Thousand Saints in One Act . . .

A<small>T</small> first they were Vermonters and up-state New York-
ers and first-generation westerners from Kentucky
and Ohio. And they were the Children of Israel, chosen by
the Lord for the upbuilding of Zion. They were an Old
Testament people, inheritors of the blessings of the tribe
of Joseph through the new dispensation. Their prophet
Joseph Smith had promised it, his mouth had spoken,
through him the Lord had covenanted with His people.
They were the flotsam and jetsam and débris left in the
wake of the Great Revival, bewildered and seeking and
salvation-bent, who had been gathered to the arms of the
true Church by the persuasive preaching of Joseph Smith
and Sidney Rigdon and Parley Pratt and Brigham Young
and the other great proselytizers.

This people had been since 1830 the witness to signs
and wonders. Their sick had been cured by the holy oil
and the laying on of hands, they had read the Book miraculously discovered and supernaturally translated through
the Urim and Thummim, they had spoken in tongues and
received the gift of prophecy, they had quivered with the
immanence of God. Heaven was their destination—Heaven
and its earthly equivalent, the Holy City of Zion built in
everlasting stones of fair colors.

For the sixteen years of the Church's first period they

had been a loosely-integrated group, alternately swelled by
proselytes and diminished by persecution and apostasy, but
even in that time their co-operative efforts had amazed the
country. They had built their Zions, their tabernacles and
their temple, and been persecuted for their pains. They
had acquired Kirtland in Ohio and Far West in Missouri
and had built Nauvoo the Beautiful in Illinois. There
they had transformed a malarial river swamp into a thriv-
ing city, the largest in Illinois, and for a while they had
grown prosperous and arrogant. The prophet had looked
over the candidates for the Presidency of the United States
and found them all lacking, and his people had set him up
as the only candidate worth a vote. But arrogance is the
other side of insecurity. Their memories were branded
with the troubles in Ohio and Missouri, with the stonings
and tar-and-featherings, the massacre at Haun's Mill, the
hatred and the murders. They had been mobbed and pil-
laged and chased, and no sanctuary lasted more than a few
years. Their millennial expectations and their exclusiveness
and their habit of voting solid on whatever side their potentate chose for them—what some might call their "un-
American" way of life—surrounded them with enemies
and in the end it was demonstrated that they could not
live in peace in the United States. Any chosen people is
likely to be looked on with suspicion or open hatred.
When the rumors of polygamy were added to the already
strained situation, the Saints had lost Nauvoo.

They saw their prophet and his brother Hyrum murdered in Carthage jail while technically under the protection of the state militia. They were driven in mid-winter
across the river into Iowa, leaving part of their number
behind to finish, grimly and without hope, the costly
temple of the Lord in the beautiful city. After Joseph's

death in 1844 they saw the schisms, the struggles for power
among the leaders, they witnessed heresy and cleavage,
watched hundreds of their fellows led away by James Jesse
Strang and Lyman Wight and the other schismatics, some
to Texas, some to Wisconsin, everywhere and anywhere.
They saw the bitter-mouthed first wife of the prophet apos-
tatize and remain behind to run her dead husband's tavern
in Nauvoo. But the whole structure did not disintegrate
with Joseph's passing. He had left it too well organized,
and he had left behind him a Quorum of Apostles and
Brigham Young, their president. Brigham at first did not
push himself to the nominal leadership of the Church; he
was content with the real leadership which came to him as
President of the Twelve.

In the winter of 1846 there were twelve thousand of the
Saints strung along the roads of Iowa, going blindly toward the great migration that Brigham ordered, their hope
set on the mountain sanctuary which he promised.

They lived in log huts on the banks of the Missouri at
Winter Quarters (now Florence, Nebraska, a suburb of
Omaha). When the time came to move on west many of
them gave up horses and mules and oxen that others better
fitted for the pioneering journey might go. The ones remaining behind planted crops all across Iowa's dolorous
miles so that those coming after in a steady stream from
deserted Nauvoo might harvest the crops for their sustenance. And in the end, wagon-train by wagon-train, company by company, they trailed out from Winter Quarters
by ox team and mule team and horse team and team of
milk cattle, the wagons crowded with chickens, ducks,
geese, cats, dogs, beehives, the children herding loose pigs
and sheep, all their earthly goods in the schooners or on
their backs. They left graves behind them, hundreds of

graves, because the black canker had gone through their camps like a scythe. They left graves beside the road, too, and piled them with stones to keep the coyotes away and went on.

They went in bitterness and in hope. The persecutions, the massacres, the martyrdom of the prophet, the bloody flux and the black canker and the desolate graves, had cemented them into a unit, and every successive wagon train for many years was like a new flight out of Egypt. The Old Testament parallel was like a bugle in the brain; some of them probably even hoped for a pursuing Pharaoh and a dividing of the waters. They had found their strength: Mormonism in exodus was a herd, like a herd of buffalo, and its strength was the herd strength and the cunning of the tough old bulls who ran the show. Brigham Young was no seer and revelator, but a practical leader, an organizer and colonizer of very great stature. He is credited with only one revelation in all his years as head of the Church, and that one is characteristic. It outlined how the Saints should be regimented for migration into tens and fifties and hundreds, with a responsible captain over each group. And when the organizational outline was completed the revelation closed with as clipped a phrase as if God were a business man dictating to his secretary. "And so no more at this time," God said. There was no more at any time. The secretary had taken over the administration of the business. If it didn't sound like blasphemy, one might say that he proved a better executive than his former employer.

Except in willingness and determination and their group strength the Mormons were a poor people, because in their flight they had had to abandon or sell for next to nothing all the property they owned. The people who

came after them, they knew, would also be poor. But the
first trains did their part to make the way easier. They
planted way stations and fields. They even dropped off
men here and there to work and earn money for the common good. They left some to run a ferry on the Platte. At
Independence Rock Brigham delegated two men to stop
off and for a fee chisel the names of wayfarers on the face
of that frontier postoffice already crowded with the initials
and messages of explorers, mountain men. Oregon emigrants, and soldiers. Nothing that might earn a dollar for
the common purse was too small to be overlooked. The
main parties inscribed buffalo skulls and left markers, and
pressed on. If they looked back at all they looked back in
prophetic visions to see the painful trail transformed into
a wide straight highway for the multitudes of Saints who
would come after.

Persecution and hardship are an exceedingly effective
trying ground. The graduates can be counted on, generally. The weak and the half-convinced and the ineducable
drop out. Throughout his career Brigham kept that firmly
in mind; he fanned the hatred of the Gentiles, he fostered
the sense of being surrounded and persecuted. It is a trick
which modern prophets and saviors have found useful.
Until people are down and out, and have someone to hate
for their condition, they do not seem likely to co-operate
for any common aim. Brigham, as poker player on a vast
scale, played off bitterness against hope, the past against
the future. He held his aces back to back, and he opened
strong and kept raising, to freeze out the grocery clerks.
It was a hard system on the rank and file, but it worked.
There were few grocery clerks among the Mormon pioneers. They were workers, doers, bearded projectiles of the

fierce religious dynamism that even yet, though grown static and in some quarters fat, has not worn itself out.

Their first act on reaching Salt Lake Valley was to plow a patch of hard earth and flood it from the waters of City Creek Canyon. The morning after the scouts arrived, even before the party under Brigham Young saw the valley, they had potatoes in the ground.

These were the people who first settled the Mormon Country, and though they have been called many things, many hard things, they have never been called bad settlers. They were as indefatigable, obedient, stalwart, and united a people as the world ever saw. Their record in the inter-mountain region is a record of group living, completely at variance with the normal history of the West. The American Dream as historians define it did not fit these whiskered zealots. Theirs was a group dream, not an individual one; a dream of Millennium, not of quick fortune. A good many wagon trains had gone westward from the Missouri before the first Mormon companies, and the mountain men had been in the Great Basin and around its borders for a generation before 1847. After the gold strike at Sutter's Fort in 1848 there were so many scramblers to the West that the population of California jumped one hundred thousand in a year. But the dream that pulled those adventurers across the Great American Desert and around the Horn, though it was a potent dream, was totally different from the Mormon dream. Even the Indians caught onto the difference fast: they knew two races of white men, the Mericats and the Mormonee.

No sooner were the bastions of the City of Zion anchored solidly in the alluvial slopes below City Creek Canyon than the dream began to expand. Here would be the City of the Saints. How about the *country* of the Saints? For that too Brigham had a plan, and it was no picayune or humble plan. It was a plan of empire.

Less than two thousand Saints landed in the valley the first year, with ten or twelve thousand more to come from the temporary settlements in Iowa and Nebraska. The entire membership of the Church then totaled somewhere around twenty-five thousand. But they were not enough, not nearly enough. Brigham's first move was to make arrangements for more. He did it by amplifying and extending the missionary system which had already worked well for Joseph while the prophet was building Nauvoo. Brigham did not content himself with sending missionaries to the most likely spots like the British Isles. Within two years after his arrival in Zion he had dispatched trusted men to England, France, Switzerland, Italy, Scandinavia, South and Central America, India, Australia, the Sandwich and Solomon Islands. Mormonism had been conceived on a grandiose scale. It was meant to cover and inherit the world in the great and terrible last days. Under Brigham Young it became in fact a world-wide movement.

At the same time that he was collecting his pools of potential manpower, Brigham was extending the boundaries of his empire, exploring its possibilities, locating likely townsites. The double problem of proselytizing thousands of Saints and of finding places to settle them in Zion occupied most of Brigham's time from 1847 to his death in 1877. It would have occupied all his time if the United States had let him alone to work out his plans as he wished.

Exploring parties went out, at first mainly southward and westward, and in the wake of the exploring parties went picked trains of colonists. Sometimes Brigham called for volunteers to settle a particular spot—and got them.

Sometimes he drafted a selected group of families—and they threw up everything and went. Colonists were in effect on missions for the Church; they could not and would not leave until officially released. At whatever personal sacrifice, they went, and they went on a careful and planned schedule. They took with them the supplies that Brigham specified, and among the settlers were always representatives of the trades and professions most essential to the spot being settled. Always too the party had a fiddler, because dancing was almost one of the ordinances. It was pleasant recreation for the Saints, and from Brigham's point of view it was indispensable as a builder of morale. Fiddlers, carpenters, blacksmiths, masons, teachers, farmers, sometimes miners and smelter workers, they went out on Brigham's orders. Every train was hand picked for the spot it was to settle, and if it showed signs of being too weak, or of being in danger from Indians or crop failure or lack of supplies, Brother Brigham sent on reinforcements.

There is a curious law of vagrancy among the early statutes of the State of Deseret. A vagrant is defined as "any person residing within the limits of this state who has no visible means of support." A man convicted of this misdemeanor was put to work on public projects long enough to pay the costs of prosecution, or not less than twenty days. The law, moreover, was strictly enforced and rigidly interpreted. A vagrancy charge was likely to be laid against "all loafers who hang about the corners of streets, court houses, or any public place, who have no business, *whether they have property or not.*" Partly, that law was aimed at bothersome Gentiles, and offered an easy legal method of making them feel unwelcome, but it was invoked against the few drones of Mormondom too. Taking advantage of the oddities of the law which he had dictated, Brigham asserted that if these loafers could find no way to employ their time profitably, he could find a way for them, and drafted them to go out and strengthen new settlements in the hinterlands. One way to make them work was to put them in a position where they had either to work or starve.

Brigham Young was a colonizer without equal in the history of America. In a desert that nobody wanted and that was universally considered a fit home only for coyotes and rattlesnakes, he planted in thirty years over three hundred and fifty towns and created the technique and made the surveys for others. One hundred of those towns were colonized in the first ten years, when transportation was fearfully difficult and expensive, when the nearest source of many essential supplies was over a thousand miles away. Methodically, as if he were sticking pins in a map, he founded villages at all the strategic points of his empire, and by 1855, eight years after the arrival of the first pioneers, he had virtually taken possession of a territory larger than Texas. He had spread the towns out from Salt Lake City through Salt Lake and Weber Valleys, reached down into Utah Valley, jumped the Wasatch to colonize Sanpete Valley southeast of Salt Lake. He had planted a precarious outpost on the Colorado River at what is now Moab, had overleaped the Weber Valley settlements by two hundred and fifty miles to establish a mission colony at Fort Lemhi in the Salmon River Mountains of Idaho. He had frozen out Jim Bridger and the mountain men and founded a pair of supply stations, Fort Bridger and Fort Supply, on the transcontinental trail in Wyoming, thereby assuring himself control of the eastern approach to Zion. He had sprung clear across the Great Basin deserts to locate the Mormon Station, now Genoa, under the shadow of the

Sierra on the emigrant road to California. More important
than any of these was the string of settlements running
south and west from Salt Lake City along the Spanish
Trail, later known as the Mormon Road and now Highway 91 from Salt Lake to Los Angeles. There was a special
reason for the colonies and missions at Fillmore, Parawan,
Paragonah, Cedar City, Harmony, Santa Clara, Las Vegas,
and San Bernardino. Most of them were stages in the Mormon Corridor, the outlet to the sea.

San Bernardino had been planned as an outfitting point
for Saints journeying to Zion. The trip by wagon across
the plains was difficult and dangerous, slow and expensive.
Brigham conceived of a route by boat to Panama, across
the Isthmus by whatever means could be made available,
and by boat again up to San Diego, which would be the
principal port serving the Mormon Empire. The trail
from San Diego to Salt Lake City was comparatively easy
and comparatively safe, and could be traveled at any time
of the year. By means of its use, Brigham hoped to keep
the influx of Saints steady, instead of having the heavy
immigration arrive in the valley during a few weeks of the
late summer and fall.

An extension of the whole Pacific-port plan in the sixties
opened another possibility, that of boat transport up the
Colorado from the Gulf of California to a point just above
the present Boulder Dam. Brigham sent Anson Call to
build a warehouse at Call's Landing in 1864; a group of
Salt Lake business men organized a warehouse and merchandise company to undertake the Colorado waterway
business. Two Gentile-owned steamboats, the *Esmerelda*
and the *Nina Tilden,* had already succeeded in fighting
their way up the current to a point near Call's Landing.
If the railroad had not come in 1869 there is every proba-

bility that Brigham would have succeeded in creating some sort of river traffic on the Colorado in spite of the difficulties of swift water, rapids, and canyons. But when it was certain that the railroad would come through he quietly abandoned both the river project and Callville. That was a secondary matter anyway. The empire had been blocked out almost ten years before; it had already started to crumble before Anson Call was ever sent to build his warehouse.

These are the limits of the empire Brigham picked out on the map by 1855: Fort Lemhi in Idaho, Forts Bridger and Supply in Wyoming, Moab (the Elk Mountain Mission) in eastern Utah, San Bernardino in California, Genoa in Nevada. From Salt Lake City to Genoa it was five hundred and fifty miles of absolute desert. From Salt Lake to Fort Lemhi it was three hundred, from Salt Lake to Fort Bridger one hundred twenty-five, from Salt Lake to Moab two hundred, from Salt Lake to San Bernardino something over seven hundred. It was a largish slice of country to settle from a supply point which was itself in starving straits part of the time, and with a population which by 1855 could hardly have been above thirty thousand.

Communication until 1870 was by wagon or Pony Express, and the difficulties of hauling in from the East the iron and leather and cloth and machinery and manufactured goods necessary for existence were so enormous that Brigham was forced from the beginning to add a third project to his double plan of proselytizing and settlement. He had to add the project of self-sufficiency. Home industries were not merely pleasant; they were essential, and in the devising of home industries with few of the facilities for industrial development the Mormons showed considerable ingenuity. They chiseled grindstones and millstones from the cliffs, built sawmills, woolen mills, tanneries. And though Brigham consistently refused to let his people prospect for or work deposits of precious metals, he was practical enough to know that iron and coal and lead were as necessary for a self-sufficient economy as wheat and corn. The Mormons very early found and attempted to develop all three kinds of mines.

The history of early Mormon mining of base metals and coal is a history of laborious failure, actually. For years the Deseret Iron Company, a Church corporation, tried to work the immense iron deposits in Iron County, near Cedar City. They imported men skilled in the manufacture of iron from England and Wales and France, built furnaces and kilns, poured their money and their labor unsparingly into the work. But the ore was recalcitrant, for all its richness, and there were not enough facilities for chemical research on the frontier to find out exactly what was the matter. The product never emerged as really good pigs of iron. Even so, the pioneers of Iron County made a good many thousand pounds of metal, manufactured a few crude implements and articles of household use, and wrought nails. There are houses in Cedar City yet that are held together with handwrought nails from Iron Mountain.

The settlers had the same bad luck with the lead mines near Las Vegas. Sent out, as the members of the "Iron Mission" were sent out, specifically to do a job for the Church's self-sufficiency program, a party of miners and smelter workers tried for several years from 1855 on to produce a workable quality of lead. They made some and shipped it north, but it was brittle and flaky and full of impurities, and eventually the Las Vegas project too was abandoned.

For a good many years isolated parties passing the mines and furnaces used to stop off long enough to smelt out a little brittle lead for ammunition, and there is an ironic story connected with the unsatisfactory stuff they molded for their bullet pouches. The ores from which the Mormons were trying to make lead had lead in them, to be sure, and plenty of it, but the "blackjack and dry bone" that hindered the smelting of pure metal, and that the Mormons had piously cursed for several years, were heavily silver-bearing galena. Nobody knows how many bear, elk, deer, coyotes, and Indians got their quietus with a silver bullet.

The iron and lead industries failed, not because the ores were of poor quality or because coal was lacking for the smelting, or because the smelter men were unskilled, but simply because the Mormons were too far out on the frontier, too far from research laboratories, too far from really expert advice. The manufacture of sugar from beets, which Brigham promoted and gave a great deal of time to, failed for something like the same reasons. The expensive machinery purchased in France and shipped across to New Orleans, up the Mississippi and Missouri, freighted across piecemeal by wagon train and set up in the valley, was almost a total loss. The alkali soil did something to the chemistry of the sugar beet that not even the French sugar-makers Brigham imported with the machinery could solve. It was several decades before beet sugar manufacture became a notable part of the economy of the Mormon Country and justified Brigham's vision. Meantime the Gentiles had a long period when they could jeer at Brigham's much-advertised business sense.

In smaller matters the self-sufficiency program succeeded admirably. The Mormons had to make their own cloth, their own leather, their own everything, and did it. Even the notorious pipe-organ was home-made. The Saints even, contrary to the Word of Wisdom which forbids the use of tea, coffee, tobacco, and liquor, manufactured their own whiskey and beer, and in "Dixie," down in Utah's south-western corner, made wine from their own grapes, all of it largely for sale to the Gentiles from the emigrant trains and the mines. "Valley Tan," a term of derision first applied to the inferior grades of leather made in Salt Lake, later came to be a blanket epithet for anything home-made and hence inferior, and in particular was the name of a singularly destructive variety of whiskey, also known as leopard sweat.

As a whole, the self-sufficiency plan did not flourish as notably as the proselytizing and colonization, though tanneries and woolen mills did get along, and the ingenuity of isolated communities out in the badlands did contrive from the materials at hand countless substitutes for manufactured goods. But the barter system was onerous and the supply of States' goods small for many years, even though Forty-niners hot for the gold fields disposed of much of their gear at a loss, stripping for speed across the desert, and though the dragoons who left Utah for participation in the Civil War sold off at auction—again at a loss—their entire store of equipment and supplies. Four million dollars' worth of goods went at that auction for a hundred thousand dollars, which left a favorable balance of trade to the Mormons for the moment. Still the heavy industry of the empire did not prosper, and the supply of cash was small, eked out though it was with tithing office script and various other substitutes for money like the co-operative script of Brigham City. The coming of the railroad, break-

ing down the exorbitant freight rates from the states, took
a considerable burden off the backs of the Saints.

But all that time, through the fifties and sixties and seventies, the colonizing went on, the proselytizing went on,
the Saints abroad were exhorted to gather unto Zion, and
they came—across the Atlantic to New Orleans or New
York or Boston, across the Middle West or up the Mississippi and Missouri to the outfitting points at Kanesville
(Council Bluffs), Iowa City, or Florence, across the plains
by wagon or mule or ox team, to arrive finally and be distributed to their patrimony in some corner of Zion, their
numbers swelling the growing communities and their labors adding pin after pin to Brigham's map of empire.

And Nothing Shall Hinder or
Stay Them . . .

THEY were British converts from the Black Belt collieries, broad-spoken proselytes from the dying towns of Cornwall and Wales; they were Manxmen and Norwegians and Danes and Swedes. They were the technologically and spiritually unemployed, many of them, the economically-stranded people of Europe's back doors, to whom the Church offered both material and spiritual rejuvenation, a chance to own and cultivate a little farm, an opportunity to start over again—most of all an opportunity to assure themselves Heaven by gathering to the valleys of Zion and building up the Kingdom. The religious motivation was the more important, but the economic should not be ignored. These were the same sort of people, living in the same sort of circumstances, as those who in 1844 made economic history by creating the Rochdale Co-operative system in Toad Lane. In that one Lancashire town of Rochdale in 1841, according to a Parliamentary report, there were fifteen hundred people existing on forty-five cents a week. It does not take much inducement to leave that kind of living for the hopeful new, and the Mormon missionaries found their richest field of labor among the millhands and miners of England. They had both inducements: another deal for the economically under-privileged, a hope of heaven for the spiritually depressed. Many of the proselytes from those English towns would have waded through fire to reach the sanctuary in the mountains, and some of them almost literally did.

Money was a problem. Most of the conversions were made among the poor, and though the richer brethren of the foreign missions were put under heavy contribution they could do little to pay the expenses of hundreds and thousands of emigrants. To help those unable to pay their own way, and to hasten their arrival in Zion, Brigham organized the Perpetual Emigration Company, whose funds, gained partly from tithes and contributions and partly from such legally earmarked sources as the fines from the stray pound and a percentage of the take from ferry concessions, were loaned to foreign converts on the agreement that they would be paid back after the settlement of the newcomers in the West.

It was an efficient system. A Cook's Tour had nothing on it. The mission agents of the Church at Liverpool chartered ships and loaned money and arranged passage. The proselyte had little to do at first but be present. He was ushered on board, made a member of the company (sometimes by baptism), freighted across to an American port, taken across country or up the rivers to the outfitting point. Agents escorted him all the way, took him to his last civilized stop, equipped him with a wagon and team and a carefully-selected load of supplies, organized him into tens and fifties and hundreds according to Brigham's one revelation, and started him West.

His own contribution began there. The more-than-thousand miles from the Missouri to Salt Lake Valley was a painful and dangerous journey, especially for trains with great numbers of women and children and old men. Wagons were heavy, the road was bad, the range was a fickle source of horse- and cattle-feed, the journey could be taken only from about May to October. Three months was good time for a wagon-train on the road; the initial company under Brigham Young took three and a half, and it had only three women and two children. Most of the emigrants, because of the heavy loads and the necessity of saving the scanty wagon-room for women and children and the sick, had to walk the entire distance. The convert made his contribution, sure enough. He was pretty well seasoned by the time he reached the valley.

Because of the cumbersome and expensive ox-team method of importing new Saints, the funds of the Perpetual Emigration Company had many demands on them, and the debtor converts were often unable, however willing they were, to repay the loans within a reasonable time. There were hundreds of Saints clamoring to come, but the money to bring them was missing. So Brigham tried a newer and cheaper plan. He sent letters to the mission heads in Europe, notified his agents in Boston and New York and Iowa City. His plan was simplicity itself. If you could not afford heavy wagons and oxen, if you had the converts but not the means to equip them, cut out the wagons and oxen, put the converts under a heavier contribution. If their faith was strong they would come; if it wasn't strong Brigham didn't want them. They would be escorted to an outfitting point as before. From there they would walk to Salt Lake City, pushing or pulling their rationed supplies and limited belongings in wheelbarrows and pushcarts.

I have been over that route, or its modern equivalent, many times, by car, by bus, by streamliner, by thumb. I

have driven it in thirty hours and hitch-hiked it in a day
and a half from Iowa City to Salt Lake. But I think that
if I had been asked to walk it in 1856, on skimpy rations,
pulling my duffle and perhaps my family in a handcart,
with hostile Indians possible most of the way, it would
have tried my faith. Apparently a trial of faith was just
what the emigrants wanted. They not only agreed to Brigham's plan; they jumped at it, and not by dozens but by
hundreds. They were already, before their ship had left
Liverpool, part of that irresistible line of force that Brigham Young had set up, already dedicated to the annealing
and unifying dynamism of the great Idea.

Archer Walters was a carpenter from Sheffield. He made
a fair living and lived moderately well, even with the price
of living gone sky-high because of the Crimean War. His
wife, an ex-mill-girl, had brought him five children, and
his life had settled into a comfortable groove. But sometimes he wondered about the hard times, and sometimes
he wondered about God. He was a serious man, Archer
Walters, but he had his thoughts and he had his dreams
of some place that might be better. Also he was a devout
man, concerned about his soul and the souls of his family,
and he was intelligent enough to see that many of the affairs of this world were unaccountably out of line.

Then the Mormon missionaries came to Sheffield, and
he heard them speak. He was impressed by their single-
hearted devotion to their belief, by the apparent serenity
of their lives. He went again, and they talked of the valleys
among the mountains where the godless were not, where
each man received according to his labor and his deserts,
and where communities of Saints were co-operating to
build the Kingdom. It was far away, the land of Deseret,

and hazed by the imagination, but it was the Lord's land, given to His anointed, and he yearned toward it. He was baptized on September 3, 1848, and ordained a priest on April 1, 1849, and brought his family into the Church with him. From there on his dreams had a focus. Somehow, sometime, the Walters family would be gathered up to Zion and the road would be straight and forever. "If I can but reach the Valleys of the Mountains, in the land of Zion, with my family, that they may grow up under the influence of the Gospel of Christ, then I shall be satisfied, though I give my life in the effort."

In the fall of 1855 came an Epistle from Brigham Young to all the mission heads. Archer Walters read it and pondered. "Let all Saints who can, gather up for Zion, and come while the way is open before them; let the poor also come, whether they receive aid or not from the P. E. Fund; let them come on foot, with handcarts or wheelbarrows; let them gird up their loins and walk through, and nothing shall hinder or stay them. . . ."

The cost of transportation from Liverpool to Iowa City, with the provision of a handcart and rations at that point, was nine pounds per person. Archer Walters did some mathematics, talked with the Elders, and ended by putting his family on the train for Liverpool. On March 22, 1856, they boarded the chartered ship *Enoch Train* along with five hundred and twenty-eight other Saints all bound for the valleys of the mountains. Four hundred and thirty-one of the passengers owned only their luggage, and their passage money had come out of the fund.

The voyage was long and tiresome, with contrary winds. Everyone was sick in the Irish Channel, and not even the Birmingham Band and the deck dances could bring them out. Captain and crew were kind, but traveling on a shoestring meant lean meals and little variety. Some of the Saints stayed sick all the way to Boston. An old lady died and was buried at sea. A child was born and named for the *Enoch Train;* another, a girl, arrived and was christened Rebecca Enoch. A little boy killed himself falling from the upper deck. The Saints strained their eyes for America, grumbled about the food, attended meeting, prayed and sang and danced on deck to the Birmingham Band, a little frightened at the cold moonlight and the endless long wash of the North Atlantic under the brittle stars.

Then Boston, and a welcome, a celebration, gifts for every Saint on board from charitable Boston ladies, and an efficient agent who shepherded them into a train to New York. (They landed at Boston to escape a dollar head tax exacted at other ports.) With scarcely a halt, hardly a look at Babylon, they shifted to a train for the West, and on May 12 they were camped outside Iowa City preparing their carts and belongings for the long hike. It was cold; wind and rain storms blew down the imperfectly-pitched tents of the tenderfeet. A number of families were down with fever.

Under the date of June 4 appears an entry in Archer Walters' *Journal* which runs like a *leitmotif* through the whole record: "Made coffin for a child dead in camp." As carpenter, Walters had plenty of those jobs. He became, in fact if not in name, coffin-maker to Israel.

On June 6 he made another child's coffin, and from then on he was a very busy man. The company finally crawled out into the dead heat of the Iowa prairie on June 8. Walters' daughter was so sick she could barely walk. The handcarts demanded frequent repair, and Walters often worked for hours after the camp was pitched and for hours before they started rolling again the next morning. He was supposed to be captain of his tent, responsible for the eighteen people under him, but he confided to his *Journal*, a little ruefully, "They were a family of Welsh and our spirits were not united." His wife, crowding the edge of exhaustion and worrying about her sick daughter and her sore-footed other children, developed a strong tendency to what the *Journal* charitably describes as "ill-temper." On June 28, when a high wind blew down all the tents and soaked the sleepers, Walters rose in the morning to write glumly, "I thought of going through needful tribulation, but it made me cross." Anybody but a Mormon would have had a stronger word than "cross" for it.

And always there were the coffins. June 15: coffin for William Lee, aged 12, and another for Sister Prator's child. June 17: coffin for Job Welling's son. June 21: coffin for Brother Bowers. June 26: coffin for Emma Sheen, aged two and a half. July 2: coffin for Brother Card's daughter. July 26: Brother Henry Walker struck by lightning in the very middle of the train. Buried without coffin because no boards available. Aug. 17: Brother Missel Rossin found dead by the side of the road. Aug. 31: Brother Stoddard died. Sept. 2: Walter Sanderson died. Sept. 8: Brother Nipras died. Sept. 14: Sister Mayer died. . . .

But they walked it. They killed rattlesnakes by the side of the trail, they labored and sweated over the continually-broken carts, they bucked wind and rain and diarrhea and the constant deaths, they waded rivers, some of them a dozen times, and they climbed the long hill to South Pass and over it and on across the Green River Valley with the dust blowing over them and the wind already freezing with unseasonable winter. Their rations were cut, and cut again, and the children whimpered with sore feet and hunger. But they walked it. At the end of September they came out of Emigration Canyon with the remnants of their five hundred Saints, the patched remains of their hand-carts, the creaking and dry-axled wagons in which the heavy equipment had been hauled. They arrived with tears and thanksgiving after a walk of fourteen hundred miles. Some days they had walked as much as twenty-eight miles, and with all their handicaps of the aged, the halt, the women and the children, they had beaten every wagon-train on the road. Nobody had passed them; they brought their own express of their coming. The town turned out en masse, and Archer Walters and his companions, with their heads up and their eyes full of the miraculous valley, stepped briskly into the city escorted by a company of lancers, William Pitt's brass band, a long queue of car-riages bearing Church officials and ladies and old-time friends from England and Scandinavia. More than seventy of them had died on the way, but they had attained their millennial home.

Archer Walters died of dysentery two weeks after he and his family arrived in Salt Lake, but he undoubtedly died satisfied. He did not live to inherit his mountain valley in the flesh, but his immortality is established. His wife and his five children all survived the migration. His children, among them, had thirty-seven sons and daughters. His de-scendants now, eighty-six years after he turned pilgrim, number more than five hundred.

I have chosen to follow Archer Walters not because his story is the most exciting but because it is as typical as any that can be found. His handcart company suffered many deaths, but no more in proportion than an average wagon-train suffered. The first three handcart companies which came through in 1856 had no more severe a time than al-

most any company crossing the plains. But the two companies who followed them later in the summer are another
story.

Those companies, under Brother Willie and Brother
Martin, were advised by the Church agents not to set out
at all until spring, because they had got a late start from
England, their carts were not ready for them when they
reached Iowa City, many of them were old and lame and
infirm. But even the warning of the experienced agents,
even the blandishments of the people of Iowa City, who
offered them high wages if they would stay and work
through the winter, could not keep them back. Their
minds were full of the vision, and they would go. They
cobbled the carts together, many of them of green wood,
with wooden axles and no tires, and pulled out, the Willie
company on July 15, the company under Martin on July
28.

The story of those two caravans of Saints is a story of
tragedy second in western history only to the tragedy of
the Donner Party. The only thing the Donner Party did
that the handcart companies did not was to eat their dead
companions. The Mormons, apparently, were better prepared to die. Their hope was fixed on Heaven, not on the
golden shore.

The Martin company had the worse time. They were
constantly in fear of Indians, because the Margetts party
and the Almon Babbitt party had been massacred only a
little time before. They labored on past the burned wreckage of Babbitt's carriage, living on a daily ration of one
pound of flour per person, and very few groceries to accompany the flour. On September 7, a full month before
winter could have been anticipated, they had a severe
frost. All along they had had their quota of deaths; now

the quota began to rise. At Fort Laramie they traded watches, rings, everything they had, for extra provisions, but even so the rations had to be cut to three-quarters of a pound of flour, then to a half pound, then even lower. There was a law of diminishing returns against them. The harder the way became, the less strength they had to get over it. The more their bodies clamored for food and warmth, the less food and warmth there were. The greater the need for haste, the slower their pace became.

Across the Black Hills there was little food for the cattle hauling their six wagons, and the handcarts broke to pieces on the rocky trails. On October 19 winter hit them at Red Buttes, the last crossing of the Platte. Some of the men lifted women or children and staggered across, many of the women hiked up their skirts and plunged. They had no sooner made the other side than a blizzard struck them. They camped and did their best to stay warm. By this time their loads had been reduced, in the interest of speed, from seventeen to ten pounds apiece. In the desperate effort to get through at all they had sacrificed blankets, greatcoats, anything heavy. Dropping with fatigue and exposure, they struggled on through the snow toward Devil's Gate. In the evenings men sat by the inadequate fires and died without a word, sitting up. Men, women, and children lay down under their ragged blankets and never rose again.

Where the road left the Platte for the Sweetwater the snow finally stopped them, twelve to eighteen inches of it. Their feet were frozen, their shoes used up. They had only two shovels for the whole camp, and to pitch tents at all they had to shovel out with frying pans and tin plates, whimpering, dog-tired, ready to lie down and let the cold take them. When they tried with numb hands to hang onto the ax long enough to drive the tent pegs into the ground they missed the pegs, splintered them, broke them from the frozen earth and with set faces groped for the splinters to get the ropes down somehow, get some sort of shelter up against the bitter wind. That night more died. The next day more. The next night still more.

They were camped patiently at the Sweetwater bridge, five miles from Devil's Gate, living on their draft animals and dying in tens and dozens, when the relief wagons Brigham Young had dispatched from Salt Lake found them. Those first wagons had some supplies, but not enough, and even the wagons were none too safe in the deep snow three hundred miles short of the valley. Twenty men were left with most of the carts and luggage to winter at Devil's Gate. The rest hurried for Salt Lake. Children and sick persons were put in wagons, but the rest still had to walk, many of them shoeless in freezing weather. Rocky Ridge—South Pass—over the divide in a howling blizzard on November 18, but by that time more relief wagons had met them and all could ride, huddled under the slimsy shelter of the canvas and feeling the wheels lurch and sink and climb over the snow-hidden road. More of them died; the rest pressed on. On November 21 Green River, on the 23rd Fort Bridger, on the 24th the cedars of the Muddy, and glorious big fires for the first time in weeks. On the 26th Echo Canyon, and a child born. Both mother and child lived. The child was wrapped in the sacrificed underwear, the holy garments, of one of the relief party, and was named Echo. If his name meant anything, if there was in his post-natal memories any echo of what his mother must have borne with him over the bitter road, he must have had a haunted life.

Then on the 27th the Weber River, on the 28th East

Canyon, on the 29th Big Mountain, the wagons crowding in desperate haste over the backbone of the Wasatch, making thirty-five miles a day through the roughest kind of country, and on Sunday, November 30, they came down the wintry canyon into the warmer weather of Salt Lake and were home.

Those, that is, who got there were home. But perhaps the uncounted dead who lay along the trail (one Church historian estimates the number of casualties at one hundred forty-five out of five hundred eighty) were home too. Some of them were rocked over against the wolves, some of them lay where they had died in the snow, but none of that mattered. They couldn't help build the Kingdom, but they could in the last days inherit it in bliss with their kindred around them. They could rest in the assurance that their sacrifices had sanctified them in the eyes of the Most High. Brigham Young preached a sermon in which he told his people that the scattering of those saintly bones by the coyotes meant nothing. They would arise on the Day in a new and shining garment of flesh and be renewed in Heaven along with the Holy City that they never got to see.

In Our Lovely Deseret . . .

ALMOST from the beginning, in spite of Brigham Young's determination to shake the dust of the United States from his feet and leave the mobocrats and Gentiles far behind, Mormon and Gentile were mixed in Salt Lake Valley. The wilderness to which the Saints fled betrayed them. One blow, the Treaty of Guadalupe Hidalgo, put them back in the country they had fled from. Another, the discovery of gold at Sutter's Mill, threw them squarely in the path of empire, and from that moment until the end of the century two ways of life clashed in the stronghold of the Saints. They clashed, and in many ways they still clash, yet in a curious way they were necessary to each other. Emigrants striking for the gold fields were in desperate need of a resting place, a supply point, before attempting the desert by the Mormon Road, and they found at Salt Lake the milk and garden truck and fresh teams they needed. The Mormons, on the other hand, were very poor, short of equipment, short of hard cash with which to buy what they needed in the States, and they found in the gold seekers a lucrative market, a sellers' market. Abhorring the Gentiles, hating them for past persecutions, a world away from them in ideas and ideals, they still could not afford to shut their gates upon them. Some of the Gentiles stayed in the valley, opened stores to get in on the emigrant trade; because they had cash with which to buy in the States, the stocks in their stores were frequently fuller and more varied than those among the Saints, so that even while the Church fought against the infiltration, thundered from the pulpit against the importation of the Devil into Zion, it had to concur in the economic truce that mutual dependency had brought about. Just as it had decided earlier that it was cheaper to feed the Indians than fight them, so it finally decided that it was more profitable to milk the Gentiles than to shut them out.

In effect, it was an armed truce. Gentiles often complained in letters to their home newspapers, or in their published accounts of the journey across the continent, that the Mormons discriminated against strangers, threatened them, impounded their stock and charged them a fee to get it out again, even sometimes murdered them for their wagons and goods. The Mormons on their side protested that the Gentiles were rowdy, dishonest, vicious, and worse; that they tried to corrupt Mormon women, created disturbances, accepted hospitality and later bit the hand that had fed them.

Those difficulties were enhanced by the Federal officials sent to Salt Lake after the designation of the region as the Territory of Utah in 1850. Although Dr. Bernhisel, the Mormon lobbyist in Washington, had succeeded in getting Brigham Young appointed territorial governor, there was a sprinkling of Gentiles among the other officials, so that the political organization of the territory was arrayed against itself just as the economic and social order was. The Mormons had wanted statehood. They tried, as a matter of fact, a half dozen times, from 1849 on, in the hope of relieving themselves of the political camp-followers and carpet-baggers that territorial status forced upon them.

They did not make it until 1896, and then they made it only at the expense of the cherished religious ordinance of plural marriage, and their unsuccessful efforts to get recognition of their claims only added to the antagonism they felt not only against the Gentiles in Utah but against the whole United States. Those hostilities resulted fairly early in two incidents, the Mountain Meadows Massacre and the Mormon War, one tragic and one comic, which brought the difficulties to a head in 1857.

The Mountain Meadows Massacre need only be mentioned in passing, since it is one of the few episodes in Mormon history that is well known outside of Utah, and since Edwin Corle, in the *Desert Country* of this series, has already summarized it with admirable objectivity. It was a hard thing to be objective about at the time. There was little doubt in anyone's mind, whether he was Mormon or Gentile, that the Mormons had stirred up the Indians against the Fancher party of emigrants passing down through southwestern Utah on their way to the coast. There was no doubt that the Indians had run into hot opposition and had been about to give up, and that John D. Lee, Isaac Haight, Philip Klingen Smith, and others of the priesthood in southern Utah had organized an expedition, pretended to come as rescuers, and then massacred all but a handful of children under a flag of truce. It was a bloody and nasty business, outcome of years of bitterness at the Missourians and the murderers of Joseph Smith, capstone to a structure of hatred and misunderstanding that had been building for a long time. The Gentiles immediately assumed that Brigham Young had ordered the extermination of the party; the Mormons, unsure of just how deeply they were involved, kept their mouths shut or blamed the Indians. Besides, they already knew that a punitive expedition was being sent out against the territory by the federal government to "put down insurrection." They were already practically in a state of war with the government without the Mountain Meadows Massacre. They hung together and kept mum. The trouble that a group of fanatic brethren from Cedar City had brought upon the Church was less important than the trouble that the whole Church was in with the government.

That trouble had come on gradually. It was part, actually, of the whole secession problem that was finally solved by the Civil War, and the excuses adduced on both sides were apart from the real issue. The Gentiles picked up polygamy and the un-American priesthood government of the Territory of Utah and clamored for the extirpation of those evils. The Mormons protested against being saddled with unfriendly, incompetent, and immoral federal officials. The real issue was that the Territory of Utah did not wish to be a part of the United States and everybody knew it. But no one would recognize it. Many of the officials and the army officers engaged in putting down the "rebellion" in Utah during 1857 and 1858 rushed four years later to join the Confederacy.

In 1847 Brigham Young had publicly said, "Give me ten years and I shall ask no odds of the United States." That was plain enough. So were the events in Utah during the next ten years. And on July 24, 1857, ten years to the day after Brigham's arrival in Salt Lake Valley, Brigham stood in the "bowery" at the head of Big Cottonwood Canyon, where the Saints were holding a Pioneer Day Celebration, and informed his people that Albert Sidney Johnston was leading an army of several thousand regulars to invade Zion.

Brigham asked no odds. He prepared his people for war.

Later that day, when he asked the ten thousand Saints assembled in the canyon if they would support his measures,
there was not a dissenting voice.

The Mormon War is one of the odd episodes in American history. The United States, mainly because Utah had
had difficulty with its appointed officials and because politicians, in response to popular clamor, had to do something about polygamy, accused the territory of treason and
rebellion. The territory retorted by accusing the United
States of treason for sending an armed expedition against a
peaceful territory. There had been in 1856 a great revival,
a purging, a flood of re-baptisms, among the Saints; they
were united and belligerent, and they still had the Nauvoo
Legion, practically a private army. They threw up breast-
works in Echo Canyon, sent instructions to all the officers
of the Legion, warned the rank and file Saints to be ready
to burn down their houses and move at an hour's notice.
Brigham promised that if the soldiers ever reached the
valley they would find nothing but ashes.

It was not much of a war, and what there was of it the
Mormons won. Their guerrillas under Captain Lot Smith
and other Nauvoo Legion officers drove off the army's
stock, burned its supply wagons and sent the wagoners hik-
ing back toward the Missouri, delayed the invader until he
dug in near Fort Bridger and postponed the invasion until
better weather and safer supply lines were forthcoming.
There was not a man killed by gunfire, hardly a shot fired
except by guerrillas to scare the army's mules into stam-
peding, but the end of 1857 found the Mormons still defiant behind the barrier of the Wasatch.

By spring, when real shooting might have developed, the
situation had changed. Governor Cumming, the recent ap-
pointee to Brigham's old position as head of the territorial

government, had joined Johnston in Wyoming. He, as well as Delaney R. Eckles, the new chief justice, and P. K. Dotson, the new United States marshal, favored a conciliatory course, using the military only to enforce the laws. Johnston, irritated by the lack of success which had attended the first act of the invasion, and even more irritated by the ironic gift of salt which Brigham Young had sent to the marooned and half-starved soldiers in Camp Scott, was for marching in and subduing the impudent Mormons with a strong hand. At that juncture there arrived at Camp Scott an old friend of the Mormons, Colonel Thomas Kane, who had come all the way around by Panama and out from California to reason with both Brigham and the army. Eventually he and Cumming promoted something like a peaceable settlement. Brigham called back his people, already in exodus deeper into the wilderness, and canceled the scorched earth policy he had ordered. He allowed the soldiers to march into the territory under the rather humiliating terms that they would establish their quarters at least forty miles from Salt Lake City, in order to prevent incidents between the soldiers and the Saints. Then, according to one report, he took a contract to furnish lumber for the building of Camp Floyd, southwest of Salt Lake, and cleaned up fifty thousand dollars on it. Even if the Gentiles were dragoons, it was more profitable to milk them than to keep them out.

That little "war" and the policing of Utah by United States troops did a number of things in Mormondom. Though it did not in the least put a stop to the bickering and jockeying of the warring factions, and in fact increased them by giving federal appointees an opportunity of calling on the troops for every conceivable reason, even the holding of federal court, it did establish an outsider in the

Governor's chair which until that time had been occupied
by Brigham Young. That is, it split the government, making the people technically responsible to a lay government
while in fact they were still ruled by the priesthood with
Brigham at their head. Until Johnston's army, ecclesiastical and political government had been virtually one, and
long after the Mormon War isolated communities went on
as usual dispensing secular justice through the bishops'
courts and the Quorums of the Priesthood. In Salt Lake
City, after 1858, those two kinds of government were increasingly divided, and just after the outbreak of the Civil
War three years later the insistence of the Saints on clinging to their theocracy brought into being one of the
strangest pieces of political machinery the country ever
saw—a ghost state with a ghost government.

The original petition to Congress for the admission of
the State of Deseret in 1849 had claimed all the territory
from the crest of the Rockies to the crest of the Sierra and
from the Oregon line to the Mexican border, with a long
strip of the Pacific Coast near San Diego thrown in for
good measure. The Congressional action granting territorial, not state, government whittled off the whole southern
section and made it into the Territory of New Mexico, and
another bill passed at the same time took away the seacoast
and gave it to the new state of California. That was only
the first of a number of reductions in the area the Mormons claimed. In 1861 the creation of Nevada and Colorado snipped great blocks off both east and west, and another slice was taken to be given to Wyoming in the year
1868. In 1864 Nevada got another strip, in 1866 still another. The Mormon War, moreover, had weakened the
Mormon claim to many of the outposts, since upon notice
of the coming of Johnston's army Brigham had called in

the San Bernardino residents, the Carson Valley Mission; Lemhi and Las Vegas had already folded. Forts Bridger and Supply had been burned by Mormon guerrillas before Johnston stuggled into the Green River Valley.

Those outposts lost in 1857, as well as the slices taken off by Congressional action in the next few years, were never regained, but the Mormons were a long time admitting that they were gone. They had been the first Anglo-American farmers in all that country—in Utah, Arizona, Idaho, Wyoming, Nevada, New Mexico. For a time in 1846 and 1847 they had made San Francisco practically a Mormon town. By 1851 they had had more than five hundred of their number firmly planted in San Bernardino. And unless they were called in by specific Church order, they were the kind to stick. They could colonize and make a living out of ground that an ordinary frontier farmer would have scorned to camp for the night on. And they resented the deliberate chiseling off of sections of land which they had first broken. In 1862, when they held a third constitutional convention in the hope of sliding into statehood on the wave of agitation to admit non-slave states, they were jubilantly proclaiming that the United States was doomed to destroy itself, and they were grimly determined to keep up their claim to all the empire they had founded. The government of the State of Deseret, outlawed since 1850 when the territorial government was set up, was quietly revived, and for eight years, without legal status, without recognition, without a fifth of its claimed territory, with only a nucleus of its claimed constituents, it went on functioning under the rose.

According to Dale Morgan, who has made the most extended study of that ghost government, it was organized and kept in operation probably as a gesture, as a secret bond to hold the Saints together and remind them that one day they would have their rights and the fulfillment of prophecy. Perhaps Brigham meant it as a mark of respect to the prophecies of Joseph Smith; there is some reason to suppose that Brigham himself expected the Lord to restore to the Saints their plundered lands. The name "Deseret" was a symbol in the Mormon Country. It was a *Book of Mormon* word, signifying "honey-bee." It symbolized the tradition and the dream, the laboriousness and the golden hope of final heavenly culmination, that the Saints brought into the Great Basin. And by Mormon reasoning there was sound prophetic basis for the feeling among the rank and file that the long struggle for autonomy would soon be successful. Joseph Smith's most famous prophecy had foreseen war between the states, beginning in South Carolina. After the states had destroyed each other the Millennium and the gathering-up of Zion could take place in the true spot approved by God, in Jackson County, Missouri.

For those reasons, the ghost of government kept alive in Utah from 1862 to 1870 represented more than mere defiance, more than a game of outwitting the United States. It represented the tradition, the preservation of the sacred fire, the mystic and under-cover unity of the Lord's people regardless of political sub-division.

In practice, as in theory, the ghost government was insubstantial. Because it had no legal jurisdiction over the land and people it claimed, its acts were as ghostly as the body which made them. The membership of the legislature of the State of Deseret was man for man the same as that of the legislature of the territorial government. All, naturally, were good Mormons, since the Gentiles could muster only a handful of votes. They were elected separately, in a special Church election; they met a day or two after the closing of the regular assembly and passed the same laws—only they applied those laws to the whole Mormon Empire instead of to the depleted region known as Utah. And the executives and judges were not the political jackanapes sent out from Washington. They were the high priests of the Church. Brigham had had to step down as territorial governor to make way for appointees more amenable to instructions from Washington, but he never really stepped down. He merely stepped back out of sight, and all during the life of the ghost government he was the ghost governor, just as in fact he was absolute dictator through his churchly power. Mormondom suffered the forms of territorial government to be put upon it, but those forms were like an entirely unnecessary belt worn by a person whose pants are already held up by suspenders.

Perhaps it would be more accurate to call Deseret a shadow government rather than a ghost, because though it itself was powerless, the thing which cast it was not. That thing was the theocracy, which through the fifties and sixties was the most potent and absolute government any part of the United States ever saw. Though it had many similarities to the theocratic government of early New England, it went further, because it had more enemies than Indians and a few scattered heretics to contend with. It was in constant conflict with both the people and the government of the United States, and it developed its methods accordingly. Like everything the Mormons did, it was done thoroughly.

Put it this way: Within the United States, almost a hundred years ago, existed a dictatorship as complete in its power as any in contemporary Europe. Though it lacked

the ruthless aggressiveness and the arrogance of the dictatorships we know, and though its aims, being intimately
bound up with a Christian faith, were in no way comparable to those of the dictatorships of our day, it never-
theless functioned efficiently in every walk of life, and in
the course of its history picked up about every practical
trick that authoritarianism ever knew. I say that without
intent to prejudice the Mormon Church or to question
its loyalty. All this is history, and dead; the bitterness that
once adhered to the Mormon question is sweetened and
forgotten in all but the most unreasonable breasts, and
the methods that the Mormons developed to defend and
project themselves have with time dwindled to a few surviving habits of superficial importance. Still, some of those
habits are striking, and they all look back to the system
which began under the Prophet Joseph and reached its
full power in the first generation of the Mormon occu-
pancy of the Great Basin.

The Mormons were never, in their Church organization or in their social patterns, what we think of as democratic. They were a sociological island of fanatic believers
dedicated to a creed that the rest of America thought either
vicious or mad. They were led by a prophet whose word
was irrevocable law, even if that word transgressed the
laws or the moral taboos of the country at large. Their
loyalty, in other words, was first of all to the Church and
the Prophet, its leader, and that unswerving loyalty gave
rise to a theocratic and patriarchal form of government.
We are so accustomed to use the word fascist nowadays to
designate that particular frame of mind that we are likely
to think of early Mormonism as a proto-fascist society. It
was no more fascist than communist, but it was authoritarian. The ultimate power rested not with the people but

with the priesthood who promulgated and interpreted the direct word of God. And the word of God had sometimes to be promulgated by coercion and defended with force.

Here was a group of people full of fanatic zeal, zealously willing to submerge their individualism for the good of the society. Here was a private army of considerable size, known first as the Host of Israel and later re-organized in Nauvoo as the Nauvoo Legion—an army trained and equipped and ready at the word of the potentate. Though the Legion was technically part of the Illinois State Militia, it was in fact Joseph's own private force.

Here also was a secret police as effective and terrifying as any dictator could wish. Though the Church has persistently denied that the secret group of avengers organized by Brother Avard in Missouri ever had any official sanction, and has insisted that the group broke up almost at once because of the members' horror at Avard's illegal plans, there is no doubt that in Far West, Missouri, the formation of the Host of Israel was paralleled by the formation of the secret police known at first as the Daughters of Zion. ("Arise and thresh, O Daughters of Zion; for I will make thy horn iron and thy hoofs brass; and thou shalt beat in pieces many people; and I will consecrate their gain unto the Lord.") That body, led by such redoubtable champions as Orrin Porter Rockwell and Bill Hickman, was both a personal bodyguard for Joseph Smith and a kind of secret task force. The Gentiles, from that day to this, have blown up its exploits into ogrish proportions, but there is sufficient evidence to indicate that the activities of the avengers did not stop with the Missouri troubles, and that the denials of the Church leave a good deal unexplained. Certainly the Gentiles *thought* there was such an outfit; under the names of

Destroying Angels and Sons of Dan, or Danites ("Dan shall be a serpent by the way, an adder in the path that biteth the horse's heels, so that his rider shall fall backward") it was known and feared for a long time through the intermountain West.

It serves no purpose to irritate old sores and insist that the Danites upon higher orders eliminated many an enemy of Mormonism, and it makes no great difference whether the unpleasant but necessary jobs of secret police work were done by a formal organization, as the *Confessions* of John D. Lee attest, or by a few handpicked strong-arm men. But it would be bad history to pretend that there were no holy murders in Utah and along the trails to California, that there was no saving of the souls of sinners by the shedding of their blood during the "blood atonement" revival of 1856, that there were no mysterious disappearances of apostates and offensive Gentiles. Perhaps even those incidents were purely unofficial and spontaneous acts of devout Mormons, the Mormon equivalent of lynch law and vigilantism, and reveal not a deliberate plan of the priesthood but unbridled zeal among the Mormon people. The massacre of the Fancher party at Mountain Meadows certainly seems to have been undertaken in that mood. But Lee's *Confessions,* the autobiography of Bill Hickman, and the body of incriminating evidence against Port Rockwell, as well as a whole flood of anti-Mormon books of the period, seem to make a fairly sound documentation of the activities of the Danites.

No religious group, especially if it is persecuted, is likely to escape its period of terrorism, and no revolutionary group either. Mormonism was both fanatically faithful and revolutionary. It was furthermore a product of the American frontier, never notable for its tenderness about the shedding of human blood. The objections of the Gentiles—and they were loud—were stimulated partly by fear, partly by political chicanery, and partly by the fact that the Danites, when they murdered anyone, murdered in cold blood, for a purpose, perhaps on orders. That seems a logical conclusion of group psychology. When you work not for yourself but for a cause, you have no right to kill for anything but the cause. Among themselves, the Mormons were always an extremely law-abiding people, even by Gentile admission. To their enemies they were sometimes a scourge.

But private armies and sworn loyalties and an instrument of vengeance in the Sons of Dan were not the only tools of Mormon authoritarianism. The Church had its symbols, with all their emotional connotations, from the mystic embroideries on the temple garments to the beehive symbol of state industriousness. It had its uniform, the symbolic underwear known as "garments," worn by all married Saints, and so sacred that a really pious Mormon is supposed never to let his body be quite out of contact with them, even, according to satiric Gentiles, in the bathtub. It had its controlled press, its official organs of news and opinion like the *Deseret News* and the *Millennial Star*, both of them extremely long-lived publications. The *News*, published in Salt Lake, has been going since 1850, the *Millennial Star*, published in England for the benefit of Saints abroad, since 1840, and their policy as Church organs has not changed materially in all that time.

Mormonism had its encirclement myth and its *Drang nach Osten;* it believed that the Saints were a chosen and superior people. (It would be a feeble faith that did not think that of itself.) It had its typical undemocratic elections, yes-no elections sustaining or refusing to sustain the names proposed by the Quorum of the Priesthood. Within the Church the members have never had even the right of nomination, and even yet, at April or October Conference, it is possible to go into the tabernacle in Salt Lake when an election is in progress and get a shock from seeing the forests of hands, ten thousand in one motion, go up on every name. It takes courage for a Mormon to dissent. One gentleman who rose in the tabernacle a generation ago and asked for an accounting of Church funds was unceremoniously thrown out and disfellowshipped. No accounting was ever made.

Authoritarian methods could be tracked down to tinier and tinier details: self-sufficiency, barter system, regimentation, group responses, discrimination against hated or feared races, youth movement, the dispatch of agents (missionaries) to spread the doctrines in far lands, the belief that ultimately the faith will inherit the whole earth. During the course of the years the authority of the priesthood has been somewhat weakened; the secret ballot, superseding the Mormon signed ballot which allowed the priesthood to make sure at any time how any given member voted, has made for considerably less unanimity in political elections, and the infiltration of Gentiles into the larger cities and towns and into the mining and industrial areas has brought in influences which often nullify the pressure of the Church. Generally speaking, it is the country Mormon who can be depended upon to do as he is told, and the so-called "Mormon counties" which can be predicted without recourse to the Gallup poll.

Those Mormons obey because their whole habit and training of life predisposes them to obedience. They are no people regimented against their wills into an iron-clad system. They will defend their system militantly, because by and large it has been good to them. By and large it has been responsible, despite its assumption of power over the individual. Call it a benevolent despotism. It is not a democracy, even yet, except in terms of state and national politics, and its essentially fundamentalist hostility to free thought has driven a good many of its sons and daughters into something like exile, but it cannot be called either deplorable or unwholesome any more than any other fundamentalist faith can. After all, it satisfies its people, or most of them.

The ghostly government of the State of Deseret still wields its unpublicized but effectual sway over three quarters of a million farmers and merchants and professional men and laborers in the Mormon Country. Even when the Mormons built ghosts, they built for the ages.

Shibboleth . . .

𝖽 𝟪𝝏 𝟥 ꡏꡕꡋ

IF you had been a child in a Mormon school in the eighteen sixties, you would have been required to read that. You would even have been required to know that it meant "I see a cat," and to write some sort of reply in kind. You might have nudged the tow-headed girl ahead of you and scribbled on your slate, with the tenderest school-days' shyness, 𝖽 ꡂꡒ ꡗꡜ , and been thumped by the teacher, not for the orthographic crime you had committed, but for inattentiveness.

And if you had been an adult Mormon in those years, a recently-arrived convert of foreign extraction, you would have been studying in the *Deseret News* articles in these eye-tangling chicken tracks, with directions for making them give up their horrid secret. You would probably have been told in Sunday Meeting, if you hadn't already heard it from the tabernacle pulpit, that the English language you had been painfully acquiring since your landfall in America was a linguistic mistake of the first magnitude, a morass of unpronounced and unpronounceable consonants, sneaky diphthongs, c's that ought to be k's or s's, th's that might be either hissed or gurgled, gh's that might be anything from a grunt to complete silence. You new

100

proselytes, Danes and Swedes and Norwegians and Englishmen and Germans, would have been urged to study the
Deseret Alphabet, a magic instrument by means of which
all this confusion could be cleared up at a stroke and your
path to linguistic felicity made straight and easy. It would
be awkward if, in the imminent gathering-up of Zion, none
of the newly-arrived Saints could read or spell the language
that Zion would speak. Devote yourself, therefore, to the
study of the new alphabet, an invariable system of characters whose sounds were always the same, as inflexible as
numbers. You could always depend on 2 to mean 2. You
could also depend on ♉ to mean the sound "k."

It is an odd spectacle to see the Saints, six years after
their occupation of Salt Lake Valley, isolated from the
world, scrabbling for a meager living in the sagebrush,
fighting crickets and grasshoppers and locusts and drouth
and mountain fever—a poor and uneducated people faced
with a harsh environment and an unbroken land—busying
themselves with so academic a problem as the inadequacies
of the English language. It is so bizarre, on the face of it,
that historians and travelers were led to make guesses at
obscure politico-theological reasons behind the invention
of the new orthography for Mormonism. They guessed,
among other things, that the Mormons wanted a secret language, to prevent their blood-curdling records from being
looked over by unfriendly strangers. They guessed that the
Mormon leaders wanted to keep their flocks from the profane literature of the world. They hinted at dark practices
that were best recorded in invisible ink in an exclusive
code.

Actually, although all of those reasons have some weight,
the explanation for the invention of the Deseret Alphabet
is neither so darkly sectarian nor, on the surface, so inter-

esting. But from another point of view it is more interesting than if it had represented Mormon abdication from the United States and the secular government and orthography of man. Like the ghost government of the State of Deseret, like the careful and Heaven-dictated formula for the Mormon village, like the burning sense of dedication and the Canaan-dream which made the Mormons create city after city, community after community, and bear up under their Biblical wandering through the wilderness, the Deseret Alphabet fits the pattern of the up-building of Zion, the preparation for the Millennium. And like most of the millennial activities of the Saints, the idea was not a Mormon invention. It was something in the air, something caught from the religious and intellectual revivalism of the middle nineteenth century.

When Brigham Young got interested in the reform of the English language, and suggested it to the regents of the University of Deseret—a pitiful little clot of basic learning with an elaborate organization of boards and advisers and aims—he was completely in character as a nineteenth century reform leader. He was more than an ecclesiastic; he was part of the whole revivalist movement which looked for the reform of the churches, the individual, the nation, which advocated the purging of the salt of the earth in preparation for the last days and the inheritance of bliss. It would have been odd if language had been overlooked during the reform agitation that flowed through the nineteenth century. As a matter of fact, it had been started on the sawdust trail to redemption about the time that Joseph Smith was locating the Golden Plates and laying the cornerstones of the Church of Jesus Christ of Latter-day Saints. Pitman's *Stenographic Soundhand* had caused a stir in 1837. His *Phonographic Journal* had appeared in 1842.

Shorthand and phonetic spelling reform were in the wind, first in England and then in America, where Benn Pitman established a shorthand school in the forties. Five years after the board of regents of the University of Deseret met and plotted an alphabet in which every sound should have its invariable symbol, Graham's phonetic alphabet was due to appear.

This was a wind that blew not only from England to America, but all the way across the plains to a desert valley hidden among the mountains. The Saints, no matter how hard they tried to escape, were linked with the world and the world's concerns.

They had more reasons for a phonetic alphabet than some. Their great floods of proselytes came from England and Scotland and Wales, but there were many from the Scandinavian countries, and some from almost every corner of the globe. The English converts were ill-educated, the others were almost without English. The amalgamation of the diverse nationalities was a problem, and the difficulties of English spelling and pronunciation were a hurdle. Small wonder that Brigham should adopt the current methods of simplification and purification. A private alphabet, moreover, would be one more tie to bind the Saints into a group. Brigham was statesman enough to know the welding power of language. There was probably also, as the *Deseret News* suggested some years after the beginning of the experiment, a feeling that the "yellow-covered" literature of the Gentile world might be thus kept from the hands of young Saints. And there was undoubtedly, behind the initial interest and the practical incentives, the obscure drive of the millennial preparation.

The alphabet that the regents devised and Brigham Young approved is a curious hodge-podge. The British world-traveler Captain Richard Burton, he who had pried into the holy mysteries of Mecca and who tried unsuccessfully to wheedle out of Brigham a look at the Mormon Endowment House, noticed the similarity of the alphabet to Pitman's symbols. The historian Bancroft thought he saw similarities to the "reformed Egyptian" characters of the Golden Plates, a page of which Joseph Smith had reproduced in *The Pearl of Great Price*. An eastern editor, commenting with kindly interest on the linguistic experimentation going on in Zion, was reminded of the Ethiopian alphabet in the back of Webster's Dictionary.

Anyone trying to track down the sources of the Deseret characters is due for a painful and probably fruitless search. The "reformed Egyptian" is a blind alley—no parallels exist there. There are specifically eight resemblances to Pitman characters, but the symbols never represent the same sounds as they do in Pitman. And there is a resemblance or two, perhaps accidental, with the Ethiopian alphabet, which is also purely phonetic. But the net result of scratching among the hieroglyphics is the conviction that the Deseret Alphabet is an eclectic job, the handiwork mainly of one George Watt, stenographer and secretary, who had introduced Pitman's phonography to the Saints in Nauvoo and had been an official Church reporter ever since. With the help of Parley P. Pratt, W. W. Phelps, and other regents, Watt made up an alphabet of phonetic symbols, thirty-eight of them, and presented it to the board.

It was no mere speculative gesture the Mormons were making. They seldom stooped to idle speculation. When they took up speculation it was with a practical end in view. The end in this case was the introduction of the new orthography in the schools of the territory. In 1855 the legislature dutifully voted an appropriation of $2,500 for the casting of a font of type. The discussion that had been going on about the project in the *Deseret News* took on a tone of solid and progressive optimism. Arguments about the relative merits of the phonographic and phonetic styles of language reform gave way to exhortations that one simple, standard language be adopted against the imminent gathering-in, one orthography be readied for the coming crisis.

The alphabet had a hectic and interrupted existence. The troubles with the federal government, the Mormon War, the squabbles with territorial officials, constantly interrupted the reform movement. Through 1859 and 1860 Brigham Young's journals were being kept in the alphabet, as well as some of the Church records. A first and a second reader were printed in 1868, and the publication of the *Book of Mormon* in Deseret symbols was projected, though it was not to be accomplished until 1869.

But the children and the teachers complained. The flat monotony of the tailless characters made hard reading. Most Mormon kids were not vitally interested in schooling during those years, anyway, and the teachers were too often either amateur volunteers or underpaid starvelings. Reformed English practically died on the vine, in spite of Brigham Young's example and encouragement, though one product of those years has preserved it for posterity in numismatic collections. Gold coins made in the valley from California dust in 1860 exhibited a crouching lion and around him in Deseret Alphabet characters the legend, "Holiness to the Lord." In that one gold piece are shown two strands of the Mormon bond with other revivalist and reform movements. The alphabet comes from the same climate of perfectionism that produced the shorthand and phonography of Pitman and Graham; the legend is the old battlecry of the hell-fire evangelist Finney which he carried into Oberlin on banners 9 feet high in 1835.

Though the alphabet struggled through the later sixties, there were signs of dissolution in the 1870's. Some of the priesthood, still sold on the idea of a perfected language, proposed that Pitman's system be substituted for the cumbersome local alphabet, and it was voted to publish the *Book of Mormon* in Pitman symbols. Still, the priesthood and the regents decided that for local consumption Deseret would do, and plans were made to go ahead with it. But Orson Pratt, on his way to England to arrange the *Book of Mormon* translation into Pitman, was stopped by news of Brigham Young's death, and with the passing of the Lion of the Lord all orthographic tinkering died quietly. Utah was now linked by rail and by telegraph with the rest of the world. It was apparent that the gathering-in of Zion was not going to be immediate. There would be time for foreign converts to learn the usual English, and there were other ways of uniting the Mormon people than making them struggle through a difficult alteration of their language habits.

Like most of the practical methods the Saints took to prepare for the millennium, simplified English got postponed and ultimately forgotten. Few copies of the three books which composed its entire literature even exist now. Few people even in Utah ever heard of the Deseret Alphabet. It is a collector's item, an artifact from a prehistoric barrow, a relic of the time when Manifest Destiny and the Hope of the Kingdom washed up together on the shore of the West, and Manifest Destiny, with history and probability and industrial and numerical strength on its side, swallowed the smaller wave. Until the expectation of glory comes again, the English language will have to depend on I. A. Richards and the multiplying semasiologists for its reconstruction, and the perfect world will wait not upon the millennium but upon the triumph of Marx or Machiavelli or Henry Luce, prophets of another dispensation.

Arcadian Village . . .

ARCADIA is a hard place to find, but if you drive down Highway 89 between Bryce Canyon and Zion National Park you will pass the place where it used to be in the 1870's and 80's. It doesn't look like Arcadia now. It looks like a pleasant little Mormon town strung along the valley of the Virgin River, sleeping peacefully under its red cliffs, shaded by its maples and mulberries and smoke trees, surrounded by its gardens and orchards. It is a village of between four and five hundred people hardly distinguishable from dozens of other Mormon villages. It is a nice town to stop at for a coke on a hot day, and in summer it smells of ripe peaches. But Arcadia? Not quite.

As a matter of fact, it never did look like Arcadia from the outside. It looked like a rather flimsy fort made out of deal boards during most of the eleven years of its heyday. But it came closer to being the perfect village than any the Mormons ever founded; it wedded utopian economics to millennial theocracy and got a result which for a long time (as utopian societies go) looked like the realization of man's ancient dream. It eliminated completely the fear of poverty and want; it furnished to all its members the amplitude of food, shelter, and clothing whose possession, according to some ways of thinking, ought to remove every source of human quarrelsomeness. It managed to bring its several hundred members into a communism of goods, labor, religion, and recreation such as the world has seen only in a few places and for very short times, and to do it without loss of gaiety or good nature. The life was strenuous, but it was also wholesome; it brought content. The number of people from that town who lived past eighty is good statistical evidence that heaven-on-earth does not breed the will to die.

They called it Orderville, not because of the meticulous orderliness of its community life, but because Joseph Smith, in an early revelation, had dreamed of an ideal social and economic system which he called the United Order of Enoch. All property was to be consecrated to common use, each man holding a stewardship for as much as he needed to support his family, and each putting his surplus back in for the benefit of all. That first United Order was put into practice in Kirtland, Ohio, and in Missouri, but it had to be abandoned after a short trial, partly because the hostility of the surrounding Gentiles interfered with economic experimentation, partly because there were no leaders strong and capable enough to hold together the Missouri Order when Joseph Smith had headquarters far back in Ohio, partly because the rich hung back from consecrating their property, and the poor flocked in in the hope of getting an inheritance. Joseph reluctantly put the idea away, telling his people that they were not yet ready for the practice of that divine institution, but that the day would come when it would be practiced in its fullness.

Brigham Young never attempted to re-establish the United Order on Joseph Smith's terms. To support the priesthood, who work in the Mormon Church without pay, but whose families sometimes needed support when the head was away on a mission, Joseph had instituted the "lesser law" of tithing, and Brigham was content to leave the Church resting on those foundations until the influx of Gentiles, the seizing of much of the merchandising business by Gentiles and apostate Mormons, and the panic of 1873 forced him into economic tinkering. Then, to whip the Gentiles and to stir up the weakening solidarity of his people, he turned both to co-operatives and to Christian communism. He and other Church leaders organized vigorously, beginning in St. George, which was by then a kind of "winter capital" of the Mormon Country, and building up local Orders all the way up the valleys.

In most towns the second United Order succeeded no better than the first one had at Kirtland and Independence. Many Mormons, especially in the northern towns, had grown wealthy; they were reluctant to endanger their prosperity by pooling their property. And for some reason —perhaps because he himself was dubious about the reaction of the leaders, and meant the Order only for the rank and file—Brigham did not insist upon communist economics as a divine command, and he never abrogated the "lesser law" of tithing, which according to the Prophet Joseph would be given up when the Saints were ready for the real Saintly way. The United Order, for Brigham, was an economic expedient, and though many communities obediently tried it, some with great enthusiasm, there was not the zeal that theocratic compulsion might have brought. The Gentiles, moreover, fought both the United Order and the co-operative Church stores which immediately preceded it, because such a Mormon coalition meant the eventual strangling of all Gentile enterprise. Zion's Cooperative Mercantile Institution, formed in 1868 to break the hold of Gentiles on the trade of the territory, did fifteen million dollars' worth of business in its first five years. After 1873, also, it acted as a covering institution for local industry, promoting goods produced under the revived Mormon program of self-sufficiency. And the Z.C.M.I. sold shares of its stock to no one who was not in good standing in the Church, paid up in his tithing and possessed of a good moral character. It was almost as hard to buy into the Z.C.M.I. as it is to get into the Temple. No wonder the Gentiles fought it. No wonder they fought the United Order, which was even more closed to outsiders and which rendered whole towns ineligible as buyers of Gentile goods.

It was not, however, the Gentile opposition and ridicule that broke up the second United Order in most towns. It was dissension from within, signs of a cracking in the insularity of the Mormon population. Both rank and file Mormons and Gentiles noticed that the Church leaders, for all their talking, did not come forward in any numbers to consecrate their property to the Lord, or even to Brother Brigham as trustee-in-trust for the Lord. Imperceptibly, year by year, their wealth had grown, and even though they had followed Brigham's advice and stayed away from the gold fields, they liked well enough the prosperity that a generation in the valley had given them. They stalled, and for once the small Mormon caught on and stalled too. In most towns the Order lasted only a year or two before bickerings, recrimination, bad management, or anger over imperfectly-kept accounts broke it up.

But in the remote settlements, especially in the southwestern part of Utah, in the corner of Nevada adjoining, and in the pioneer colonies founded a little later along the Little Colorado and the San Juan, the United Order had a fair trial. Almost invariably, in settlements where all were poor, it worked. In Orderville it lasted with conspicuous success for eleven years, and hung on in altered and diluted form for some time after that. It is only necessary to look at the history of the families who settled the town to see why it was likely that co-operation would be taken more seriously, practiced more diligently, and clung to more tenaciously among them than among other groups.

For one thing, they had been tried over and over again in the faith. Some of them had been involved in almost every hegira the Mormon Church ever made. They had lost their property and even some of their friends and relatives in the Missouri troubles, and had been driven back to Illinois. They had built in Nauvoo and been chased out again, across to Winter Quarters and on over the plains to Salt Lake Valley. They had built again in the valley, and at Brigham's orders many of them had uncomplainingly pulled their stakes to go and colonize other settlements along the west slope of the Wasatch. In 1865 they had been called again, this time to the Muddy Mission in what is now Nevada.

They were not pioneers of the itchy-footed and free-elbowed sort. They had no claustrophobia when the population got to be ten to the square mile. After all their wanderings they wanted to settle down, but they did not complain. For the third or fourth time they sold their land, turned their little wealth into seed wheat and plows and covered wagons, packed up the flour and ammunition and machinery that Brigham instructed them to take, and started out. There was no gold field in their mind's eye, not even a land overflowing with milk and honey. They were headed for a desert outpost where the chances were fifty-fifty they would starve to death.

Still, they went, and they went singing. The towns they

founded, the Moapa Valley towns of Overton and St. Thomas and St. Joseph, later became famous for the quality of the garden truck they produced, but the pioneers found them no Canaan. The Indians were inquisitive and bothersome and light-fingered, the insects and the drouth and the uncertainty of irrigation were trials. And almost as soon as they had established themselves on the Muddy and become a way station on the Mormon Road to California, they found themselves cut off from their roots. The Moapa Valley was in 1866 taken away from Utah and added to Nevada. Nevada levied taxes; the Saints protested that they were paying their taxes in Utah. It was four years before an official survey definitely established the line, and the taxes owed to Nevada were four years behind.

The colonists appealed to Brigham to be released from their mission. If the railroad had not come, if the possibility of holding the empire's corridor to the sea had still been open, if the Colorado River route for bringing in supplies and converts had not faded out, Brigham would probably have counseled them to stay. But Brigham's plans had changed. The direction of planned settlement had shifted toward the Bear Lake country and southern Idaho. So Brigham advised them to abandon their villages and come back.

Now for the fourth or fifth time they gave up what they had seized from the desert. Some of them, worn out, trailed back to their old homes in the valleys. But two hundred of them went, again on Brigham's suggestion, to Long Valley on the Virgin River, where they re-settled the town of Mt. Carmel, abandoned in 1866 because of trouble with the Navajo.

They were not even yet through moving. They had been at Mt. Carmel four years when Brigham instituted the

United Order. Most of them wanted the Order, welcomed
it. A good many less-seasoned settlers in the town did not.
In the end, to avoid a break-up before the program could
get well started, the bulk of the Muddy settlers and others
in agreement with them picked up and moved two miles
and a half up the canyon to found an entirely new town
on communist principles. They had suffered and sacrificed
too much to be fiddling away their time in disputes with
their neighbors. They were the shock-troops of Zion, and
they had taken a beating in the Lord's name for a long
time—thirty years, some of them. They had, without their
own knowledge, done their archaeological duty on the
Muddy, leaving their town of St. Thomas to be drowned
under Lake Mead and preserved in the ultimate sandstone
along with the lost pueblo of the Ho-ho-kim. They did
their sociological duty at Orderville, carrying to its logical
extreme the group psychology of Mormonism. They lived
their doctrine in its fullness; by one means or another, the
work of their hands was marked for immortality.

If anyone had been mad enough to ride down Long Valley in the late seventies or eighties before five o'clock in
the morning he would have found, quite naturally, that
Arcadia slept. The sun comes fairly late over the walls of
the canyon, and before sunrise the valley lies in a clear
gray light so transparent that every leaf on the river cottonwoods is distinct, the timbered hillsides are sharp-edged
and shadowless. The wind has not yet begun to stir.

The bottom is lush with orchards and fields, green with
that vivid and almost unbelievable green observable only
in places where vegetation is a lucky local accident. But
the town is a disappointment. A high board fence encloses
a block of land thirty rods square. The only break in the

wall is a gate on the south side. Inside the enclosure, the place improves, though it is still curiously like a barracks. Along east, north, and west is a solid row of shanties, their high blank ends forming the outside wall of the town, their inner ends fronting on a wide sidewalk shaded by maples, mulberries, poplars, boxelders, tamarisks. In the center of the court a larger building, twenty-five by forty feet, lies down behind a high flagpole as if tethered to it. For all the regimented look of the place, it seems peaceful in the gray light. Let it sleep, this hollow square that resembles a tourist cottage camp before the earliest tourists are awake. It is only five o'clock, after all.

But out of the door of one of the shanties comes a large man with a cornet in his hand. He glances at the floating scarves of cloud over the east rim, cocks his eye at the scarred hillside above the town, spits in the dust, and puts the horn to his lips. This is Thomas Robertson, the blacksmith, the official dawn rooster, and his cock-crow is a Mormon hymn, "O Ye Mountains High." He blows not only loudly but with a certain sedate enjoyment, and when he has finished he blows air through his horn and wiggles the keys and goes back inside.

Within a few minutes people are stirring. A handful of girls and another handful of women hurry across the square and disappear into the central building tethered to the flagpole. The building stretches itself and wakes. Its breath goes straight up into the air. All along the rows of shanties men, women, and children appear. Men and boys in gray homespun and floppy straw hats and heavy cowhide shoes cut through the gate and around to the north side, where the corrals and chicken coops are. A woman emerges to hang a half dozen diaper cloths on the line between her shanty and the next. Down in one corner a girl is singing, continuing the hymn with which Thomas Robertson awoke the town:

> *Oh, Zion, dear Zion! Land of the free,*
> *Now my own mountain home*
> *Unto thee I have come. . . .*

There is a buzzing, a preparatory hum, throughout the village, like the hum you hear when you put your ear to a beehive. There are greetings, windy yawns, snatches of laughter. Out of one door bursts a boy with another boy chasing him. Staggering with laughter, he circles a smoke tree and tries to cut back, but his pursuer catches him, and they wrestle. They lie on the ground pounding each other perfunctorily, they roll aside and rest, they rise to hands and knees and go after each other again like a couple of pups, rolling in the dust. A woman calls them sharply from inside.

By seven o'clock there are people who are already through with their morning chores, and who hang around as if waiting for something. Promptly at seven it comes. Thomas Robertson steps to his door again and blows another hymn, "Do What Is Right, Let the Consequence Follow." Nobody worries much about the consequence. What is right, at that hour, is breakfast. They break in hurrying queues toward the central dining hall. Robertson, without waiting to blow air through his horn, hangs it up and ties into the line.

Three rows of tables stretch the length of the dining room. It is rather like an immense boarding house, the plates turned neatly over the knives and forks and spoons. There are no tablecloths or napkins, but the wood of the table is scoured soft and smooth and white. The Bishop, Thomas Chamberlain, waits until the room is quiet and then offers prayer. One more preliminary, the hymn "Lord, We Come Before Thee Now," and the last hurdle is cleared. The plates are turned over, the five cooks in the kitchen begin ladling out the food, the six girl waitresses carry it in.

The waitresses do their work quickly and with seriousness, especially the three younger ones, eleven or twelve years old, to whom it is a sign of growing up to be admitted as junior waitresses. People eat fast. Do what is right, let the consequence follow. There is work to be done. They push back by couples and threes and clear out. Eventually Auntie Harmon, who is childless and hence is put in charge of the whole swarming multitude of children, gets the place empty and calls the kids. They come in a rush, duck their noses briefly toward their plates, and fall to. When they are done it is their duty to go up and say, "Please, Auntie Harmon, I'm done," and she will say, "Well, get along to your mother then." Sometimes a boy, excited because today a bunch of them are to be admitted to the garden for gooseberry picking, bolts out the door still chewing, pokes his head back to choke out a strangled "Please, I'm done," and vanishes.

The waitresses lug the dishes back to the kitchen for the cooks to wash, scrub up the tables and benches, dump clean white sand on the floor and scour it around, sweep it up again. (Soap is too precious to be wasted on floors.) An hour before lunch is ready, they are through, and go out in a giggling, secretive group to pick wild roses for lunch. If they put one rosebud under each plate they will need only about four hundred.

At twelve o'clock Thomas Robertson will stop work in his smithy outside the stockade, reach down his cornet, and tootle a luncheon hymn. The five women in the kitchen and their man helper, all of them serving a week's kitchen police, will have the three great boilers on the brick furnaces bubbling with food—three bushels of potatoes in one, several bushels of hominy in another, gallons of water gravy in another. The bread, baked every night by two male bakers in the ovens built under the kitchen—three hundred pounds of flour a day mixed in a mighty wooden trencher—is stacked ready. And from everywhere, from fields and orchards and corrals and chicken coops and tan· nery and furniture shop and cooper shop and shoe factory and grist mill, the queues will come hurrying again.

At six Robertson will roll down his sleeves, take off his leather apron, close up his smithy and lift his cornet and blow, and at supper there will be another prayer and another hymn, probably "Come, Let Us Sing an Evening Hymn." The dining room will fill and empty for the sixth time, the last straggling child will snatch a crust and disappear. Then the dining hall will lie down behind its flagpole and sigh like a run dog and drop its head between its paws and sleep again until the five o'clock bugle, unless there is a dance that night, or an entertainment, or amateur theatricals.

Whatever he did in Arcadia, every member of the community had three times a day to sink himself in the common life of the village. The punctual and communal meals brought the town's life to a point; they enlarged and stabilized and tested and tempered the co-operative spirit of the Saints. No matter how much neighboring towns laughed at community dining, no matter how many stories they told of troughs which carried the refuse of the adults' meals down to the children, no matter how visitors raised their eyebrows and wondered how one could stand eating

always in a boarding-house bedlam, the people of Orderville liked it, and they stuck to it until a flood ruined the
bakery ovens in the basement, and even after that, in the
dying years of the Order, many of them yearned for the
good old days when private life was reduced to a minimum
and public life expanded to fit the principles of Saints who
were brothers in fact as well as in faith.

Orderville was more than a hundred miles from a railroad then. The terminal of the Denver and Rio Grande
Western branch line—called the "Wooden Shoe Line"
sometimes because of the Scandinavian peasants working
their fields in sabots—was at Marysvale. But it was not
mere isolation from the world that let the communal village thrive where so many similar experiments in towns
only a few miles away failed miserably. For one thing, you
couldn't hold anything back on the Orderville brethren,
consecrate part of your property and save out a nest egg.
If you went in, you went in whole hog. For the sum of
one dollar and other good and valuable considerations you
signed over your entire wealth, even to pots and pans, to
the Board of Directors as Trustee-in-Trust, and you got
back shares in the company plus a flat wage and credit at
the Order store. You were expected not to overdraw your
wages, but if you had to you could. You were also expected
to produce a surplus, but if you didn't it was all right. At
the end of the year all debts were canceled and all sur-
pluses absorbed and everybody started fresh.

No one could say that another got more than himself,
because skilled and unskilled labor were paid alike. There
were no plutocrats and no charity cases, and for a long
time no bad feelings of any consequence between members. When they founded their town they were earnest for
co-operation—so earnest that most of them were *baptized*

into it. A new member was carefully quizzed by the board. Did he believe that the Lord had advised him to join this co-operative life? Was his family in agreement with him? Did he train his family in the fear of the Lord? Did he practice kindness and piety in his family life? Did he have any debts? Did he swear or use profane language? Did he break the Word of Wisdom? Did he steal or fail to return things he borrowed? Did he tell dirty jokes? Did he abuse dumb animals? Could he keep his temper? Was he willing to work according to his strength and ability at whatever task the board should assign him? Would he promise to avoid all lying and backbiting and slandering of brothers and sisters?

If he did and was and avoided all those things, they welcomed him in, turned his property into the common pool, and gave him a job, for which he received credit of a dollar and a half a day. His wife was worth seventy-five cents, as were his boys from eleven to seventeen. Daughters were not much of an economic asset. Between ten and thirteen they drew twenty-five cents, and under ten half that much. No money, of course, ever changed hands. There was no money to change. Credits and debits went down in the company's books. Board for adults cost about fifty dollars a year, with children's meals at half or three quarters of that amount. A man's clothing was debited at $17.50, a woman's at $16.50 annually. If at the end of the year a member's accumulated wages exceeded his spending, he signed a waiver and gave the surplus back to the common fund. And the oddest thing of all—for years not a single wife in Orderville, apparently, ever rose to say witty and acid words about the annual adornment budget!

A good many of the women of Orderville were plural wives (Bishop Chamberlain, for instance, had five), but

there seems to have been hardly a trace of the female bitterness that marred the domestic arrangements of good
Saints in other quarters. Sometimes, in order to obey counsel and marry a second wife, a man would have to build
another house, or establish part-time residence in another
town, because he didn't dare bring a second wife into the
same house or the same village with the first. But in Orderville people lived higgledy-piggledy in the uniform frame
shanties and the net result of polygamy at close quarters
seemed to be merely a wider and more varied circle of
acquaintance for each woman.

The structure of the town was even stricter than that of
the City of Zion, just as the town life carried to such extremes the most idealistic Mormon perfectionism that the
Orderville brethren were almost aliens in the midst of the
surrounding Mormon society. In Orderville, and in some
of the less successful United Order villages like Kingston,
Allen's Camp, Sunset Crossing, and Bunkerville, the Mormons approached closest to the community life of the
Pueblos. They were peaceable, domesticated, virtually self-
sufficient.

It is difficult to find anything that the Orderville brethren were compelled to buy, aside from arms, ammunition,
and a minimum of machinery. In the town itself, or on the
farms and ranches the Order acquired in the canyons, out
on the Arizona desert, and down in the semi-tropical lower
valley of the Virgin, practically every necessity was grown
or manufactured. The orchard and vegetable garden, just
outside the square, produced peaches, apricots, grapes, cur-
rants, gooseberries, garden truck, watermelons. From the
hillsides came timber and firewood, and up the valley a
few miles was a coal mine. Down near Washington, on the
"Cotton Farm," they grew cotton that was ultimately proc-

essed in their own mill. At Moccasin Springs, between the Vermilion Cliffs and the Grand Canyon, there were great fields of sugar cane and the simple machinery and vats for making molasses. Sugar they could not manage, but what they could not manage they did without. Molasses, poured over crumbed-up bread, satisfied the sweet-tooth of the children. Candy could be made from the green skimmings of the cane. Peaches and other fruit could be boiled down in molasses for preserves.

At various farms the brethren raised wheat, corn, and oats for their needs. Up the side canyons from the town there was good grazing for the beef and dairy herds, and as the flocks grew they traded a rifle and ammunition to a Shivwits chief for perpetual grazing privileges on Buckskin Mountain (the Kaibab Plateau). By 1881 they were paying taxes—and tithes—on five thousand head of sheep. They were making their own clip, carding and spinning, weaving their own cloth in their own mill. Women in the tailor shop made clothes for the community; other women braided wheatstraw for the characteristic floppy hats. Men stripped bark from the scrub oak and stacked it for the tannery where all the town's leather was made. The shoemaker's shop was busy the year around making rough unlined cowhide shoes, harnesses, saddles. There were dyeing vats for the coloring of cotton and wool cloth with homemade dyes like madder, indigo, kinnikinnick, logwood powder, greasewood. A crew of soap-makers burned cottonwood logs for ashes, leached the ashes with water, added grease or oose plant to make the harsh soap that all washed with.

They were an ingenious and industrious crowd. The furniture shop made chairs, tables, bedsteads, bureaus, for all the shanties in the village. (Some of those pieces are hunted by antique-collectors now.) They had grist mills and saw mills, and in Brother Carling, who possessed a lathe, they had a combination Santa Claus, lapidary, and resident artist. Just before Christmas Brother Carling devoted his days to turning toys, dolls' heads, gadgets, while women sat in his shop and stuffed bodies for the wooden or plaster-of-paris heads he made. At odd times during the year Brother Carling could be induced to melt down the infrequent dimes that came into the clutches of girls, and make rings out of them. He ran a night school and taught the rudiments of drawing and painting. It is pleasant to speculate on what the work of Brother Carling might have developed into if Orderville had gone on for let us say a century, untouched and unhindered by the world outside. Like everything else in Arcadia, art and the love of beauty were rudimentary and simple, but they were present. Witness the rosebuds under the dinner plates.

Orderville never had a luxurious existence, and it never quite attained a whole-hearted peace with the neighboring towns. It was too successful; the pressure from outside was growing; the isolation that surrounded it was not proof either against ideas or against federal officers looking for "cohabs." Self-sufficiency was an ideal which at first was almost realizable, but the fact remained that Orderville existed under the laws of the United States, and in the midst of a society increasingly imitative of the world outside.

Other Mormons did not cheer when the Orderville brethren picked off the best grazing land by locating springs and water-pockets. They did not cheer when they noticed that by pooling labor and capital the Orderville people produced more and produced it more cheaply than an individual could. They did not refrain from laughing a little contemptuously at the sternly simple regimen of Arcadia, at the straw hats and the homespun and the cowhide boots. Like the Amish, like the colonists at Amana or Homestead in Iowa, like the Dukhobors and the Mennonites, the Ordervillians were clannish, not only because they had cultivated the group spirit to a point where it had no place for outsiders, but because they felt the ridicule that the outsiders heaped upon them. To a certain extent, the United Order of Orderville, by creating a self-sufficient microcosmic society in the midst of the Mormon macrocosm, put itself in exactly the same position that the whole Mormon Church occupied with respect to the United States. There was no persecution, no violence, but there was some bad feeling and a good deal of ridicule.

What killed Orderville? Was it the pressure from outside or weakness within? Could it have survived if its isolation had been more complete, or would it have broken down of itself?

It is difficult to answer these questions. Certainly there was one weakness in the structure of Orderville, and one which in combination with outside difficulties helped to break the village up. The founders of the village had forgotten one thing: they had made no provision for young men growing up in the Order. They had no property to consecrate, and as a result they held no shares in the Order and could expect nothing but the opportunity of working for a dollar and a half a day payable in food and shelter. And while they went on working for a subsistence, the boys from St. George and Washington and Kanab and Leeds and Harmony worked as teamsters for the silver mines at Pioche or Silver Reef and got paid in solid shining money twice as much as the Orderville boys got in credit. Young men of Arcadia looked resentfully upon the swaggering youths from other towns, and in their hearts envied them. The smart alecs wore store clothes, Stetson hats, silk handkerchiefs, riding boots.

In addition to that complaint, which the board might possibly have been able to adjust without the loss of more than a few of the young men, there arose difficulty over those who consistently overdrew their credit. The industrious began jawing the slothful. Skilled workers, looking around the country which was then in the midst of a boom from the Pioche and Silver Reef mines, discovered that in most places skilled labor was worth twice as much as common labor. They proposed that the wages be adjusted; the board wrote to the Church authorities asking advice, and the authorities advised them to adjust the wages. Immediately there was a counter-complaint. Some were getting more than others. The fine equality of the original community was gone, and it would never come back.

Orderville might have weathered its difficulties but for three things, none of them blamable upon the board. One was the opening of the silver mines and the sudden flow of easy money in the surrounding towns. Another was the error of the hierarchy in advising the adjustment of wages for skilled labor, an error that admitted the growing profit-motive in all Church affairs. The third was the polygamy prosecutions under the Edmunds-Tucker Act, and the coming of deputy marshals snooping for "polygs" and "cohabs." The men with plural wives, who were in effect the natural leaders of the town, fled to the underground. Wives lived as widows; second, third, and fourth wives stripped off their wedding rings (the absence of a ring ceremony in the Mormon wedding service harks back to that period of the persecution) and stayed out of sight as much as possible. There was little chance for the leaders to work out any solution for the inheritances of young men or the knotty question of wages. Orderville was caught in the larger war that Mormonism was waging with the United States, was actually a martyr to it.

By 1885 it was clear that the old perfect society was gone. The farm lands were sold off to the members at auction, only the livestock, the tannery, and the factory being held back as capital stock in the company. As late as 1889 the company paid dividends, and it was financially independent to the very end.

But the bond that had held it together, the capacity for abnegation and social living, was gone from the time the outside world began to crowd the valley; from the time when Orderville youths first noticed consciously that the Kanab punks wore fancy cowpuncher clothes, and that the St. George smart alecs had money to jingle in their store pants; from the time when the first Orderville girl saw out of the corner of her eye the brilliance of the silk neckerchief around the outsider's throat, and let her eye stray to the clumping and sullen clumsiness of her Arcadian swain; from the time when the annual allowance of $16.50 for clothes began to rankle in the bosoms of Orderville's fair.

One of the most important things that Orderville forgot, one of the things it would have had to settle if it had hoped to survive after the polygamy persecutions died down, one of the things it might have known from the beginning, was that the perfect society may starve, may freeze, may be chased and outlawed, may do almost any number of things almost permanently, but only for a very short time, during the very height of its initial enthusiasm, may it dispense with ornament. Brigham Young should have known that, but he never learned. He was always grousing about the fancies of his harem and fulminating from the pulpit against giddy fashions. He kept up that tirade for more than thirty years, but the fact is there as recalcitrant as a stone in a shoe: Fashion, as much as anything else, killed Arcadia.

Mammon's round.

Chief President of the Islands
of the Sea . . .

HERE are two things to remember about early Mormonism: it was conceived as a world movement, destined to inherit the globe; and it was a revealed religion, filled with miracles, prophecies, revelations, and the other evidences of God's active participation in the affairs of men. Between them, those two characteristics have produced some strange aberrations, and even some schisms, in the Church.

The acceptance of miracles and revelations, for one thing, gave rise to a string of upstart prophets who set their dreams over the orders of the priesthood. There was James Jesse Strang, who took a party of recusant Saints into Wisconsin after Joseph's death, later moved them to Beaver Island in Lake Michigan, and there built himself a kingdom with himself in the saddle as potentate, prophet, revelator, and high priest. He instituted polygamy and lived the life of Riley until apostates and Gentiles from the mainland invaded his island, scattered his people, killed him, and permanently broke up the ideal society Strang had created.

That was in 1856, twelve years after the mob had killed the original prophet of Mormonism. In that same year, in

Utah, the Saints were going through a hectic reformation, being dispossessed of devils, receiving the gifts of the spirit, repenting and being re-baptized, talking in tongues, and hitting the sawdust trail generally. One victim of that emotional upheaval was Joseph Morris. Like Joseph and Strang, he heard the voice of God speaking to him, calling him to a great work, and on the strength of those intimations he applied to Brigham to be installed in the inner circle of the priesthood. Brigham treated him like a crank, though he did not threaten him as he had threatened Gladden Bishop's reformers-from-within. Disgruntled, Morris had revelations telling him that Brigham was unworthy to lead the Saints any further, and gathered together a group of ecstatic followers below Weber Canyon, which God told him was to be the true Kingdom. There he kept a couple of secretaries busy taking down revelations in both Danish and English, many of them directed against Brigham and his quorum. Eventually a posse was sent to shut him up. The Morrisites barricaded themselves and fought it out, but were eventually overpowered as ruthlessly as the Missourians had overpowered the Saints a few years before. Morris and several of his followers were killed, a number were fined and jailed, and the rest finally found sanctuary at Soda Springs, Idaho, under guard from General Connor's California Volunteers.

There are two dissident prophets, each with his own burning dedication and his own appointed kingdom. But neither reached so high, or had such grandiose dreams, or came so close to succeeding, as Walter Murray Gibson, adventurer and impostor extraordinary.

Before he ever came into the orbit of Mormonism he had led a fantastic life. He was born on the Bay of Biscay, educated in South Carolina. By the time he was twenty-

one he had been married and divorced. For a time he was
a United States Government representative in Guatemala
and Costa Rica; later he was master of the revenue cutter
Flirt, carrying secret cargo to the East Indies. While he
was in the Indies he brought the natives to a near revolt,
and precipitated an international incident. The United
States' published report of the investigation runs to over
three hundred pages. Gibson was cashiered; his explanation was that he had had dreams of being a "potentate in
the east."

His disgrace did not cure him of those dreams. A little
while afterward he was approaching the eastern committee
of the Mormon Church with the proposition that the persecuted Saints be moved to the South Sea Islands, where
they could be fruitful and multiply without interference.
The elders refused his proposals, but Gibson was not discouraged. Apparently he saw in the Mormons an instrument peculiarly suited to a person of his own talents. During the Mormon War he appeared in Utah and made the
same proposition to Brigham. It was clear, he said, that
even in the West the Mormons could expect to be driven
and hunted. Why not take them to the Pacific, where a
vast empire could be built up? But Brigham was then in
a fighting, not a running mood. He too turned Gibson
down.

Still he persevered. The Church had had missionaries in
Hawaii since 1850; they were now all in Salt Lake, called
back because of the trouble with the United States. They
knew the islands, spoke the language, and could tell a curious man a good deal in a short time. Gibson took pains
to meet and talk with them. When he had got what he
wanted he had himself baptized into the Church, and appeared before Brigham again, this time as a brother in the

faith. He did not now advocate the moving of the entire population; all he did was talk fast enough to convince Brigham that he had intimate knowledge of the islands, and worm out of him a commission on parchment to be a special worker in that field. That sort of commission might have given an ordinary man a few little prerogatives and got him access to the best homes. But Gibson was no ordinary man. He made that little slip of paper into an empire.

He arrived in the islands in 1861 and went about his job with admirable caution. First he posed as a literary man, and delivered lectures to willing groups. When he had been around enough to have a grasp of the language, he declared his mission. He had, he said, been sent by Brigham Young to be "Chief president of the islands of the sea, and of the Hawaiian Islands, for the Church of Latter-day Saints." To prove his claim he had the parchment, by now all done up in ribbons and seals and badges. He was glib, he had a monumental presence, he spoke with alternating thunder and sunshine in his voice. The natives were awed.

They were not really hard to awe, or at least the Mormons had never found them so. They took to Mormonism more eagerly than any people among whom the Saints had labored. Representatives of other sects had worked among them without great effect, but the Mormons took them by storm. Wisely laying aside the Word of Wisdom, they let the natives smoke all they wanted. No other missionaries were that liberal. The Mormons were not too proud to go out into the villages and live with the natives. That too was good. And they had one thing that no other religion could offer. God had spoken to them, not two thousand years ago away off in Asia Minor, but yesterday, the day before, last year, and in the very islands themselves. Here was fresher news, later dope. The Hawaiians liked the idea

of God's contemporary presence, and they were impressed
by such miracles as the revelation which let George Q.
Cannon learn the Hawaiian tongue in one stroke. That
was an impressive matter. So was the history the Mormons
taught them, that the peoples of the islands were of the
blood of Israel, a branch of God's chosen people, brothers
to the Lamanites, and would partake of the ultimate salva-
tion which God had promised his dark children.

From a Wednesday to a Monday two elders baptized a
hundred and thirty converts. By 1852 there were six hundred native Saints, and by 1896 there were destined to be
eighty-three branches of the Church, forty-three meeting
houses, and just short of five thousand members, about
one sixth of the native population. An unofficial estimate
in 1925 guessed that about a third of the native population
was Mormon. They were good Mormons, too. The Church
even got them to work as part of their religious practices,
and their zeal is indicated by what happened to Clarence
E. Dutton when he was investigating the Hawaiian vol-
canoes for the United States Geological Survey in the
eighties. He came down with his pack train through a village full of half-naked savages, and was promptly clapped
in jail for driving donkeys on the Sabbath.

Gibson didn't have all that to work with in 1861, but
he had a good nucleus of already-converted natives, and he
found plenty more who fell all over themselves to hear the
eloquence of the Chief President. He made himself exactly
what the Hawaiians wanted him to be. He stalked like an
emperor, he made the natives come into his house on
hands and knees, he put the *Book of Mormon* in a hollow
stone and told it abroad that to touch it was instant death.
By playing upon all the local superstitions and taboos, he

became almost a god. The Hawaiians called him Father, and brought him tributes of produce and money and goat-skins and fish. For a fee ranging up as high as a hundred and fifty dollars he would make his loyal subjects elders, priests, bishops, or apostles, and with the money he bled from his adorers he bought half the island of Lanai, where he started drilling all the able-bodied men in the tactics of war so that they could attack and subdue the peoples of other Pacific islands and spread the empire.

All this he did in three years. When in 1864 a group of elders arrived from Salt Lake to look into the rumored doings of the Chief President, he was absolute potentate in his little kingdom, worshiped as a god. In his inner sanctum was the framed parchment from Brigham Young, with its brave ribbons and badges and seals, but the natives had practically forgotten that Brigham Young existed. The commission had become in effect a personal letter from God to Gibson, and Gibson was a higher power than any number of Brigham Youngs.

It took the investigating elders a good long time and cost them a great deal of effort and argument before they convinced the natives that they had been duped. But even after they succeeded, even after most of Gibson's flock was weaned away to Oahu, where the Church establishment was strongest, the Chief President still had his half island, duly recorded in his own name. For a time he ran sheep on it. Later he was elected to the Hawaiian legislature, and was selected by King Kalakaua as his Prime Minister. With or without the personal letter from God, he was destined to be a satrap.

He was the power behind the Hawaiian throne for a long time. Not until 1887 did the people catch up with him and throw him out, twenty-six years after his modest entrance into the local scene. His death in San Francisco was the poetically-just death of the penniless exile, but that is hardly the important thing about Walter Murray Gibson. The important item in his fantastic biography is his illustration of the old sour truth about causes and faiths: that an unscrupulous impostor can lead any gullible and believing people by the nose, and lead them for long times and distances, before they are willing to give up their faith for the harsher vision of reality. Both Joseph Smith and Brigham Young have been accused of being just that sort of impostor. Brother Joseph certainly aspired to become the man on the white horse, and he flashed a gaudy General's uniform around Nauvoo and set himself up as a candidate for the Presidency, but no real study of the record can fail to reveal that to both Joseph and Brigham there was a side which was responsible to and even tender of the people. Neither of them ever stooped to the kind of bare-faced swindling that Gibson practiced. They were leaders, and they liked their jobs, but they were also men with a social vision that compensated and corrected their desire for personal aggrandizement.

And what a footnote to the potency of the Mormon dream the career of Walter Murray Gibson makes. Even in the hands of a cheap crook, even out in the lost islands of the Pacific thousands of miles from the temple and the personal authority of the priesthood, the faith was dynamic and successful. It made converts by the thousand, and some of those converts were so filled with the dream, so agitated to be properly baptized and to undergo the ordinances in the temple, that they threw up their island paradise and took the long trek to Zion in search of another Heaven.

It is one thing to bring in converts from England or Scandinavia; the economic motive and the current of a whole period operated there. But these Hawaiian brothers and sisters went only to be surer of Heaven, and that meant virtually giving up the world.

The Gathering-up of Zion . . .

IT was Arbor Day, 1899, a bright day with little wind. On the east the bare slope of the Stansbury Range was misted with new green; the sun lay hot in the valley and on the low Cedar Mountains to the west. In the little settlement—a typical mile-square Mormon village of a couple of dozen houses, a chapel, a school—a crowd was gathering. There were overalls and shirtsleeves among them, but most were frock-coated as if for meeting. Even the brownskins were dressed up, and teeth glinted, hands waved, heads nodded. The babble of voices, English and Hawaiian and a mixture of the two, went up in the still air. A horse pawed dust in the wide street and backed nervously against his buggy shafts. For a block along the street buggies and wagons stood in line, many of them the two- or three-seated light spring wagons with fringed white tops that the Gentiles already knew as "Mormon buggies."

A man climbed on a wagon box and lifted his hands, and the babble fell away, dropped to silence. With his hands still lifted, the man asked a blessing in English, repeated it in swift and liquid Polynesian. The heads around him bowed, then came up, and Elder Richards began in English again. The Lord, he said, had blessed this people and this plantation until it had grown prosperous. He would continue to bless it if all would anchor their lives

136

in work and prayer. Ten years ago this colony of Iosepa had been a barren desert; now it was becoming an oasis, a place of gardens and homes. That transformation had taken hard work by the members and careful nursing by the guardian Church. But the thing was being accomplished, and today there would be a big step taken toward making Iosepa a real oasis, a garden in the desert. He prayed again that the Lord would bless them and the work they were to do today.

As he stepped down he spoke to two Hawaiians standing near, and they began lifting down nursling trees from the next wagon. The whole crowd moved forward to pick up shovels. Boys came staggering with buckets of water. A hole was dug, a tiny walnut tree planted in it, soaked, and tamped down. One wagon with its workers went up to the other end of town and started planting in methodical rows. Before the Hawaiian colonists and the visiting churchmen from Salt Lake stopped that day they had planted three hundred walnut trees, three hundred fruit trees, a hundred ornamental trees, and a good many shrubs. As a last duty they moved down en masse to the pest house, a mile and a half south.

The pest house stood alone on the flat—treeless, shrubless, flowerless. One smudge of bright green marked the spring, but all around the building the ground looked blasted and bare. Before the door, set at a wobbly angle in the hard earth, stood a peeled spruce flagpole on which the inmates ran up the flag when they needed anything. There was no sign of life about the place as the crowd straggled up and stood quietly. Silence settled down. The laughter and talk that had accompanied the planting in the village died, and even children stood soberly, staring at the weathered and symbolic pole, its flag wrapped around the base. No one inside needed anything.

Bishop Harvey Cluff nodded to the workmen, and they drove their shovels into the ground, already dry for three or four inches down. It crumbled in hard white clods under the shovels. At the window of the pest house a brown face appeared, and a murmur went up from the watching Hawaiian women. The face disappeared.

All around the house they planted shade trees, small ones, but the best and sturdiest of the lot. At the end they prayed again, Bishop Cluff standing close to the door and speaking loudly so that those inside could hear. The door opened a crack as he prayed, but no one showed, and when he had asked God's blessing on all the company and their works, and especially on the stricken people inside, the crowd moved away, still soberly, toward the village that with its new trees looked like a baby orchard. The ground under their feet as they passed along the edge of the barley field was sodden from the irrigation ditch, and the corrugated, regular beet field was black with its overnight soaking, its channels glistening spottily with brown water.

As they looked back there was satisfaction in the sight of the slender green-tufted saplings they had planted around the house of sickness, but the gaunt flagpole still dominated the yard. Only when the last straggling walkers were a quarter of a mile away through the sagebrush did anyone appear outside the house. Then a woman in a red dress came out and stood silently looking after them. Another joined her, then a man. They did not answer the waves of people who looked back.

That was Iosepa, and the pest house around which shade trees were planted in 1899 was the only leper colony in the history of the Mormon Country. Of the three inmates,

J. M. Kaulenamaku died in July of that same year; the two women lingered, noduled and ulcerated and outlawed in their barren little shack, and died at some date which even the Church archives seem not to have recorded.

As for the colony itself, the oasis in the Skull Valley desert, it is a ghost town, abandoned twenty-five years ago and sold by the Church to the Deseret Livestock Company. Most of the trees are gone, blown out in the winds that made Skull Valley a little dustbowl in the thirties. The country has gone back to the grazing that it was used for in the earliest days of Mormon settlement, and most Utahns now do not know that for almost fifty years there was a colony of Hawaiians in the state, and a leper colony to go with it.

Iosepa did not exactly fail. It merely adjourned. But it must have been a mighty relief to the hundred-odd Hawaiians when the Church completed the temple at Laie on the Island of Oahu. Some of those Hawaiians had been in Utah since the sixties, working as day laborers, baking in the dry desert summers, freezing in the winters, hanging on painfully and faithfully because the temple work they did gave them a fool-proof ticket to the Heaven they craved. It was the temple which had brought them; they went back gratefully when a temple was built in their own islands. From the beginning they were strangers in Utah, strangers to the climate, to the life of pioneer farming, to the language, to the. social structure they were asked to adapt themselves to. Their mortality was high, their status hardly better than that of the Indians.

They were, in effect, wards of the Church, and even after the authorities bought the Skull Valley ranch and settled them there, they were in constant need of supervision and care. Unlike the Anglo-Americans and Scandinavians who

settled other valleys, the Hawaiians were not given plots
of farm land and town lots in their own names. Iosepa was
a plantation, and the laborers were paid thirty dollars a
month in goods for their labor. It was actually a pretty
good plantation. In one year the proceeds of the ranch in
barley, hay, and livestock totaled twenty thousand dollars.
But the brownskins were still strangers in the land they
tilled, no more a part of Mormon society than the Goshutes who lived a few miles south of Iosepa on a tiny reservation.

They were strangers in the land, despite their faith and
their absolute childlike loyalty to the Church. More than
one of them must have stood sick for home amid the alien
corn. The outbreak of leprosy in 1896 caused a tremendous explosion of journalistic hysterics from the Salt Lake
Herald, but it was never really serious. Three people got
it, and all three died, and that was all. But the leprosy outbreak was symbolic; it was an outward mark of the inward
sickness, the longing for the jungled mountains and the
white beaches of home. The Hawaiians made a heroic effort to be pioneer Mormon farmers, but they never were
a part of the society that tried half-heartedly to assimilate
them. In the end the Church realized that. It paid the fare
back home for those unable to pay it for themselves—a
kind of Perpetual Emigration Fund in reverse—and let the
colony break up. Of all the Hawaiians at Iosepa, only one
remained behind, and he remained only because he was in
the army at the time.

That was the first and last attempt of the Church to
Mormonize people of other than European blood and
settle them in the Utah valleys. Zion is a white man's country. Even though the Hawaiians are still believed to be of
the blood of Israel, a branch of the lost tribes who settled

the islands of the sea, they are not now being brought to Zion for the gathering-in. Zion is spread to include them; the institutions are taken to the heathen in orthodox missionary style—to Hawaii, to the Friendly Islands, to New Zealand and Australia, to Polynesian and Tahitian and Maori and Bushman—and in the last days they will be brought together by the Lord for the reuniting of the seed of Israel.

And Iosepa has gone back to sagebrush and bunch grass, and cattle graze over the dusty acres where the brown colonists labored in the vineyard of the Lord.

Myth and Legend . . .

FOLK literature, the scholars tell us, is likely to spring
out of a society which is homogeneous in environment,
occupation, and customs. Folkways produce their own peculiar folk literature and folk beliefs. But Mormonism
does not seem on first glance to have created any notable
folklore. Balladry, which flourished elsewhere in the cow
country, does not seem to have been enriched from the
valleys of the mountains, though there are hundreds of
cattle, sheep, and horse ranches on the fringes of the arable
land. The ballads the cowpunchers sing are those imported from Texas, New Mexico, Arizona, or Wyoming—
"Strawberry Roan," "Ridin' Old Paint," "Blood on the
Saddle." The Mormons are a singing people, and always
have been, but their creative energy seems to have spent
itself on hymns, which are often folksy enough. They are
exhortations to a life of strict piety, didactic celebrations
of the Word of Wisdom, glorifications of peculiar Mormon
institutions, or rather smug self-gratulation on being God's
chosen people. But balladry of the usual western sort is
missing.

So is the bumptious frontier journalism characteristic
of the rowdy West. Only in the mining camps and in railroad towns like Corinne, founded and inhabited by Gentiles, has there been heard the glad warcry of the Press,

going forth to battle with inkhorn, horsewhip, and der-ringer. The Gentiles in Salt Lake City had their *Vedette*, a rabidly anti-Mormon sheet, and the mining camps, as elsewhere in the West, produced their two or three or ten short-lived newspapers and their dozens of word-slingers-in-the-grand-manner. But the Mormon towns and villages did not. A good many of them still have to see the first news sheet come off a local press. The whole of San Juan County, the largest in the state of Utah, can boast of only one paper, and that is owned and operated by outsiders.

The *Deseret News* serves the orthodox, and always did. It is official, it comes from headquarters. It is also digni-fied, even a little solemn. It does not stoop to wisecracks, personal backbiting, humorous complaints of the editor to his empty purse, or any of the stock in trade of frontier journalism, and except for occasional tart replies to Gen-tile criticism it never did so stoop. Put up against the papers from Bingham or Park City it is a humorless and didactic sheet. By and large, it matched the people it served.

No balladry, no gentlemen of the press. It is hardly the West at all. Even the minor art of swearing was not culti-vated to the extent that it was elsewhere. Occasionally one meets a Mormon with the knack of putting swear-words together, and sometimes one encounters a speck of inter-estingly-local profanity in the milk of Mormon human-kindness. I have not heard elsewhere the typical Mormon "I'll be go to hell," and I have never found even in learned treatises the characteristic "Bear's ass!" with which a native of Cache Valley expresses disgust. What swearing there is among Mormons in general is likely to be fairly tame, and this in spite of the fact that both Brother Brigham and Heber C. Kimball, his right-hand man, were notable swear-ers and threateners from the pulpit. They were always offering to send their enemies to hell across lots, or give them a dose that would puke them worse than lobelia. A little of that fresh and vigorous tradition remains, though in the staider communities it is likely to be buried under a layer of piety like sausages put up in lard, and to emerge only on great occasions. The story is told of a pious brother in one of the rural settlements who forgot for some reason to milk his cow before he got dressed for Sunday meeting. Rather than change to overalls, he tucked up his coat tails, folded back the lapels of his Prince Albert, and sat down gingerly on the stool. The cow was "ringy." She kept looking around suspiciously and switching her matted tail across the elder's Sunday shirt. He compressed his lips and tied the tail to her leg. For a while he milked steadily, and then in one disastrous motion the cow kicked the bucket into his lap and upset him on the dirty stable floor. The elder, legend says, rose slowly to his feet. His stature grew from second to second, until he stood on tiptoe with the pressure of wrath in him. His hands made futile clawing motions down the stained lapels of his coat. Finally he found words. "If I wasn't a man of God . . . If I wasn't the Bishop of this Ward . . . If I wasn't a member of the Quorum of the Priesthood in this Stake . . . If I didn't have duties and obligations to live up to . . . If I wasn't called upon to put away wrath and bind the evil passions . . . I'D BREAK YOUR GOD-DAMNED NECK!"

But even where Mormon swearing has been preserved best, it is mild by comparison with the sulphurous art of the mining camps. It lacks the imagination and the humor, just as Mormon place-names are likely to lack the profane and impious descriptiveness of Gentile names. The one exception I know is Cohab (short for "Cohabitation") Canyon, near the Capitol Reef National Monument, and even that may have been applied by the deputy marshals.

Mormon swearing is mild, generally. Mormon place names are stolid. Mormon journalism is solemn. Mormon singing neglects the ballad for the hymn. The gentleman in Hemingway's story who, listening to Salt Lake City on the radio, got the impression that the city was clean but dull, was not entirely wrong. But the piety that submerged the usual folk arts has fostered others. The peculiar theology of Mormonism, plus the superstitious conviction that Heaven was close and that angels walked among men, has produced a body of story midway between myth and legend, profoundly didactic and within certain circles implicitly believed.

Here are a few:

1. *The Heirs of Madoc . . .*

In 1858 a party of eleven Mormon elders, led by the "Mormon Leatherstocking" Jacob Hamblin and guided by a Paiute euphoniously named Naraguts, left Santa Clara on the Virgin River. For objective they had the Hopi towns south of the Colorado. For purpose they had the verification of a legend almost as old as America.

They traveled across the then-unknown desert past the places that later would be Short Creek, Moccasin Springs, Kanab, down to the flank of the Kaibab Plateau. From here they cut eastward down House Rock Valley and across the Marble Canyon platform to the Crossing of the Fathers, where Escalante and his party of Spaniards had found a ford in 1776. It was a difficult passage; Escalante's hewn steps in the cliffs helped them some, but when their pack mule ran off with all their food south of the river they were in trouble. For three days they struggled through the canyons without food, until they came upon signs of cultivation and found an overlooked squash in a field. A little later they made their way into Oraibi and were taken in by the Hopi.

Their crossing of the Colorado was probably the first crossing by white men at that spot since the year of the Revolution, but that was not particularly important. Jake Hamblin was to act as Brigham Young's scout and Indian-missionary for a good many years, and to discover crossings of the Colorado at several points. As Mormon Leather-stocking he has a permanent and respected place in the history of the West. But what made this 1858 expedition unusual was not Hamblin or his demonstration of a route across the formidable barrier of the river. Exploration was only a partial reason for the expedition. Another reason was explained by the presence in the company of Durias Davis, a Welshman. The mission that Davis was entrusted with was inextricably tied up with Mormon mythology; the legend of the Welsh Indians which he came to examine was part of the whole climate of superstition and speculation that had produced the *Book of Mormon* twenty-eight years before.

Joseph Smith had answered the question of who were the American Indians to his people's satisfaction, but there were scoffers in the world who did not believe the story of Lehi and his sons, who fled Jerusalem at the Lord's command in 600 B.C. They had come after long journeying to South America, a land appointed for them, and there they had split into two factions, one led by the virtuous Nephi, and the other by the vicious Laman, both sons of Lehi. After multitudinous wars, dethronings, pursuits, captures, sinnings and repentings, and after the passage of approximately a thousand years, the white-skinned Nephites were utterly wiped out by their sinful brethren, who had very early been cursed with dark skins for their wickedness, and who had reverted to barbarism. Before that last battle near the Hill Cumorah in New York state, migration had brought both Nephites and Lamanites through the isthmus and into North America. Moroni, son of Mormon, was the last survivor of his people. He hid the golden plates containing their history deep under the earth, to be rediscovered in the Lord's own time by the chosen prophet of the New Dispensation.

That story explained the Indians as a remnant of the lost tribes of Israel who had been cursed with a dark skin and doomed to labor in darkness and to run wild in the forests. In the New Dispensation the Gentiles would discover the true faith, according to Nephite prophecy, and bring the blessings of God back to the Lamanites, thus confirming the earliest blessing which the Lord gave to the family of Lehi.

Because of that story and that prophecy, the Mormons did their best to convert the Lamanites and make farmers of them. The Indians were not wolves to be destroyed, but souls to be saved, as they were to the Jesuit and Franciscan missionaries in the Southwest.

That story also explains Brigham's curiosity about the Hopi. Members of the Mormon Battalion, marching from the Missouri to the Pacific twelve years before, had brought back tales of ruined cities in the Rio Grande Valley, had taken those cities as proof positive of the truth of the *Book of Mormon*. The Ho-ho-kim, the Old People Who Left, were the Nephites, the ruins were the ruins of their cities. And the Hopi, whom the Mormons called the Moquis, lived in towns; they tilled the soil, raised squash and beans and corn, showed signs of a higher civilization than the miserable Goshutes or the thieving Paiutes or the warlike and nomadic Utes and Apaches and Navajo. Were the Hopi living in the echo of that long-vanished civilization? Had they any tribal memories, were they aware of their possible origin?

That was one question. Another, and the one which prompted the inclusion of Durias Davis in the exploring party, was a slightly disturbing one. If Davis found Welsh words among the Hopi, the theory that their civilization was patterned on the Nephite culture might be undermined. Either way, Brigham was curious. If the town-dwelling Indians to the south of the Colorado were the Welsh Indians about whom rumor had been in the wind for two hundred years, it ought to be investigated. There is no knowing Brigham's feelings on the subject, or what he would have done to explain if the Hopi had turned out to be Welsh. They would have offered an alternative explanation, not a substantiation, to the *Book of Mormon* account of the aboriginal culture. Let it go at the fact that he wanted to find out.

How much of the Welsh Indian story Brigham knew is doubtful, but he could easily enough have known most of it, since the earliest converts to the Church had contained Welshmen, and Welshmen are peculiarly imaginative and tenacious makers of legend. If Brigham knew most of it, this is about what he knew:

He knew that in 1169 Owen Gwynedd, Prince of Wales, died leaving nineteen children. One of them, Hywell, the illegitimate son of an Irish mother, seized the throne and was challenged by his legitimate brother Davyz, whereupon a third son, Madoc or Madawg, became disgusted at

the unnatural strife within his family and resolved to put
the whole thing behind him. He set sail with three ship-
loads of companions (some accounts say two) in the year
1170. He sailed due westward, and eventually landed in a
new world, presumably the southeastern coast of North
America. Leaving a party of colonists behind, he beat his
way back to Wales, gathered together a larger company,
and set sail again with ten ships (some say eleven). His
navigation was not accurate enough for him to hit the spot
where he had left his colony, but he struck the continent
all right, either somewhere in the Carolinas or at the
mouth of the Mississippi or on the east coast of Mexico.
From those two immigrations of the Cymri came a race of
white Indians with beards, a numerous, warlike, civilized
race who have had laid to their account the Ohio mounds,
the ruins of the Southwest, the Aztecan and Mayan cultures, and anything in general that did not seem clearly
the handiwork of the Indians known by early explorers
and trappers and settlers.

The Reverend Morgan Jones, in 1660, had reason to
bless the foresight of his countryman Madoc five hundred
years before. He was making his way back to Virginia from
Port Royal, South Carolina, when he and his companions
were captured by Indians and informed that they should
make ready to die. The Reverend Jones, in a fit of despair,
lapsed into Welsh. Some versions of his story say that he
prayed, but his own account gives him no better than a
lament: "Have I escaped so many dangers, and must I now
be knocked on the head like a dog?" A warrior of the Doeg
tribe (Doeg—a corruption of Madawg?) surprised him by
answering in Celtic, and the Reverend Jones' life was
spared. These Indians, he said, entertained him for four
months, and he conversed with them and preached to them

in Welsh. They lived on the Pontigo River, not far from Cape Atros. Jones was willing to conduct to the spot anyone who wanted to investigate, but apparently no one wanted to.

The Reverend Jones, one may guess, was as sad a liar as his illustrious countryman Geoffrey of Monmouth, who palmed off his fictions about King Arthur as sober history and directly created one of the three great "matters" of medieval story. But Mr. Jones did not invent his whole tale. He could have got the hint from books, from Hakluyt, from Peter Martyr, from Harcourt's journal of his voyage to the Guianas, from various histories of Wales. The tale of Madoc may be the most sober history in the world—at least the part of it dealing with his departure from Wales. And all the Welshmen who after Morgan Jones interested themselves in the Welsh Indians needed only a hint from some tall-talking frontier trader to blow the story again through the world. Some pointed to the white-god myth of the Aztecs, the fact that the Aztecs worshiped the cross, the supposed incidence of Welsh names in Mexico, to support the theory that the men of Madoc landed in Mexico and gave their civilization to the Indians there. Others affirmed that somewhere in Kentucky there was a tribe known as the Paducas who spoke Welsh and were whiter than other Indians. Off in Missouri somewhere, rumor said, lived a tribe of white and bearded Indians with an advanced civilization. They called themselves Mandans, which may have been a corruption of Madawgwys. Both these tribes, according to people who had visited them, had a book which they kept wrapped up in skins and which they were very anxious to know the meaning of. That, said the legend-makers, was a Welsh bible. Two army officers reported that they had conversed with Indians who spoke fluent Welsh as their native tongue. The scholar Catlin, in his *American Indians,* noted that the canoe of the Mandans was utterly unlike the canoes of any other Indians, and corresponded almost exactly with the Welsh coracle.

Though there is just enough possibility of a germ of truth in all this to make it piquant, most of it must be looked at with Geoffrey of Monmouth in mind. Geoffrey, because his country had been beaten and dominated, invented for it a glorious past and a hero who would never die. One suspects other Welshmen of coveting for their country the glory of discovering the new world. And anyway the nineteenth century was a speculative century. A dream or a fantasy caught the attention of men more then than now.

That was what Brigham might have known. As settlement pushed westward the homelands of the Welsh Indians moved on ahead of the frontier, and there was as much reason for suspecting the Hopi—more, really—than any other tribe of having white ancestry. But the expedition was a disappointment. Durias Davis found no Welsh words on Hopi tongues. He concluded, from his talk with the old men through an interpreter, that the Hopi originally had come from Mexico, and that some of their legends indicated knowledge of the Montezumas. That left the Welsh Indian legend up in the air, but it matched well enough with the story of the Nephite migration northward through Mexico, and in effect substantiated the *Book of Mormon.* With that the party had to be content.

That should have settled the question. But it didn't, quite. Legends have the quality of growing up again. They

are never quite eradicable. When Hamblin went again to
the Hopi in 1862 he brought back three Indians to visit
Salt Lake and have their eyes opened. Almost the first
thing that happened to them was that they were pounced
on by a group of Welshmen who buttonholed them and
tried to make them admit that they spoke Celtic. The
Hopi pretty definitely didn't.

Yet in 1878, twenty years after Durias Davis failed to
discover anything Welsh in Oraibi, a Mormon missionary
named Llewellyn Harris went among.the Zuñi and found
new hope. He listened to Zuñi legends and got about this:
Three hundred years before the Conquest, white men
landed in Mexico and told the Indians they came from
beyond the eastern sea. From these white men the kings
of Mexico were descended. In time white and Indian blood
was so mixed that all trace of the white men was lost except
for a few Mexican legends and a few Zuñi legends and a
few Welsh words "among the Zuñi, Navajo, and Moquis."
So there we are back at the assertion that the Hopi may
be Welsh. Brigham and Durias Davis might as well have
saved their trouble. What people want to believe they will
believe, especially if they are Welshmen or Mormons. If
they are both, there is nothing short of dynamite that will
remove a superstition.

There is a curious variant of the Nephite-Welsh myth
connected with the naming of Montezuma Creek and Recapture Creek in San Juan County. San Juan has notable
cliff and cave ruins, and is only a short distance from Mesa
Verde. One of the first Mormons to penetrate that country
was Peter Shirts, who from being alone too much or other
cause dreamed up the story that Montezuma, after his capture by Cortez, escaped to the north (here comes a Welsh

king of the Indians) and was overhauled by the Spaniards on Recapture Creek. It is a pleasant story, but rather more fanciful than its parent myth.

2. *Walkers, Talkers, and Dreamers . . .*

The Scandinavians and Welshmen and Channel Islanders who formed a sizable part of the Mormon population came of superstitious stock; their blood was infected with the virus of myth and legend, and the peculiar qualities of the *Book of Mormon* and Mormon theology encouraged rather than discouraged the growth of such beliefs. It is necessary to remember always that God spoke directly to Joseph Smith, that the Holy Ghost invaded the homes of men, that miracles and revelations and the gifts of the spirit and the exorcism of devils were commonplaces among the Mormons for fifty years and are by no means extinct even today. A Mormon village is hardly complete without its elders who cure the sick by the laying on of hands, or an old Scotch grandmother with the gift of second sight, or a woman who has been moved by the spirit to speak in tongues, or Scandinavians who see the "gänger," the walkers-after-death. According to some writers on the Mormons, more than one man was blessed by Joseph Smith in the early days and told that he would never be touched by an enemy bullet. Porter Rockwell, Joseph's personal bodyguard and one of the most redoubtable of the Sons of Dan, had his hair singed and his clothes pierced, and once took off his coat to shake slugs out on the floor after an affray, but the word of the prophet was good. His hide was never so much as broken by a bullet.

Mormonism, historical and contemporary, is shot through with a theology that to outsiders looks like the wildest superstition, and a superstition that has almost become a theology. It is a composite and complicated web, product of the ignorance and witchcraft of the frontier, the pseudo-science of amateur anthropologists and sociologists, the ignorance and superstition of the under-privileged people of Europe who became converts. Mormonism virtually pre-supposes a literal belief in the Bible, the *Book of Mormon,* and the revelations of the Prophet Joseph. I shall not soon forget a discussion I had with my landlady when I was in school in Salt Lake. I had been reading Robert Ingersoll and she had been listening to the sermons at the Spring Conference of the Church, and it is a question which of us was more horrified at the unexpected abysses of the other's mind.

The superstitions imported from Europe with the converts differ little from those of other sections of the United States, except that they are perhaps more tenaciously believed, and sometimes acquire local forms. Witches have been stoned in the Mormon Country, but water-witches are still accepted in the back country, and the seers who find lost articles are more numerous than elsewhere, and have a more solid theological justification. The beliefs of Europe, New England, and the frontier melt naturally into the Mormon system and take coloring from it. If a Norwegian grandmother in Sanpete or Sevier valley sees in dreams the uneasy spirit of a dead relative, it is not likely to mean that he was murdered or improperly buried, as it would have meant in the old country, but that he has some sin on his conscience or has never been properly baptized or wants to have some temple work done. That kind of walker is quieted easily enough. Let the grandmother take the next opportunity to be baptized for her dead relations, and all is well.

More interesting because more intimately connected with the body of special Mormon belief are the superstitions and supernatural manifestations which arise directly out of the revivalist tradition.

Speaking in tongues, for example. The technique is simple. A man, woman, or even child is moved by religious ecstasy to arise and speak in a gibberish popularly supposed to be the confusion of languages visited on the builders of the Tower of Babel. Always, except in the infrequent instances when it is a deliberate hoax, tongues come upon the speaker during a moment of great religious excitement. Testimonial meetings have been classical places for such outbreaks. Either a wretched consciousness of sin or a glorious awareness of virtue may bring it on. It is spontaneous, hair-prickling, like the stream of talk of a manic depressive. It goes on at a rattling pace, and sometimes leaves the victim either exhausted or unconscious. Its effect on the audience is equally startling. The spirit is catching, and people leap up to interpret what has been said. The interpretation is usually a stern reprimand to sinners, an exhortation to walk in the ways of God and leave off wickedness, or a prophecy of dire punishments if the community does not mend its ways.

As a psychological aberration speaking in tongues is not greatly different from other emotional releases, bacchic or cataleptic or hysterical, common among any highly emotional religious group. Mormonism has never since its first years used the sawdust trail technique best exemplified in modern times by the Holy Rollers; it has never encouraged the emotional excesses of the camp meetings, has never rolled on the earth and bitten the dust and then settled it with repentant tears. Its missionaries have customarily displayed a commendable rationality and logic and decorum. But that process of talking with tongues, like the device of the testimonial, has remained in the Mormon mind and even yet, infrequently, comes out. For one thing, it is mentioned in the *Book of Mormon* as a manifestation of God's presence. It also has fairly clear relationships with the miraculous translation of the Golden Plates. It is part of the submerged body of Mormon lore that once in a while embarrasses the Church authorities, so that several times the Church has been at pains to discountenance some babbler as a fraud, in the same way that it discourages or repudiates revelation unless it comes to the ordained revelator, the President of the Church.

Mormonism as an organization no longer likes to be a religion apart. In practice, if not in overt theory, its thesis now is that it is a faith like any other faith, one which Mormons believe to be true but which they are too well-bred to force upon others unless those others are interested. For outside consumption it exploits its similarities, not its differences. Public relations are an important branch of Church activity, and a bunch of fanatics having revelations or talking gibberish not only undermine the authority of the priesthood, but give the Church a black eye outside.

Still the really zealous Mormons, of whom there are many in the provinces, go on believing in something like the old way. At Torrey, for example, which is on the road to the Capitol Reef National Monument in southern Utah, there is a museum likely to prove more interesting to many people than even the incredibly gashed and colored canyons of the monument. Until 1937, when Congress set aside the area, Torrey was far off the main lines of travel, and preserved the habits and psychology of the little Mormon towns well after they had been diluted elsewhere.

The country is spectacular and almost inaccessible; it is close to one of the former hideouts of the romantic outlaws known as the "Wild Bunch." The terrain is so broken and eroded that even yet parts of the monument have not been explored, and in 1940 a party discovered a natural bridge that had remained hidden for sixty-five years, though it was only three miles from the town of Fruita. In country like that, habits linger.

Two people in Torrey exemplify old-line Mormonism, or did until old Charlie Lee died. Charlie was the son of that John D. Lee who was executed in 1877 for his part in the Mountain Meadows Massacre, so that he came by his zeal honestly. He was a whiskered old patriarch with a wild eye, and for years was the recipient of dreams and visions and manifestations. He was a notable finder of lost articles, but his principal visions had to do with the uncovering of ancient artifacts from the many cliff-dwellings around the Reef. His collection, which was one of the best a few years ago but has since his death been dispersed and distributed, included all sorts of Basket-maker and Pueblo artifacts, bows and arrows, grinding stones, baskets, pottery, and especially some very rare bullhide shields. Most of them he found through dreams and visions.

The other museum in Torrey is owned by Bishop Pectol, who some years ago had the honor to find incontrovertible proof of the *Book of Mormon.* Bishop Pectol does not claim to be divinely directed where to hunt for things, and he does not talk much about his most prized find, either because it is too precious for profane eyes or because the Church has asked him to keep quiet. The find itself, a deerskin marked with the mystic temple symbols of the Church, is reported to be locked in a strong box in the Church offices in Salt Lake. Those symbols, of course,

are Nephite in origin; they prove that the Nephites were
the builders of the ruined cities throughout the Southwest,
and they prove that the Nephites did have the true religion
as the *Book of Mormon* sets it forth. The deerskin has
been seen by few people, and since the Church has not seen
fit to display it in the Church Museum in Temple Square,
it must be either very sacred or very dangerous. One old
gentleman who saw it before it was sent to Salt Lake re-
marked that maybe the temple symbols were on it, if you
looked right, but if you looked just the regular way it
looked as if the mice had chewed it.

Charlie Lee and Bishop Pectol represent Mormonism at
its most emphatic stage of belief. They, and men like them,
are still the best exhibits in their own museums, if one is
as interested in the living as the dead.

3. *The Perpetual Patriarchs . . .*

The stranger came to the corral gate just as Niels Nielson was finishing up the chores. He was an old man who
looked like a tramp, and he was driving a ratty team.

"Howdy," he said.

Niels Nielson nodded, leaning on his manure fork. The
stranger was travel worn. His rig was covered with dust,
the wheels stuck with red clay.

"Wondered if you could put me and the team up tonight," the stranger said. He didn't ask it. He said it, and
waited. Nielson tipped back his hat to scratch his head.

"Yeah," he said. "Sure, I guess so. I haven't got any hay
for your team, though."

The man sat quietly on the wagon seat. "Come a long
ways," he said. "From way down the valley. Eighty miles,
must of been."

Nielson looked away to spit on the ground, his face perfectly straight, but he thought, Eighty miles in that old rig, with that team. In a pig's eye. He raised his head again. "You might get the Bishop to put the team up," he said.

"Where's he live?" The stranger remained slumped on the seat, the lines slack over the bony hips of the horses.

Nielson stuck the fork in the ground by the corral bars. "Just up the street," he said. "I'll go on down with you." He started walking, and the stranger flapped the lines and creaked after him.

The bishop was willing. "Sure," he said. "Turn 'em into my pasture. I'll feed 'em with mine in the morning."

"I thank you," the stranger said. "I'd appreciate it."

Nielson helped him unhitch and spank the weary horses through the pasture gate. Dust flew from under his hand when he slapped the off horse on the haunch. "Well, come on," he said. "Mother'll be having supper pretty soon. Got any baggage you want to bring along?"

"No," said the stranger. "If you could lend me the loan of a towel and some soap I'd appreciate it."

"We ain't got much, but we got that much," Nielson said.

They walked together up the street, stepped across the ditch and around to the kitchen door. Mrs. Nielson was putting crocks of milk in the cellarway. "Mamma," Nielson said, "can you find soap and a towel for this man? He's staying overnight."

Mrs. Nielson's eyes flicked from her husband to the stranger, and two little downward lines appeared at the corners of her mouth. "Yes," she said briefly. She went into the house and in a minute came back with a towel and a slab of homemade soap. "Basin's right there," she said. "Water's in the pump."

She and Niels Nielson went inside. "Where'd he come from?" she said.

"Just drove up. Said he'd come eighty mile. You should of seen his team. The Bishop's got 'em in his pasture." He chuckled a little, tonguing a cracked lip.

"Aren't you kind of liberal?"

The stranger was splashing in the basin outside. They could hear him snorting. Nielson met his wife's look. "Now, mamma," he said. "That's all right." He went into the other room.

In a few minutes the stranger came in, his shirt collar still rolled down and his hands and arms scrubbed to the elbow. Mrs. Nielson stood curiously in the kitchen, and he smiled at her. His teeth were good.

"It warms the heart to find hospitality," he said, with a little inclusive bow that took in even the twelve-year-old boy staring from the other side of the room. "I stopped at several places in this town, and not one of those families was willing to take in a tired traveler and his worn-out team." He rubbed his hands together and smiled at Mrs. Nielson again. His voice was deep and calm and a little oratorical. "But they will regret their selfishness," he said. "There will come a day when they will wish that they had not been so close they couldn't help a stranger in need." His hands rubbed harder, as if he relished the prospect. "Those people will see signs and wonders," he said. "I hate to think what is going to happen to those folks."

Over the stranger's shoulder Niels Nielson saw his wife's eyes open wide and the lines at the corners of her mouth deepen. He frowned at her, and she turned to set the table.

They ate in the kitchen—a bowl of bread and milk apiece, with a loaf and a crock ready for refills. Niels Nielson apologized for the fare. "We ain't got much," he said. "You're welcome to what we have, but it ain't much."

"Hospitality," said the stranger, "sweetens the meat."

Supper opened the gates of the stranger's talk. He expanded. He grew voluble. Sitting with the family after the meal, his caked and curling shoes stuck out comfortably in front of him, he spread himself. He told of places he had visited all over the world—Vienna, Budapest, Stockholm, London, New York. He had traveled the length and breadth of America hundreds of times. Niels Nielson sat and listened, and a little wrinkle of humorous disbelief grew between his eyes. From time to time he looked at his wife. What a blowhard, they said to each other silently.

"You ever been in Kansas?" Mrs. Nielson said suddenly.

The traveler turned and beamed upon her. "Oh, yes. All over the state. You know Kansas?"

"I come from there," she said. Her face took on a completely blank, stupid expression. "I was wondering how the folks back in Atchison were. You ever been through Atchison?"

"Know it very well," the stranger said promptly. "Know a good many people there, matter of fact. You ever know a family name of Birrell?"

Mrs. Nielson looked at her husband. "Birrell?" she said. "I don't . . ."

"Lived just around the corner from the bank," said the stranger. "Very kind, very hospitable family. Two young daughters, must be about fourteen and sixteen now."

"Well," she said, "I . . ."

"Smith?" the stranger said. "Henry Smith? His wife has

just passed away, poor man, leaving him with three young children. Very sad. Very sad case."

"How long since you been in Atchison?" Mrs. Nielson asked weakly.

"Let's see . . . year, year and a half. Say, you know the James family?"

"Walter James?"

"That's it!" he said, and slapped his leg. The dust rose thinly. "Walter James. How long since you've seen those folks?"

"Land," Mrs. Nielson said, flustered, "it must be fifteen years. Walter James' daughter Sue and I used to be best friends. What's happened to her?"

"Married," the stranger said. "Married and the mother of four sound young ones. Last I saw her she still looked like a girl, just as young as young."

"And still that long black hair?" she said. She was sitting a little farther forward. "I remember it used to come clear down below her waist. She could sit on it."

"Not a gray hair in it," the stranger said. "She coils it up on top of her head somehow. Beautiful hair, just like a young girl's."

Mrs. Nielson laughed a little jerkily. "Well, isn't that the *oddest!*" she said. "Imagine meeting someone that knows Sue James. Who'd she marry?"

The stranger scratched his head. "Let's see. Butler, was it? Brown, Billings, Brewer . . . ?"

"Not Bill Brewer?"

"The same. William Brewer."

Mrs. Nielson dissolved into a fit of weakening laughter. "Imagine!" she said. "Why, Bill Brewer was about the rattiest, no-accountest, beatenest, timid little squirt of a boy. He must be four years younger than she is."

"Grew up into a fine man," said the stranger. "First-rate man. Prosperous, good family man. Well liked everywhere."

She shook her head, still laughing. Then she stopped laughing and looked at the traveler. She looked from him to Niels, and her forehead was knitted. "Well, I certainly have to apologize," she said. "Tell you the truth, I thought you were stringing us with all that talk about your travels. And here you know Sue James! Well . . ." Her forehead smoothed out, puckered again. "What threw me off right from the start," she said, "Niels told me you said you'd driven eighty miles today. How could you do that, with a scrawny team?"

The stranger had been smiling benignly upon her all through her apology. "That team," he said, "ain't *quite* as bad as it looks." He smiled more broadly, as if enjoying something secret and pleasant. Mrs. Nielson shook her head again and started to stand up.

Involuntarily the breath wheezed in her throat as the pain hit her, and her hand grabbed at her side. She staggered, threw a helpless look at Niels, and started out of the room, bent over, her hand still clutched in her side. Niels half rose, but the stranger's voice stopped him.

"Are you in pain?"

Mrs. Nielson turned and grimaced from the doorway into the kitchen. "I've had it for quite a while," she said apologetically. "They seem to think I have cancer."

The stranger sat still, looking up at her with the shadow of the benign smile still on his face. Then he stood up, and both Mrs. Nielson and her husband noticed the quiet dignity in his movement. "You will never have pain there any more," he said.

After a moment's staring, Mrs. Nielson went out back

to the toilet, and in the toilet, as she told people later, "something passed her, it looked like cancer that they operate nowadays for," and her pain vanished. Still bewildered, but anxious now to do everything for the stranger, a little afraid of him and vastly puzzled, she went into the house and told her boy privately to go over to the neighbor's to sleep. The stranger would have to have his bed.

The boy scowled, kicked the floor, hung around. After a while he beckoned his father into the kitchen. "Do I have to give up my bed for that old tramp? Probably he'll leave crumbs in it and everything."

Niels looked at his son, thought a minute, and went back to consult with his wife. It wasn't quite fair to turn the kid out of his bed. Maybe they could make some other arrangement. But before he had a chance to catch his wife's eye the stranger, who could not possibly have overheard the conversation in the kitchen, stood up. "You tell your boy he needn't be afraid of me leaving crumbs in his bed," he said. "I'm a clean man. Besides, I don't want his bed. I can make me a layout here on the floor."

Nielson, after a minute's baffled wonder, went after some quilts.

Early in the morning Mrs. Nielson, miraculously free from pain, rose and put herself out for the stranger's breakfast, but he seemed preoccupied and ate little. Eventually she gave up urging him and asked him if he wouldn't like to take a lunch along.

"That might be all right," he said.

He took the lunch she fixed for him, smiled all around the family, and raised his hand in a gesture of blessing. The same dignity that they had noticed when he spoke about Mrs. Nielson's pain came upon him. "You will never want for bread," he said. "May God bless you."

They watched him start off down the road. Within a very few minutes some relatives came up the same road. "Did you notice the man with the scrawny team as you came up?" Mrs. Nielson said. "He was the strangest man."

They looked at her blankly. "What team?" they said. "We didn't meet any man with a team."

Mrs. Nielson gasped, but not with pain this time. "Why, there wasn't any other way he *could* go!" she said. "He started out just a minute ago. You'd have had to meet him." She looked at them with her eyes widening and her mouth opening. The traveling, the prophecies of what would happen to the inhospitable families, the curing of her pain, the way he seemed to know everything that everyone thought, the blessing when he left, the mysterious disappearance. . . .

"Oh, my goodness!" she said. "He must have been one of *them!*"

The stranger was, presumably, one of *them.* The Nielsons all believe it; so do the neighbors of the Nielsons in Manti. They are all honest people, they do not tell lies and are not in the habit of imagining things. And since 1928, when the visitation occurred, they have been able to point to the bad luck afflicting the people who turned the traveler away, and to their own increased prosperity. They can point to the fact that Mrs. Nielson never had a recurrence of her "cancer." And they know for a fact that the stranger started down a road that offered no cover, and in a very few minutes absolutely disappeared. He could not possibly be anyone except one of the Three Nephites, the perpetual patriarchs.

There is hardly a town in the Mormon Country which has not, at one time or another, had such a visitation, and there is not a completely devout Mormon but believes in these three old men who wander the world eternally until the second coming, giving blessings, healing the sick, admonishing the delinquent, delivering spiritual messages. Very infrequently two or three have appeared at once. Generally they come alone, and though the descriptions that people have given of them vary considerably, there is a discernible unity in the legend.

The Nephites are old men, usually described as having snowy-white hair and long beards; they are often poorly dressed, always well-spoken and mild; sometimes the mark of their immortality is on them in the form of a beautifully soft and fresh complexion, or the snowy whiteness of their "garments," or the waxen look of their bare feet. Almost always they come in the guise of travelers asking for food or a night's lodging, and their customary thanks is to heal a sick person, bless the household, or promise prosperity or health. Most of the people who have seen them have not been aware at the time that they were entertaining immortals. Some of the hosts have been surly and ungracious, and been upbraided for it. One woman even offered a Nephite a cup of coffee, and was sternly rebuked for breaking the Word of Wisdom. But when the Nephites leave there is an invariable sign of their supernatural state. They depart in the fresh snow and leave no tracks, or they start out an open road with no turnings and mysteriously vanish. Then it dawns on their hosts who they are, and they reverently remember every detail of looks and clothing, every word the strangers said.

If the experience of the Nielsons were unusual, it would mean little. But it is anything but unusual. A. E. Fife, who has written the best scholarly study of the legend to date, collected in a very short time and a very limited area forty-three such stories, and Hector Lee of the University of Utah, who is now working on an exhaustive paper, and who kindly allowed me to take the Nielson story from his files,* has collected dozens of similar visitations and is constantly running into more. A number of my own acquaintances have either encountered a Nephite themselves or have had a relative visited.

Both Mr. Fife and Mr. Lee note the similarity of this Nephite legend to that of Ahasuerus the Wandering Jew, to the story of Joseph of Arimathea, to the legend of St. John the Divine. There is no space here to follow their tracking down of the folk-tale analogues. But it may be useful to look at the passage from the *Book of Mormon* which, once the Saints were well settled in the valleys of the mountains, gave a peculiarly Latter-day Saint cast to the old floating legends converts had brought from northern Europe.

The Mormon scripture runs thus: Immediately after His ascension from the Holy Sepulchre, Jesus appeared to the Nephites on the continent of South America, administered to them, taught them, chose disciples, told them that they were a people specially chosen by God to know the true gospel. He raised a man from the dead, cured the sick, went through a kind of new-world reproduction of His career in Judea, and then prepared to return to His Father. Before He left He gathered His disciples around Him and asked them to name their desire. Nine of the twelve asked that when their span on earth was done they be gathered immediately into the Kingdom. Christ blessed them and told them that when they were seventy-two years old they would have their request.

---

* I have fictionized the Nielson story somewhat and invented a few details, but the outline is exactly as the family told it to Mr. Lee.

And when he had spoken unto them, he turned himself unto the three, and said unto them: What will ye that I should do unto you, when I am gone unto the Father? And they sorrowed in their hearts, for they durst not speak unto him the thing which they desired. And he said unto them: Behold, I know your thoughts, and ye have desired the thing which John, my beloved, who was with me in my ministry, before that I was lifted up by the Jews, desired of me. Therefore, more blessed are ye, for ye shall live to behold all the doings of the Father unto the children of men, even until all things shall be fulfilled according to the will of the Father, when I shall come into my glory with the powers of heaven. And ye shall never endure the pains of death; but when I shall come in my glory ye shall be changed in the twinkling of an eye from mortality to immortality. . . .

So the three loving disciples had a change wrought in their flesh so that they would not be susceptible to pain, cold, hunger, or bodily change, and they have remained from that day to this, going among the sons of men and dotting the i of their Master's teachings. They are responsible for some of the oddities and some of the pleasant customs among the Mormon people. To them, hoboes in the Mormon Country (there are, fortunately, very few, because most of the Mormon Country is off the railroads) have reason to give thanks. A stranger, particularly an old and ragged stranger, is not likely to be turned away from a pious Mormon's door. If the Mormon Country were on the road to anywhere there would be crosses on every gatepost, and bums would not be likely to give a marked house the passover.

The story of the Three Nephites, which warms the hearts of the faithful from Yellowstone to the Gila, is part of that immense body of religious lore calculated to comfort a man with the assurance that he is not alone. It is related to the revivalist certainty that persons now living will never die. It is brother to the legends of Friedrich Barbarossa and Arthur and Olaf Tryggvasson, of Ahasuerus and Joseph of Arimathea and the Fisher King. It has its connections with the myths of Thammuz and Adonis and Christ. It is a footnote to the human desire for immortal sanction and immortal protection, a human invention to defy death.

Within the body of Mormon doctrine it is completely consistent with the revelations, the prophecies, the miraculous healing, the talking in tongues, the gifts of the spirit. Within that climate of belief any old man or stranger is likely to be a supernatural messenger. And even the priesthood, though it no longer openly encourages the lingering belief in such creatures as the Nephites, indirectly contributes to their perpetuation by creating the mind-set which lets them appear.

There are within the priesthood of the Church certain old men without formal duties, but with great dignity and prestige. These are the "patriarchs." Their chief functions are to read Saintly horoscopes and to give patriarchal blessings. And though they themselves are not immortal or perpetual, there are numerous instances that I know of within the past few years when they have prophesied, in the midst of a patriarchal blessing, that the blessee would live to see the second coming. And the people being blessed are likely to believe it. It is not superstition; it is a thread in the closely woven fabric of the faith, an inducement to live according to the ordinances, to accept counsel and prove worthy.

Or take it higher in the priesthood. At the general Church Conference in October, 1941, President Heber J. Grant rose to speak. He was an old man, past eighty, and he had had two strokes. He was supposed to talk only two minutes, but the occasion inspired him and he spoke with amazing strength and power for at least ten, supported by what the congregation felt to be the arm of God. He singled out in the tabernacle the military uniforms, and directed his remarks to them. These young men, draftees and enlisted men, wore the uniform of the United States, but they were still deacons and elders, still part of the priesthood. And Heber J. Grant told them in so many words that if they lived up entirely, in word and deed and thought, to the teachings of the Church, not one of them would lose his life if this nation got into war.

That condition that a man must live scrupulously according to the Word to be worthy of God's protection is a fairly fool-proof loophole, but that doesn't matter. What matters is the *promise* that is there, the *assurance* that is there. It is possible, if you're good enough, to walk unscathed through the valley of the shadow of death. That one belief renders all other signs and wonders credible. The Three Nephites become then not a charming legend but a burning proof of God's goodness, a holy wonder.

Lares and Penates . . .

THE Mormons who fled to the sanctuary of the mountains, and the converts who joined them later, were
the kind of people who naturally have large families, and
they lived in a time and a part of the world where large
families were normal. But add to their normal fecundity
the ambition of Brigham Young to people his whole empire with industrious Saints, the pressure he put on his
people to be fruitful and multiply. Though he never took
the totalitarian expedient of offering bonuses for children,
he did, either personally or through the medium of the
lesser priesthood, practically force all the well-to-do and
responsible Saints to take extra wives as they could afford
them. So add to natural fecundity and the ambition of the
Church leaders the practical instrument of polygamy. A
man might expect as many as ten or twelve children from
one wife. From three or four he could expect thirty or
forty. Add to all those forces the Mormon doctrine that it
was virtuous to bring waiting souls into the world, that a
woman's highest glory was a numerous brood, that a man's
family went with him to the Hereafter and that his glory
in Heaven was partially dependent on the progeny he
gathered about him there, and you have some idea of why
the family was of tremendous importance in the settling
of the intermountain territory, why the birthrate in Utah

during most of the years for which accurate records have been kept has been practically the highest in the United States, and why the family, despite the tremendous significance of the organized priesthood which spreads responsibilities and participation throughout the entire membership, is still the granite foundation of Mormondom. The family among the Mormons is a microcosm of the Church structure, with the father in the place of patriarchal apostle and every member allotted certain duties and responsibilities.

I say the Mormon family is large, and was even larger. Look at a few. The Woodbury family of St. George, Utah, will tell you with pride, as a testimony of the gospel, that the descendants of one William Woodbury, who left the Church in 1847, number only thirteen, living and dead, whereas the descendants of his brother Orin, who stuck with the faith and was one of the St. George pioneers, now number over five hundred not counting those who have died. That is perhaps a not-unfair contrast between Mormon fertility and Gentile sterility.

Or William Jex. Jex married Eliza Goodwin in 1854, and never took another wife. In 1921 the family numbered the two originals, eleven children, one hundred fifteen grandchildren, one hundred fifty-one great-grandchildren, and five great-great-grandchildren, a total of three hundred sixty souls. That is an average increase of five and seven-tenths persons every year for sixty-seven years. Good husbandry.

Or Christopher Layton, one-time President of the Gila and San Pedro settlers in Arizona. At a reunion in 1915, five hundred ninety-four people were present, all of them legitimate members of the family.

Or Patriarch Benjamin F. Johnson of Mesa, who died

in 1935 at the age of eighty-seven. His descendants and their spouses and children totaled over fifteen hundred at the time of the patriarch's death, and even that is probably not the largest family in the Church.

Yet when a Massachusetts woman died in 1941 leaving ninety descendants, it was spot news for the papers all over the country.

On signboards around through the Mormon Country there used to be pictures of chubby, rosy children gooing out at passing motorists. I don't know who put the signboards there, whether the Chamber of Commerce or the National Association of Manufacturers or the Church, but they were there in considerable numbers, and under each of them was the legend: "Utah's Best Crop." That was no false advertising. The entire cost of having a baby—prenatal and post-natal care and delivery, used to be more or less universally fifty dollars in Salt Lake City, and I have no reason to suppose that the situation has changed in the last few years. Apparently mass-production not only increases the bulk of the product, but lowers its price as well.

Families have been shrinking, even in the Mormon Country, for a good number of years, but the Mormon family has had so far to shrink, and the tradition of a houseful of kids is so strong, that even yet, and even among jack-Mormons, the average family is comparatively large. The birthrate for 1939 was only 23.9 per thousand, which was almost as low as it has ever got in Utah, yet it was still high enough to exceed that of every state except New Mexico. Relief headquarters during the depression had reason to pay attention to that birthrate. Mormons marry young and have many children, with the result that inordinate numbers of indigents with many dependents went on the rolls.

But size is not the only distinguishing feature of the Mormon family. It is much more than the basic unit of the census takers. It is the basic social unit, the basic economic unit, the basic religious unit, the basic educational unit, the basic source-book of Mormon history. It is, in other words, everything that the normal American family is, multiplied by about three.

Some years ago, for a fee, I assisted a good Saint in the writing of a book designed to promote faith and a reverence for the home and family among the Mormon people. The book was finished and published, and was adopted by a number of Stakes of Zion, and its use urged upon the family heads in Ward meetings, by the block teachers, in conference, in the priesthood meetings. Like almost every program, official or semi-official or unofficial, of the Church, its organization was meticulous and complete. The book was called *The Home Evening Hour;* its purpose was to bind the family together by promoting religion, education, and recreation in an informal gathering in the home one evening a week. For the guidance of the meetings, specimen programs were outlined. The group should open with prayer, preferably a prayer bearing upon the sanctity of the home. Then there should be a hymn— and Mormon hymns are full of the home spirit. Then several of the children might present a skit or recitation or song. The father (or brother or uncle or whoever was handy) might talk for ten minutes on his experiences in the mission field or some other instructive topic, illustrating by the way a point of faith or morals. Then they all might play charades. Then the designated genealogist of the family might make a report on his researches, or tell an anecdote about some ancestor. Then the children who had been charged with preparing refreshments might bring them in and serve them. Emphasis throughout should be laid on teaching the children to accept responsibility. They should be taught to prepare their entertainment or their refreshments gladly and thoroughly, and no one in the family except through disability or illness should be exempted from taking part. The meeting should break up about nine or nine-thirty with prayer and another song or hymn.

But the thoroughness of the handbook for Home Evening did not end there. For every meeting of the year there were suggested readings from the Bible and the *Book of Mormon*. And just in case the father ran short of apothegms bearing upon the home and family, we added an appendix of every such quotation we could cull from Stevenson and Bartlett under the headings of Home, Mother, the Family. Everything was there from St. Paul to Eddie Guest, and I have no doubt that all of it has been used, and is still being used, in a good many Mormon homes.

So far as I know, there is nothing quite like the Home Evening Hour elsewhere in the United States. Evening prayers and readings from the Bible go on, of course, in the Bible Belt and in scattered religious homes, but the deliberate, organized, regimented exploitation of the family spirit seems to me possible only in Mormondom. The mingling of edification and instruction and entertainment and refreshments is shrewdly and typically Latter-day Saint; it makes the Home Evening a little brother to the M.I.A., and like the M.I.A., it is a source of strength.

So the Mormon family is both a big family and a cohesive family, an institution respected and cultivated by the priesthood. It is also an institution overseen and supervised by the priesthood. Every Ward has its "block teachers," whose duty it is to call regularly upon every home in the Ward, give aid or counsel, discuss religious and economic problems, rebuke the ungodly. In the old days the Gentiles accused the Church of maintaining the block teachers as petty spies, ordered to smell out taints of sin or apostasy and report them to their Bishop. Some block teachers may well have been spies of that sort. It would be strange if zeal had not become unbridled zeal sometimes. But there is no doubt whatever that under certain circumstances they have been angels of mercy—the kind neighbor systematized and made efficient. If they find a household sick, they report it to the neighbors and start a flow of soups and gruels and neighborly assistance; they see that no one is uncared-for; they report undue poverty and suffering to the Relief Society. And they bring to every householder the conviction that the Church cares about him, that he is among friends, that he is part of a great and good brotherhood. These liaison officers between homes and Wards sometimes visit Gentile homes as well as Mormon, and do a little quiet proselytizing. Sometimes they are made butts by the godless and the Mormon-eaters, but from what I have seen of them they keep their tempers amazingly well under the fire of Antichrist. As the private soldiers in the priesthood's army they are effective and completely respectable.

The religious significance of the family is intimately linked with the functions of the Temple, and because temple work has been so important to Saints all over the world, the Church has seen fit to spread its temples, to offer the ordinances at other places besides the capital. Besides the one which tourists gaze at in Temple Square in Salt Lake there are seven other functioning houses of the Lord: one on the Island of Oahu; one at Cardston, Alberta; one at Mesa, Arizona; one each at St. George, Manti, and Logan, Utah, and one at Idaho Falls, Idaho. Almost everything that goes on in those temples, as far as an outsider can make out, is connected with the strong family feeling of the Saints.

One can be baptized or married in the temple, one can have his relatives sealed to him for all eternity, one can be baptized vicariously for the dead (generally the dead of one's own family), and one can have all one's dead relations sealed to him to insure the gathering-in of all the souls at the last trump. In the old days one could have girls or women sealed to him as brides, even before the marriage ceremony.

A child, if he has been raised in a good Mormon family and lives somewhere within hailing distance of a temple, first is initiated into the secrets when he is about eight years old. His whole family, except those who have weakened in the faith, are probably already tied to him indissolubly and sealed for time and eternity. The only thing the primary child has to do is to be baptized for himself. But let us suppose a convert, recently arrived. Suppose he is August Dehn, recently converted by missionaries in Austria and newly transplanted to Zion. He has a number of temple duties to perform, and if he is a good Saint he takes them very seriously.

First of all, to gain access to the temple and its secrets, he must be in impeccable standing in the Church, his tithing must be paid up. there must be no taint about him of dissoluteness or disbelief. The temple is a little like a hospital which collects its bills in advance. If August Dehn can satisfy the conditions he can get from his Bishop or from the Stake President a slip called a "recommend," which will insure his admission.

He is given an appointment and instructions, and at the specified time he arrives at the temple with his garments and temple apron in a little handbag. With a little group of the devout he will pray in a large room below the temple, and then will go to the dressing room to prepare himself. He has already been baptized, let us say, in the River Oder, but he may be baptized again if' he wishes. Probably he is here today primarily to insure the company of his family in the Hereafter, where the family is of as much importance as it is on earth. He will be sealed, therefore, to his wife and to each of his children, so that they will never be parted by death, or even by divorce or remarriage. If he dies and his wife marries again, the second husband has only an earthly lien on her or on her children by August Dehn.

Those are the first processes—baptism and the sealing of one's wife and family. But one owes a duty to the rest of the family as well. Perhaps August Dehn has two brothers in Austria, neither of whom has been converted to Mormonism. He does not want to see their souls condemned to a mere terrestrial Heaven. He wants to give them the chance at least of higher glory. Neither does he want to be separated from his parents, his grandparents, or any of his ancestors. As an earnest Saint, it is his privilege to give them·all a chance to embrace the true faith.

So he starts ferreting out his ancestors. Within a family which has lived in the faith a long time, all the immediate generations have been taken care of, and the genealogy book is constantly being added to at both ends by the elected genealogist of the clan. But August Dehn has to start from scratch, and he may have no facilities· for research. He goes to the Church Genealogical Office, with its staff of trained research people and its files of millions of

names, thousands of family trees. For a nominal fee the
office looks up his ancestors as far back as he wants them
traced. It does not matter in the least where Mr. Dehn
comes from. The Genealogical Office is a vine that girdles
the world.

Now, armed with a long list of unbaptized and unre-
claimed relatives, Brother Dehn will repair to the temple
again, or if he is busy will send his wife or his children.
In practice, old ladies and children do much of this system-
atic temple work. Suppose August Dehn sends his two
boys. Each with his little satchel, they will gather for
prayer, prepare themselves in the dressing room, and
finally be led into the baptismal room with dozens of
other children.

The baptismal room is dominated by its great font supported by bronze oxen. In the font, standing in the water,
is one official. Another sits up in a little stand like the ref-
eree's box at a tennis match and calls out the names. As a
child's name is called, he rises and climbs up the stairs to
the rim of the bowl. The man in the box calls the names
of the dead and chants a little prayer for each, while the
man in the bowl supports the child's head and ducks him
completely under, once for each name. The wisdom of
sending two children to go through the ordinances together is immediately apparent. The man in the box
chants at an unintelligible clip, almost as fast as a tobacco
auctioneer, though he wouldn't like the comparison. With
many dead to be baptized for, and the temple open only
on certain days, there is a rush to get through all the
crowd that is waiting, and the baptizer can make better
time with two children, ducking them alternately as the
names and prayers come rolling from the cantor's tongue.

When that ordinance is completed, the dead have in

effect an invitation to celestial bliss. If they choose not to accept the gospel, very well. They have had the opportunity. And August Dehn can rest content. He has done his religious duty by his family. If the genealogists uncover more dead relations, the baptisms for the dead can be repeated at intervals, and if August Dehn's zeal is great enough to take in more than his family, he can have a baptism performed for others as well. A good many unsuspecting people, from Hawaiian kings to Presidents of the United States, have received this vicarious rite.

Mormonism nowadays puts little emphasis on hellfire, though in the past its preachers thundered with the best. Some of them went so far as to advocate the terrible doctrine of blood atonement, the shedding of the blood of the sinner to save his soul. Mormon history contains both murders and suicides motivated by that fanatic zeal to preserve the soul. But in contemporary times the Church has contented itself with promising sinners exclusion from bliss. The Mormon Heaven is a place of layers or strata, composed of the terrestrial, the telestial, and the celestial spheres. Only the righteous inherit the celestial degree of glory; only they will see God. Hence the eagerness to insure that glory for all the family; hence the curiously genealogical bent of the temple ceremonies and the religious importance of the family. Hence the willingness of many Mormon women in the old days to accept the institution of polygamy. A woman shared her husband's glory in the Hereafter; she might anticipate greater glory as the second or third wife of an important older man than as the first wife of a young one. And even when polygamy was under fire, when deputy marshals were combing the canyons for cohabs, the women stuck by the divine institution for those religious reasons and for purely family reasons. The children of plural wives automatically became bastards if polygamy were outlawed. Once you were in the system you had to stay with it.

All during the period of the persecutions of the Mormons, Gentiles spread rumors of the barbaric rites and naked abominations that went on in the secret rooms of the temple. It was inevitable that secret ceremonies, plus the institution of polygamy, would breed rumors of that kind. No one but a Saint who has gone through his temple work faithfully could answer those charges, and Saints who are in good enough standing to get into the temple do not customarily talk. There is no reason why they should. But the Church itself, within the last few years, has released photographs of the baptismal font and the "Adam and Eve" murals for publication in national magazines. The abominations story is pretty well dead. Yet still, because the temple is the house of the Lord, and because admission to it is a boon reserved for the faithful, and because the admission of the godless would cheapen and dirty the holiness within, the rule of the recommend is in force today. Tourists hovering outside the tabernacle after the free noon organ concert must still look with wistful eyes at the granite spires next door, and must still accept the word of the guide that no Gentiles are allowed within. To a good large extent, that spot is kept sacrosanct because it is the house of the Mormon family, the fane of that spirit of pious domesticity that has always been the most notable quality of the Mormon people.

Family Reunion . . .

COME to a family reunion sometime. It is better than an Iowa picnic at Long Beach, California, and generally almost as populous. Come to one in any of the villages —say Bountiful, between Salt Lake and Ogden. A block down from the Ward House is the old homestead where the patriarch lived with one of his two families not many years ago. In his lifetime he ran the village store and housed and fed itinerant Indians and raised up a numerous progeny by his two wives. The descendants still squabble a little about which family he loved more, and which of his two houses he spent more time in. Up and down the highway are the homes of some of his sons and daughters. Others are scattered around among nearby towns, Ogden, Salt Lake, Farmington, Morgan. The great bulk of the family, however, lives within close range of the old homestead. Mormons are not, except when the Church calls them, a migrant people. They cling to the family patrimony.

One of their most regular wanderings is the annual reunion, and they will come a long way for it. They stream into town by car, on foot, by interurban railroad, some bringing chocolate cakes, some ice cream, some sandwiches, some potato salad or punch. They shake hands, they slap backs, they goo at new babies, they marvel at the growth of the children in the last year. They gather in little knots and talk under their breath about how bad Joe is looking, and about how his wife could do a lot better for him than she does. They kid the girls and talk about the peach crop and holler a welcome as new arrivals fill the Ward House.

Until the festivities start, the women are busy getting food set out and the tables set in the amusement room. They hurry with pursed lips looking for that package of sandwiches that Min brought, they brush the hair back from their faces and open jars of salad, boxes of cake, bottles of olives. Their talk goes up in a high light clatter like the tinkle of knives and forks, and the tables sag under the weight of food. Members of one family whisper together as they examine the whole freezer of store ice cream brought by Aunt Priscilla of the other tribe, and Aunt Mae, who has brought a small freezer of her own home-made ice cream flavored with fresh peaches, guesses that if Father were alive he'd speak to the other family about acting show-offish and spiteful and wanting to be first in everything.

Finally Brother Willard, son of the patriarch, brings the meeting to order in the chapel room, asks Brother Charles to open with prayer. Before Charles can begin, Brother Willard asks Cousin Anne to take her squalling baby outside for a little while. Brother Charles prays for the health and long life of all the family. If there is anything wrong with any member, he mentions that member by name. Remember, Oh Lord, Brother Zeke's wife, who has had a stroke. Shower Thy blessings on Cousin Ed, suffering from cancer. He thanks the Lord for all his blessings and for their membership in His Church, and prays that they may all prove faithful.

Nephew John, the genealogist, reports on the family tree. He has so many names now that the responsibility for vicarious baptisms will have to be shared by all the units of the family. As for the young people, let them begin filling in their family trees in their primary books as soon as possible.

Cousin Walter sings a solo. He is Mary's husband—Mary is Agnes' girl—but Cousin Walter is not supposed to be too faithful in his Church work since he came back from music school. He sings a virtuoso number that thrills the young people and sounds just a little too arty to the old ones. The older ones lean together and suggest to each other that Cousin Walter be brought over to meeting sometime soon.

Now Aunt Peg's daughters troop up on the platform and go through a prepared number, holding up their family coat of arms and taking turns explaining the heraldic symbols. The women applaud vigorously, their eyes full of the cute little figures in pinafores.

Brother Willard leads in singing, takes the whole multitude through a couple of hymns, then through "America" and "Britannia Rules the Waves." Brother Fred, the oldest brother present, then rises to speak, and there are tears in his eyes as he enumerates the blessings that have been visited on the family. He traces the family history down from one great-great-great-great who was a Loyalist during the Revolution and had to flee to Canada. From Canada his descendants worked their way southward and westward through the generations, until now they are safe in the arms of the true Church in the valleys of the mountains. He is an old man now, says Brother Fred, and will not be with them long, but so long as President Grant, in his weakened condition, continues to lead the Church, he himself can only do his part and work as faithfully as he knows how. He hopes the young people present today will always labor in the cause of right as their ancestors have done.

By this time the whole family is ravenous. They adjourn to the amusement hall, and the women rush to get the final preparations made. Every square inch of the long tables is crowded with sandwiches, ice cream, cakes, pies, salads, pickles, dressings, potato chips, olives, preserves. Families are seated together—Hyrum's, Tom's, Fred's, Willard's, Charles'—and the mothers and daughters of each branch flutter around behind, postponing their own meal until the men and children are fed. When all are in their places, Brother Fred raises his hand, surveys the tables with a grave, proud look, bows his head with dignity, and offers up so long a grace that the children snicker and poke each other and steal potato chips.

After the grace the formality breaks down immediately. The tables rock with laughter, Uncle Orson talks incessantly with his mouth full, spinning out yarns about the family, telling how Mamie, riding into Salt Lake with that young Smith fella, got held up, and young Smith was so scared he couldn't walk for an hour afterward. Smith would have got Sister Mamie sure if Bill hadn't come back from his mission right about then and got to work. Brother Joe remarks that he has three daughters in the mission field now and doesn't know how he manages the expenses. The turkeys aren't paying very well, and there was that fire in the barn. But, he says, he pays an honest tithe and the Lord provides for him and his. He has never had a stronger testimony of the gospel.

Sister Ruth, when the eating has begun to dwindle down to half-hearted pecks at tidbits, rises and asks everybody present to report on his occupation. They stand up one by one, grinning, and speak it out, bowing back into their chairs with their napkins clutched in their fists. There are farmers, business men, salesmen, a few doctors, a good many school teachers. Women up and down the tables shake their heads at the breadth of the family interests, and lean over toward their neighbors to tell about their children or their Relief Society work.

Nobody comes around with a pot of coffee. No man, no woman, leans back to light cigarette or cigar or pipe. Some of the weaker vessels, like Cousin Walter, may relax with a sigh in their automobiles going home, and reach for the comforting weed, but within the family the Word of Wisdom is rigid law. To light a cigarette at a Mormon family reunion would be the equivalent of cursing aloud in the midst of prayers.

Two Champions . . .

ANY society is to be judged as much by the men it produces as by its institutions. Though it has been said that no system is so bad that it can spoil a good man, and none so good that it can make a man any better than his maximum potential, still the society and the body of belief within which a man is born and brought up will inevitably color him, throw his peculiar strengths and weaknesses into a revealing light.

Mormonism, like any other society, can be estimated by the men it has produced—can be estimated more easily, really, because of the cohesive quality of the Mormon group and the persistently directive activity of the Church.

It would be fatal to generalize. Mormonism has created its share of bigots, parochial intolerants, and authoritarians; the very patriarchal structure of the Mormon family and the Mormon Church assures that. The Church has fostered rigidity of belief, even a brand of theocratic stateism, has consistently kept women in their place as cooks, housekeepers, and breeding machines, and has subjugated the individual small-fry Mormon to the authority of the priesthood. But that does not mean that the Mormon-eaters have said the whole truth when they have pointed out these tendencies. It is just as true to say that among garden-variety Saints one finds rather more human kindness, more neighborliness, more willingness to devote time and trouble to the assistance of their fellows, than one will find in most sections of the United States. That neighborliness is pronounced within the group, but even outside the group, now that persecution no longer breeds suspicion of outsiders, it operates. To accompany the human kindness there is a considerable amount of Bible-Belt fundamentalism and narrowness and some ignorance. There is no absolute generalization possible. Mormons are people like other people. They do not have horns. They do not usually, nowadays, wear beards. On the whole they love their families, and ordinarily they live their religion as fully as the next man. Sometimes, like other sinners, they live part of it and ignore other parts, and sometimes they live their religion on certain days and not on others.

Next door to our cabin on the Fish Lake Plateau in southern Utah there used to be a cabin owned in the best co-operative Mormon fashion by three families from Manti. Manti is a temple town, almost exclusively Mormon and with its share of village narrowness. But when these three families came on vacation they were likely to relax a little. I was stacking wood in the back yard one morning when the head of one family came out into the sun, stretching and gaping and scratching between his shoulder blades. He did not see me. For a minute he looked out over the lake, to where a flight of gulls was catching minnows in the shallows. He yawned like the tabernacle pipe organ, rubbed his hair on end and blinked his eyes. Then he went to the corner of the back porch, reached under it, and pulled out a jug. He contemplated it lovingly, rubbing the glassy shoulder, then tipped it and gurgled a long time. When he brought it down again his eyes were clearer and he saw me. He cackled. "By golly," he said, "that's the way I like to fish!"

That was a relaxed Mormon, a notable yarn-spinner, a man with a most un-Mormon feeling for the picturesque flavor of language, an ability to wink at the Word of Wisdom, a mighty capacity to laugh. But sometimes you run into an unrelaxed Saint. Driving down from the plateau that same summer, I found a bridge washed out by a flash flood. Getting to Salt Lake meant going clear around south and hitting the Bryce Canyon road at Marysvale. Because gasoline was thirty-five cents a gallon on the mountain I had not filled up, and so I went along with my eye sharp for a gas station. It was Sunday. Not a soul was stirring in Koosharem or Burrville. Finally I came into the little lost village that is now called Antimony, but that then got along with the less industrialized title of Coyote. There was a Z.C.M.I. branch in Coyote, and a gas pump, but no one answered my pounding on the door. I looked around in back, under a grove of big cottonwoods, and saw a man lying in a hammock in the shade. When I came up I saw that he was reading *Western Story Magazine*—a good sign. But when I asked him if he could sell me some gas he simply looked sideways and shook his head. I said it was an emergency or I wouldn't bother him. There was a bridge out between Sigurd and Fish Lake, and I had to go around, and my tank was almost empty. If he wouldn't sell me any gas I'd be marooned half-way to Marysvale, and I had business in Salt Lake that couldn't wait. It wasn't a bad speech. I even thought it moving. But the man in the hammock spat over the edge, shook out his magazine, and settled his shoulders more firmly against the cushions. "It's the Sabbath," he said.

There, if you want, are two extremes of the Mormon

mind. We might look, just for the evidence that is implicit
in men's characters and actions, at two higher-up Mormons, and it seems only polite to pick two of the best, two
who in addition to their theological and financial promi-
nence were representative enough to be indiscriminately
adored by the rank and file. We love, on the whole, our
own virtues, even when we see them in somone else. And
it was for their humanity, expressed in recognizably Latter-
day Saint terms, that J. Golden Kimball and Jesse Knight
were beloved.

1. *Hierarch and Mule-skinner* . . .

J. Golden Kimball gave himself a good deal of trouble
during his long life, and was sorry about it. He also gave
the Mormon Church a good deal of trouble, and was even
more sorry about that. Honestly devout, he was also devot-
edly honest, and when orthodoxy and honesty clashed he
sometimes blurted out the honest words that offended both
the Church's piety and his own. He regretted his breaks
instantly and wholeheartedly, and though the Church
never did more than admonish him and bar him periodically from the tabernacle platform, he grieved over it. So
did the thousands who poured into Salt Lake every April
and October for Conference: J. Golden was the one high
dignitary (he was a President of the Seventies) who could
keep any audience from sleep. They called him the Will
Rogers of the Church. That was a mistake. He should
never have been compared with anyone, because J. Golden
was an original.

Throughout the Mormon Country he is already a
legend. Anecdotes and stories float through every Mormon
hamlet, and there is even a kind of fraternity of story-

tellers specializing in J. Golden stories. But like all originals, he defies transcription. He was himself, no less, no more, and nobody knew it better than he.

There is the tale that he was called up into Idaho to deliver a funeral sermon. Being a pious man, and concerned to give even a man whom he knew only slightly a valid ticket to Heaven (he confessed later that he had given many a man a ticket to Paradise that he knew would take him only half way) he laid the eulogy on thick. He had arrived late, and had been hustled up to the Ward House without a chance to collect his wits or speak to the relatives of the deceased. Still, Brother Johnson was dead, and he had known Brother Johnson a little. He could speak from the heart. Brother Johnson, he said, had been a good father, a tender husband, a frugal and industrious citizen. (He saw Brother Johnson's widow and orphans on the mourners' bench, and his eyes sought the rafters while he summoned his powers of moving utterance. But when his eyes came down out of the ceiling they lighted on the object of his eulogies sitting in the second row with a broad and incredulous smile on his face. A titter rose from the back of the room. J. Golden stopped short in an impassioned sentence and glared. He swung on the agitated Bishop sitting behind him, and his high voice blew like a bugle in the hall. "Who in the hell is dead here, anyhow?" he shouted.

To the Gentiles J. Golden was notable chiefly for his habit of swearing in the pulpit. He inherited the habit from his father Heber C. Kimball, who was Brigham Young's right-hand man and who was further famous as the possessor of more wives than any man in the history of the United States. (Golden's mother herself never knew exactly what number she was; neither did Golden.) Apostle

Heber Kimball had been a prophet and preacher and pro-faner, and Golden was his lawful son. Called once to pray for his enemies, Heber Kimball had shouted, "Sure I'll pray for our enemies! I pray they may all go to hell!" J. Golden, who spent his youth running wild on a Bear Lake mule ranch, had a mule-skinner's vocabulary in his own right.

To be sure he expurgated his language before he took up Church work. At the time of his re-conversion to piety he was bossing a gang of lumberjacks in the woods, and the Bishop suggested that maybe Golden was letting the men and himself talk a little pointedly. The Bishop's orders were to stop their swearing and start praying. So Golden said one morning, "Boys, you've got to stop this damn swearing. That's orders." Inside two days he had them kneeling in the snow in public prayer, and Golden himself cleared his mouth of everything except hell and damn, which were not really swearing and which had been his father's favorite words. He really cut loose again only once, when he tried for the first time to handle six span of oxen. They were, he said later in apology, Church oxen, and couldn't understand any other language than what he had used on them. The Lord wouldn't have wanted him to stand around in the snow and freeze to death just because the Church's oxen had been raised wrong.

All through his life his friends warned him that the Church might cut him off if he didn't stop seasoning his tabernacle sermons with peppery talk. His answer was invariable: "They can't cut me off," he squeaked. "I repent too damn fast!"

He spent almost sixty years of his life exhorting and praying and prophesying through the length and breadth of Zion. The Church had no better man for the raising of funds. Once he stood on a platform and piped a challenge. "How many of you in this congregation would give your lives for the Church?" Every hand went up. "All right," Golden said. He wiped the grin off his face with the back of his hand and lowered his voice confidentially. "How many of you would give fifty cents to the M.I.A. Fund?" They squirmed, but he had them. As they went out, every individual dropped fifty cents or an I.O.U. in the collection box.

His shrewd dramatic sense told him when to soft-pedal, when to harangue, when to stop. He practiced tricks on his audiences and they loved him for it. In St. George, when he was stumping with an Apostle to raise money, the two high dignitaries showed up in town on the monthly fast day. There hadn't been an Apostle in town for a long time. His coming put a burden on the good farmers of Dixie. They were gaunt and sad-eyed as they came to meeting. Not a chew of tobacco or nip of Dixie wine had been snitched all day. The Word of Wisdom and the midsummer heat rode heavily on them. They sat glumly while the Apostle inched his way like a measuring worm through a tedious sermon. By the time J. Golden arose they were restless and a little resentful. It was a hundred and ten in the hall; they steamed slowly, waiting for the inevitable and dreaded time when the contribution box would come out, wondering how small a donation they could get away with.

"Brethren and Sisters," J. Golden said, "you have heard good counsel. I don't aim to add much to it, even if I thought I could." He paused, his skinny six-feet-three leaning forward over the pulpit. "I know times are hard," he said. "I know it's a fast day. I know it's hot as hell. But I want to prophesy, Brothers and Sisters . . ." his hand went up in a gesture of benediction . . . "I want to prophesy that if you shell out, and shell out handsome, Apostle Lyman and I will get out of town in half an hour." They paved the platform with silver dollars.

Sometimes J. Golden was sent out to bring erring communities back into the fold. Preaching of the ordinary sort had no effect on these brethren. The spirit of apostasy was in them. So Golden took a male quartet along, and at the beginning of the services posted two of them on one side, two on the other, the first two singing "Come, Come Ye Saints," and the others singing "Oh Ye Mountains High." It was a horrible caterwauling. When he had stood all he could of it himself, Golden silenced his singers and faced his fidgeting audience. "How do you like that singing?" he squeaked at them. He stuck his bald head down and wagged it. "Sounds like hell, don't it? That's the way a town like this sounds in the Lord's ears when you people don't take counsel. Now just listen to what it sounds like when you pull together."

From the first word he had them; apostasy went out the windows and the building shook with the saintly harmony.

There have been some eloquent exhorters in the Mormon Church, but there has never been a preacher among that people as human as Golden Kimball. They had, he used to say, taken him off a dunghill and made a preacher out of him, and it was almost as hard on them as it was on him. He was a weak vessel. He admitted it. No matter how he tried to keep the spirit it drained out of him sometimes. When that happened, or when his manifold infirmities got troublesome, he sometimes refilled .with substitutes. The Word of Wisdom allowed nothing stronger than Postum, but Golden knew how to get around that. He could wink at a waitress as fast as he could wink at his own or another's human frailty. Once he got caught. He was traveling with a sour and severe hierarch, and the waitress forgot her cue. She came back to ask which of the gentlemen had asked for coffee in his Postum, and J. Golden had to repent immediately.

Sometimes he repented his prophecies, too. As his father had been before him, he was a practicing prophet, and generally he was cautious enough to escape saying too much. Perhaps he remembered a time when his father had come off the tabernacle platform wiping his brow after a particularly sensational prophecy, and said to Brigham, "Brother Brigham, I'm afraid I've made a mistake." Golden didn't make too many of those, but sometimes the spirit worked on him. He prophesied over a worried young man who was going on a mission and hated to give up his newly-bought mule. He prophesied that when Brother Nicholson returned he would find that the Lord had provided for him. He would find not one but four of the best damn mules in Zion in his corral when he got back. Then he forgot about his words for three years, until Brother Nicholson came back to abuse the Lord for not keeping His word. J. Golden led him to the corral and showed him his four mules, sent him away with them. When his wife beat her head against the wall in despair at his foolishness he said to hush up. If the Lord wouldn't keep His damn fool promises then he, J. Golden Kimball, would.

And there was the time—awful in Golden's memory— when he was being bored by an interminable sermon of Francis M. Lyman's before four hundred of the Seventies in Kanab. Golden dozed. He dreamed. He was falling off a high cliff, speculating on how soon he'd hit bottom. When he landed he woke and looked straight up into the wrathful face of the Apostle. He had fallen flat along the platform at the preacher's feet. Brother Golden repented of that too—fast.

He couldn't keep himself on the straight and narrow, no matter how he tried. He couldn't help being bored at sermons. He couldn't help cracking jokes and popping out hells and damns in the tabernacle. He made fun even of prayer if it was windy or struck him funny. He spoofed everything, including the priesthood, and when they rebuked him he repented. Sometimes, he said mournfully, he felt like the little girl whose mother couldn't make her behave. She had heard too much about goodness; it was too remote, too impossible. "Don't try to make me be good, Mother," she said. "Shoot me."

For years everyone who knew Golden Kimball thought he would die any day. He was as thin and transparent as cellophane, his voice shrank to a tremulous squeak. The malaria he had caught while on a mission in the southern states put him periodically in bed, and at seventy he had hemorrhages of the lungs. But he was a tough old organism. The doctor who examined him tried to joke him back to health, pretended not to believe he was seventy. "You don't look fifty," he said. "In that case," Golden said, "what am I lying around here for? I'm going to get out of here." He did.

At eighty he was a walking shadow. People inquired about his health so solicitously that he got annoyed and broadcast a manifesto from the pulpit. "Everywhere I go among this people they look at me with sympathy and pity, and ask me how my health is. Only a few days ago I walked down Main Street three blocks, and twelve people asked me that question. I felt like kicking the last one. I want to say to you Latter-day Saints that when I am walking around, I am alive and my head works."

His head worked, all right. When I first met him in 1937 he was eighty-four, a long, gaunt, humorous string bean, bald and cackling. But there was no doubt about the quality of his intelligence. He worked on more cylinders even at that age than most of his juniors. And he was having Word of Wisdom trouble that day. He didn't feel very well. On urging, he had a cocktail and immediately repented, with a grin. After a little while he had another, and repented again, permanently this time. "I haven't got the right to drink things like this," he said sorrowfully. "I gave up the right to sin when I became a member of this Church. But I guess the Lord will forgive me. I've done enough for Him in my time so He'd better."

He kept on doing a lot for Him. In his last years the authorities kept him out of the pulpit, because he never talked from notes, and there was no way of knowing in advance what sort of impossible thing he was going to say. He didn't know himself. But whenever he did get to speak he packed the tabernacle to the doors and had people hanging to their radios for several hundred miles around.

J. Golden gave something to thousands of people in Utah and the Mormon Country. Though they may not have been aware of it, he gave them their heritage. He *was* their heritage, a salty combination of zealot and frontiersman, at its very best. When he was killed in an automobile accident at the age of eighty-six he left more sincere mourners than Brigham Young had. He also left his own funeral sermon, probably the only sermon he ever prepared in advance. It contained among other things a typical Golden Kimball anecdote. During Sherman's march to the sea General Longstreet, he said, ran into a miserable wretch soliloquizing behind a bush: "My shoes are gone, my clothes are almost gone; I'm hungry, I'm weary. My family have been killed or scattered and may now be wandering helpless and unprotected in a strange country. I love my country. Yes, I would—I would die—yes, I would die willingly, if it was necessary, because I love my country. But if this war is ever over, I'll be damned if I ever love another country!"

"I feel just such patriotism," said J. Golden's funeral sermon, rather ambiguously, "for my Church and my people." Even after his death he cracked wise in solemn places. He had loved his Church honestly, but it had been a little hard on the mule-skinner in him, and no power on earth, not even the Church, not even death, could keep him from saying so.

He said he loved his fellow men, sure, but he loved some of them a damn sight better than others. He said he was working like a Trojan to love his enemies, making slow progress but still hopeful of getting there. His worst hatred was apostasy, disloyalty to the Church he served. The proper treatment for apostates, he said, was to knock them down and repent later. In some ways he was the hammer of God, but he was the anvil too. That was a figure he liked. A man ought to be as good an anvil as he was hammer.

For all his bumptiousness, J. Golden is probably inhabiting the highest Heaven with all those Saints whose wavering faith he strengthened. If they didn't make it, he is probably the unhappiest and maddest soul in that material Mormon Paradise. "Suppose," he said once, "I do everything the Lord asks of me and by and by He says to me, 'Good boy, Golden, go on up there.' And I am exalted to the highest pinnacle and you people lag behind and fail to do your duty. What fun can I have up there all alone playing the jewsharp and talking to myself and knowing you fellows are stuck in the mud somewhere?"

There has never been a better statement or a better exemplification of the group spirit of Mormonism.

I hope he is having fun. I hope he can slip off now and again and do something he has to repent about. I hope they don't bar him from the celestial pulpit. I hope he can catch the eye of a ministering angel now and again and whisper in the angelic ear, "Slip a little coffee in my Postum this noon, will you? I've been good for so long on this damn cloud I want to make sure I'm not dead and gone to hell."

2. *Uncle Jesse . . .*

Western mining camps have always been the symbols of violence, the storied focus of all the hell-roaring, wild-eyed individualism of the frontier. They released, because of the quick wealth and the hectic tempo of living which exaggerated everything in their inhabitants, every anti-social tendency that the frontier on its way west had developed. The one hundred and one murders which occurred in one year in one barroom in Alta, Utah, are characteristic, even if they do not represent quite the norm. Mining camps attracted rough characters as a sugar-bottle attracts hummingbirds, and the rough characters generally lived up to their reputations.

But what of a mining camp in which saloons and bawdy-houses were absolutely forbidden? What of a camp in which drunkenness or the use of tobacco were causes for losing one's job? What of a mining camp in which the men worked a six-day week, observing the Sabbath discreetly and with dignity? What of a camp which possessed a church and a church amusement hall where hard-rock miners came and danced country dances and drank sarsaparilla and soda pop with their families or with girls far different from the gay ladies who frequented Bingham and Park City and Silver Reef and the Carbon County coal towns? What of a camp in which no murder was ever recorded?

Unbelievable? It would be anywhere else in the West. In the Mormon Country it isn't, quite. All that is necessary for that kind of camp is that a Mormon or a Mormon corporation with a sincere and active belief in the Church doctrines should dip into the mineral wealth that is generally, in the Mormon Country, the peculiar province of the Gentiles.

Jesse Knight did just that, and in a characteristically Mormon way. He built at least two sin-proof mining camps, and after he began to take millions out of the ground he did things with his money that by other standards than his own seemed insane.

So much depends on the point of view. Mining men have been immemorial players of hunches. In any mining town, anywhere, it is still possible to run into excited men with new jiggers and devices and doodle-bugs, descendants of the forked hazel sticks with which their ancestors witched for water in New England. With those doodle-bugs it is a cinch to discover ore bodies. Just walk around, with this little magnetic dingus held before you, and if there's metal in the ground the dingus will click or whistle or bend downward or make a noise like a cash register. Even if your mining man doesn't have a doodle-bug, he is likely to have a hunch, and he will play his hunches carefully until one of them pans out, when he is even more convinced that his hunches are sound.

Jesse Knight found his first mine by a hunch, but he

called it something else. He called it a "manifestation."
Translated from Mormon idiom, that means a message
direct from on high. There is no great difference between
a manifestation and a hunch except that the sender of one
signs his name in capitals. Jesse's manifestation told him
that there was valuable ore in the Humbug property in
the Tintic district near the present town of Eureka. It told
him further that he was going to have all the money he
wanted as soon as he was in a position to handle it properly, and that he would one day save the credit of the
Church, which was then in debt and struggling with its
creditors.

That whole manifestation came true. Jesse did find valuable ore in the Humbug, in spite of the name which incredulous and contemptuous mine operators had tacked
onto that limestone claim. He made those scoffers eat their
words so completely that even geologists have now labeled
that mineral-bearing formation the "humbug lime."

Jesse Knight was a logical man to have a manifestation.
Though he had as a young man repudiated the Church
(as J. Golden Kimball had), he had come back into it reverently after the elders, by the laying on of hands, saved
his daughter from a virulent fever. And his whole lineage
marked him as a good Saint or nothing. His grandmother's
funeral was the first one at which Joseph Smith ever
preached; his father's marriage was the first that Joseph
ever sanctified. His mother, widowed at Winter Quarters,
had come across the plains with her family and had spent
her entire life being dutiful and faithful. And when Jesse
came back to the Church he came back wholeheartedly to
the tradition of his family.

The Humbug made him rich. The second shipment of
ore he got out to the United States Smelting Company

netted him over eleven thousand dollars. It assayed 3.8 ounces of gold, 175.1 ounces of silver, and 34 per cent lead. So Jesse, playing his manifestations, bought up as much as he could of the surrounding property, the Uncle Sam claim in particular. When his tunnel was in fifty feet he told the muckers he guessed it would be a good idea to turn it to the right. Within a few feet they ran into a rich body of lead ore. Still playing his manifestations, Jesse bought the Beck Tunnel, and by mystic direction sank a shaft three hundred feet, ran a drift off it to the east, and hit an ore body forty feet wide. He bought the Colorado claim, and was so sure of striking ore in it that he built an ore bin at the same time he was driving the tunnel. The ore bin turned out to be in exactly the right place. He did the same thing with the Iron Blossom, next door. He did it again with the Dragon. Before he finished he had established a continuous ore body or channel two miles long, much of the ore lying on the floor of a lovely crystalline cave, so that a man with a shovel could simply dig up loose dirt and dig up wealth. The whole floor was rich carbonate lead silver, without waste and as easy to mine as gravel. By the time Jesse finished having manifestations about the claims in that area he was worth ten million dollars.

It was as a center for the operation of these mines that Jesse built Knightsville. At his own expense he built a Ward House in it, and an amusement hall to boot, so that his workmen would not be tempted to go down to Eureka and patronize the poolhalls and saloons. He organized a school, hired a teacher, got the miners to chip in for the expenses of education. When the two dollars apiece which the miners contributed did not quite keep the school going, Jesse applied for county help, but the county replied that there were not enough children in the school to warrant the expenditure of county funds. So Jesse went over to Diamond Camp and hired Jim Higginson, whose eight children cleared up every difficulty.

Instead of hanging around saloons and whorehouses, Knightsville spent its community effort on a basketball court, concerts, town dances, and socials. As a mining camp it would have made any mucker from Nevada or California laugh, but it got out the ore and it had a good time. Secure in his manifestations, Jesse went calmly ahead paying his men twenty-five cents a day more than the prevailing wage, and giving them Sunday off, and he bucked the Gentile operators all over the state until he convinced them that they could get out more ore by working well-paid men six days a week than they could by driving them through seven. And he canned everyone he caught drunk.

Expanding his enterprises, he built sampling plants, smelters, railroads, mills. In the second decade of the twentieth century he was probably the largest single holder of patented mining interests in the intermountain country. He had the stewardship of all the money he could want, as his initial manifestation had promised him he would. There is something very close to inspiring in the way he used that money.

First, as a long-standing obligation, he paid all his back tithing, with compound interest, for the years in which he had ignored the Church. Then, looking around for ways in which to use his money, he inaugurated a system of small loans to impoverished brethren, operating on principles very like those of the Federal Housing Authority of later date. But that project didn't please him. There ought to be a better way of helping hard-up Saints than lending them money and putting them deeper in the hole. He bought up the old co-op store in Provo and tried his hand at paternalistic green-grocering, but that, though he made the store flourish, didn't please him either.

From those beginnings he embarked on a many-sided program of social amelioration. He was a one-man resettlement plan, WPA, Reclamation Service, RFC, FHA, PWA, anticipating by thirty years many of the New Deal's social experiments, and doing it out of no obligation other than the obligation he felt he owed his Church and particularly his people. In other words, he felt his money keenly, and he turned it to social rather than personal uses. He was not its owner; he was its steward, in the best United Order tradition, and though there was no organization which would help him turn his surplus back into the common fund, he did his best to redistribute it where it might do some good.

One project dear to his heart was begun with the purchase of a large amount of land in Alberta, near Cardston, where some Saints had already settled. When President Lorenzo Snow, in his message to the world at the dawn of the twentieth century, called upon men of wealth to take up enterprises that would occupy the unemployed and relieve wretchedness, Jesse Knight was one of the few who took him seriously. First he bought a township and a half of Alberta prairie, and four thousand steers, and opened a ranch. The next year, when he went up to see how his affairs in that corner of the world were progressing, he bought an additional 226,000 acres, and closed contracts with the Canadian Northwest Irrigation Company and the Alberta Railway and Irrigation Company, binding himself to build a beet sugar factory, have it ready to handle the crop of 1903, and keep it in operation for twelve years. Then he laid out a townsite, specified that if gambling houses, saloons, or houses of ill fame appeared in the town the settlers would lose title to their land, and called for settlers.

Within two years he had fifteen hundred of them, largely young couples from the Mormon Country further south, crowded out by the fact that the amount of land and water in the Mormon Country proper allowed for only so much expansion of the population. In effect, Jesse Knight was providing a place to take care of the overflow of Utah's population, to absorb Zion's export of man-power. On Knight's townsite a man could buy ten acres of plowed land, ready for planting, at ten dollars an acre with no money due for three years. Jesse advanced the money to fence the entire tract in the best Mormon group-farmer fashion. And when Canadian officials in bewilderment asked him why he was throwing his money around settling up that particular corner of Alberta on terms so ruinous to himself, he quite simply pulled out President Snow's twentieth century message: "Men and women of wealth, use your riches to give employment to the laborer! Take the idle from the crowded centers of population and place them on the untilled acres that await the hand of industry. Unlock your vaults, unloose your purses. . . ."

Jesse was always unlocking his vaults and unloosing his purse. Shortly after he had sold out his seven electric power plants to Electric Bond and Share for over a mil-lion, making himself three hundred thousand dollars on the deal, he is reported to have wondered out loud what he was going to do with that extra money. Thirty thou-sand of it, of course, was earmarked; that went as an imme-diate check for tithing. But the other two hundred seventy thousand worried him, as money lying idle in the bank always worried him. He didn't leave it lying there long.

This time he invented a personal WPA project. Because

there was a good deal of unemployment around Provo, he undertook to build at his own expense, or at least to begin and carry until there seemed no more need for it, a scenic highline drive along the foot of the Wasatch between Provo and Springville, ornamenting it with walnut trees, grapevines, and a concrete waterway. It didn't, as a matter of fact, get finished, but it got started, and it did the job Jesse wanted it to do. By the time the worst of the seasonal unemployment had been taken care of, he had another idea. To be exact, he had a manifestation, almost the only manifestation which never paid off. Something told him to buy the mountainside east of the present Ironton plant of U. S. Steel and look for minerals in the main body of the Wasatch. When he had driven his tunnel in for a half mile without sign of pay dirt he was willing to call it quits and write that particular manifestation off the books. But there were still many men, unable to get work elsewhere, who were dependent on the drilling and mucking jobs he gave them. So he ran the utterly useless tunnel in another half mile, knowing that it was merely throwing good money after bad. Nothing ever came out of that drift but rock—and the satisfaction of having given work to a lot of needy people.

Whenever he got a hunch, Jesse branched out. He opened up coal veins, founded the mining camp of Storrs, in Carbon County, on the liquorless, girl-less, pool-less, tobacco-less model of Knightsville, with a Ward House at its core. He sank immense sums on irrigation projects in the Uintah Basin, trying to open up new lands for settlement. In the Tintic mining district he projected drain tunnels which would bleed the surplus water out of great ore bodies and create a steady supply of irrigation water to the farming valleys below. That plan never quite matured either; its principal effect was to keep people at work and to honeycomb the Tintic Mountains with drifts and tunnels.

Through all the ramifications of Mormon economic life Jesse Knight was a force. He opened banks, built sugar factories and railroads, opened up new country for farming. The more money he found in his vaults the more enterprises he branched out into. And eventually, strictly according to the first manifestation which had changed him from an obscure rancher to a fabulous and beloved magnate, he saved the credit of the Church. Then he went the manifestation one better by saving the reputations of a number of high-ranking brethren who had got a little too deep in financial jugglery. The last years of his life he spent being fairy godfather to Brigham Young University, at Provo. Whatever endowment the school has is largely due to Jesse Knight. He gave land, built buildings, handed over fat envelopes full of bonds, came to commencement and talked to the graduating classes on how to live a good life.

When Jesse Knight died in 1921 the Mormon Church lost its heaviest and most faithful tithe-payer, and the Mormon people lost one of their best friends. Uncle Jesse was one side of Mormonism at its best, as Golden Kimball was. He took seriously the responsibilities which wealth laid upon him. From his drinkless and smokeless and whoreless mining camps to his WPA and resettlement projects, he underlined the differences between Mormon and Gentile philosophies. His abiding sense of the group and the group's needs, his respect for the common man, and his concept of money as an instrument for social betterment were a reflection of that part of Mormonism—unhappily weaker than it used to be—which was unerringly prophetic.

And there is one of the curious facts about Mormonism in general: the prophetic elements of its doctrine, the advanced social program, all those points of belief and system which pointed toward a planned economy, have grown weaker in Mormondom as they acquired strength and followers in the world at large. As the Gentile society which in the beginning matched the profit motive against Mormonism's hope of Heaven begins gradually to readjust itself, having gone as far as it can go, Mormonism reveals itself as an economic empire, an empire of dollars instead of the dreamed-of empire of men. By the time the world knows enough to learn from Mormonism and other societies with a similar sense of dedication to an ideal, Mormonism has been converted to the other side. At least the Church has. But that is another story, and a later chapter.

Jesse Knight was a compromise between Big Business and the Kingdom of God. If he had lived in the days of the second United Order he would have been one of its leaders. Living when he did, he could only put sticking plaster on the world that Mormon society had evolved into. He could not help build the Kingdom; he lived in a money world, and all he could do was try to patch it up.

Fossil Remains of an Idea . . .

THIS is the story of a town. It isn't much of a town, and never was. Sometimes in summer it comes close to breaking heat records, but that is its only distinction except one. It is probably a rattier-looking town than most, certainly less attractive than the ordinary Mormon village, because of its lack of water. In summer there is hardly any way of keeping the sand from drifting in and settling all over everything every time the wind blows. There are a few windmills and a few wells, and there used to be good range for cattle, but the homesteaders who came bonanza-farming during and after World War I plowed up all the grass and turned the country into something very close to desert. Most of the homesteaders have dried out and gone, and the range will come back, but it takes time. Looked at from one point of view, it is a pretty good place to starve to death. The only really productive part of the town is owned by a man named Lauritzen, who owns all the water from the creek, is not a good Saint, and has persistently refused to give up any of his water to the drifters who came in.

The name of the town is Short Creek. It is in Arizona, almost on the Utah line, about fifteen miles as the crow flies below Zion National Park. It sits directly under the magnificent section of the Vermilion Cliffs known to early geologists as the Towers of Short Creek and to the Paiutes as Tumurru, Rock Rover's Land. There is marvelous scenery to look at, but few people ever see it, because Short Creek is off all the roads to anywhere, and because the one road in is an axle-breaker. The only way in is from Hurricane, on the Utah side. The Colorado River cuts all of Mohave County off from the rest of Arizona. It is possible to get an idea of the effectiveness of the river as barrier from the fact that Kingman, the county seat, is ninety miles away by airline, and four hundred and twenty-five by road. To cover that ninety miles in a car you have to go clear down into California, back across Nevada, and through the corner of Utah.

There isn't even a church in the town. The only churchgoers who ever lived there were Mormons, but it was too poor a community to support a Ward House. So they used the schoolhouse. They used the schoolhouse for dances, too. Old Man Colvin, who was the first settler in there except Lauritzen, used to play the fiddle while his wife Lizzie chorded for him on the piano. But there was a little trouble from the beginning, partly because Old Man Colvin was pious and wanted the dances opened with prayer and run like Ward House dances, partly because the Gentile homesteaders and cowpunchers didn't feel like throwing quarters in the tin cup if they weren't allowed to cut loose and get their money's worth. Besides, the cowpunchers were always coming up and yanking Lizzie away from the piano when there weren't enough women to go around. Old Man Colvin didn't like it. "They're a-dancin' my Lizzie to death," he said.

Nothing that can be said about Short Creek can make it sound like much of a town. There was nobody there at all before 1913; then came the Lauritzens, then a little clot

of good Saints in the village and a scattering of homesteaders out on the mesa. Short Creek was founded too late and
in too poor a district ever to become one of the model garden towns of Mormondom. There simply wasn't enough
energy left. Everybody was tired. And it was hot, and Lauritzen hogged all the water. But just the same it got to be a
sizable village at one time. It was always poor, though conditions picked up during the depression when almost everybody in town got eight, ten, or twelve dollars a month
from relief headquarters. That was the biggest boom Short
Creek ever saw, that period of relief. But all this is really
not the important thing about Short Creek. The important
thing is that for a couple of short years Short Creek was
the capital of the world.

The Saints of Short Creek, representing as they did the
relief rolls of Mormonism and living as they did in the
Arizona Strip, attached topographically to Utah and politically to Arizona and pretty generally ignored by both,
were a pretty zealously orthodox lot. They didn't believe
in traveling, because automobiles were the instruments of
the devil. Within their inadequate oasis they abjured the
world, and the troublesome Gentiles from the mesa only
hardened their fundamentalist rigidity. Their spiritual
leader was Isaac Carling, who had one of the few developed farms, with an alfalfa field, currant bushes, and a row
of peach trees. Isaac preached some fairly ornery sermons
about the Gentiles and their cigarettes and their home
brew, and prophesied a considerable number of earth-
quakes and fires and floods. But that didn't stop the Gentiles from coming into Short Creek for their good times.
There wasn't anywhere else to go. The Saints had to stand
them, just the way they stood the dust and heat and
drouth and wind. Isaac in his sermons grew solemner and

solemner, and surer in his mind that the Gentiles were going to hell across lots. And the surer he got of that, the surer he was that the faithful Saints in Short Creek were on the high road to Heaven. That assumption is nearly always a dangerous one. Something was bound to happen in Short Creek, and eventually it did.

To understand what happened in Short Creek you must go back clear to Joseph Smith and his revelation about polygamy. That revelation is reprinted in *Doctrine and Covenants*, Section 132, but in Short Creek in its heyday nobody had to look it up. Everybody knew it by heart. That revelation assured the Prophet that if a young woman were given to a·man, and she were a virgin and not promised to another, then that man was justified in taking her. And if two or three or four such were given to him, he was still justified. There was no top limit except that imposed by economic considerations. That was the way the Lord told it to Joseph, and that is the way the Church believed until 1890, when President Wilford Woodruff was forced to knuckle under to overwhelming federal pressure and issue a manifesto against plural marriage. The manifesto did not repudiate the divine origin of the institution; it merely forsook it as a Church doctrine because it conflicted with the law of the land. Polygamy was not wrong; it was impolitic.

A good many Mormons refused to accept that manifesto. Some moved to Mexico, some married new wives in secret, some married them on the high seas where the "law of the land" did not apply. But by and large there was only a scattering survival of old-line, amnestied polygamous families, and a few rebels who broke from the Church's decree, to testify by 1925 that Utah had ever been a polygamous state. And it was in precisely such places as Short

Creek that the law of God was likely to look worthier than the law of the land. Nobody in Short Creek had ever seen any of the law of the land. It was too hard for the law to get over from Kingman, and Utah law stopped at the state line. In Short Creek, where religion was nine-tenths of a man's life, and life was pretty dull even if it was nine-tenths religion, people had time to think about their faith, and a perfectly free opportunity to live by whatever faith they chose.

The idea didn't come to Short Creek from Heaven. It came from Lee's Ferry, on the Colorado, where a number of men had gone right on adding wives and nobody had bothered to stop them. The Johnson brothers particularly were well-known polygamists. Nobody wanted to stop them. Lee's Ferry was out of the world. Governor Hunt of Arizona went through the town once and somebody told him the farmers there were polygamists and ought to be prosecuted. The Governor took one look around and said, "Hell, if I had to live in this place I'd want more than one wife myself."

The Johnson boys were cousins of Isaac Carling. Both of them were fast talkers, but Price, who had been on a mission to the southern states and knew how to spread the gospel, was the real initiator of Short Creek's crusade. By 1928, in casual conversations, he had Isaac just about convinced. That was the year the Church began to take notice of the Lee's Ferry scandal, and to make it warm for the Johnsons and their friends. Isaac Carling, long and lean and solemn, went around shaking his head and saying darkly, "The Lord ain't pleased with man when he makes a law ag'in my conscience. The laws of God are higher than the laws of man, and if I got to foller one or the other I'll foller God." He talked about living "according to the fullness of the gospel," and he started casting sheep's eyes at Edna Black, though he already had one wife named Elva.

Then the whole group of Lee's Ferry polygamists cleared out and moved up to Short Creek. There were Price and Elmer Johnson, Carling Spencer, and Edner Allred, each of them with two wives. Isaac received them with open arms, but the Gentiles and the less-enthusiastic Saints were not so sure. The Gentiles were mad. Isaac had refused to allow them to smoke within fifty feet of the schoolhouse, had warned them about drinking and creating a disturbance, and was always prowling the grounds in search of sin. Now they saw him welcoming a bunch of Lee's Ferry cohabs, and they howled. But the louder they howled, the closer the faithful drew together. They had the true gospel and they would practice it in spite of the laws of the land or the pressure of the Church, which liked nothing quite so little as the rumors that were spreading out from the Strip.

Something had caught fire in Short Creek, that bedraggled and dusty hamlet under the cliffs. There was zeal and rebellion in the air. When the Church authorities in Hurricane summoned Isaac, his wife and mother, and Price Johnson and his two wives, Isaac and Price challenged the priesthood quorum to deny the revelation of the Prophet Joseph. The priesthood wouldn't, but it sorrowfully detached the whole Short Creek crowd of rebels from the Church, deposed Isaac, and reorganized the Short Creek Branch under Charles Hansen, the schoolmaster.

But Isaac and Price refused to be disfellowshiped by a priesthood which bowed down before man-made laws. For a few years they held their meetings apart from the regular meetings, but by 1935, growing bolder, they had moved into the schoolhouse and taken over. They even admitted strangers, and some of those strangers proved to be friends incognito, polygamists from the Salt Lake group led by Joseph W. Musser and John Y. Barlow. Musser and Barlow, at first merely curious, apparently decided that the fire growing and spreading in Short Creek might be made useful. Here in this singularly inaccessible spot might be the place to promote a real development of the fullness of the gospel. In the meetings and in conversation winged words began to fly around: Millennial City, First City of the Millennium. Out of their enthusiasm they got up a vision of houses blanketed in flowers, walls of precious stones, foundations of fair colors, temples shining in the sun. They forgot, momentarily, that Lauritzen still owned most of the water rights, and even if they had remembered it they could have thought up a miracle—a rock smitten by the staff, water flowing from the cloven cliffs. Musser, who edited, and still edits, the avowedly polygamist newspaper *Truth,* and who for years has been the head of a group of believers in plural marriage, went back to Salt Lake to direct things from there, but Barlow stayed, and Barlow was going to be a Moses to this people. He was an old man; he had failed in everything he had ever tried; he had been a reliefer since relief had come in, but he knew that he was chosen to lead the world straight. Five hundred families of polygamists, he said, were ready to move into Short Creek as soon as arrangements could be made. The village would blossom, and soon all of northern Arizona would be cleansed of wickedness and the Saints could build the true Kingdom in peace.

So they started to usher in the Millennium. First a mysterious stranger named Zitting appeared at the Lauritzens' door and wanted to trade "choice properties" in northern

Utah for the Lauritzen ranch and water rights. The Lauritzens, suspecting him to be a representative of Musser, turned him down. But that didn't stop the leaders from bringing people in. Ianthius Barlow, John Y.'s younger brother, arrived with two wives and families, leaving a third wife in Salt Lake to draw her relief check and forward it to him. Came Lyman Jessup with a pretty second wife. Came Carl Jentsche and a young bride, his second. Came Richard Jessup with only one wife and Fred Jessup with none at all, both of them hopeful. Came Edmund Barlow and his two. Came the two current wives of John Y. Barlow, along with the family of girls his dead first wife had borne him. Came Cleveland LeBaron of Lee's Ferry, passing through on the way to Hurricane and dropping off one of his wives en route. Came Jack Fish from Los Angeles, with a wife and family and two "widows" and a carload of household goods. Zion was being gathered in.

All the time polygamist groups in Salt Lake and Los Angeles, convinced that in the Strip celestial marriage might flourish again, donated money. The Short Creekers bought a red truck for the speedier gathering-in of the faithful, and for months it made weekly trips to return burdened down with people anxious to live excitingly in the Lord's way. It was a pretty stimulating period in Short Creek's history.

The town, naturally, couldn't hold all the immigrants. Every shack was bulging with them, six to a room. Many of them lived in granaries and sheds, and many others set up their stoves, beds, tables and chairs in the open, without even tents. One good rain would have drowned the whole bunch, but in that summer of 1936 there were no storms. They noticed it: God was tempering the winds and looking after his lambs.

Nobody in the town had anything to live on, any way to make a living, except the few who had painfully nursed up little garden patches in Short Creek's earlier years. Many of them received relief checks, but obviously the First City of the Millennium could hardly go on accepting checks from the government whose laws it was setting out to overthrow. It had to have a stable economy; it was inevitable that the leaders should revive the United Order. They didn't bother to incorporate as the earlier Orders in the seventies had. They merely organized, under the headship of John Y. Barlow, a thing called the United Trust, to which everyone was asked to donate his property, even to the last bedtick and the last broken stove leg.

The barrenness and privation of living outdoors or in crude shacks had been the first test of the faith. The United Order was the second. Some people, like Isaac Carling, gave everything they owned. Isaac even gave his garden, and submitted to being sent away to work on a farm in Utah for the good of all, while mobs of uncontrolled kids broke down his fences and violated his peach trees and trampled his vegetables. Others, with less to give than Isaac, gave it just as willingly. But some, like Jack Fish of Los Angeles, got mulish and refused to join the Order. They were a heterogeneous and ignorant and incompetent lot of people, and they liked much better to sit in the shade of Isaac's tool shed and talk about the shortcomings of their neighbors than to labor for any cause.

They tried, rather languidly, to do something. They got an old car motor hitched up to a shingle mill and in the course of the next two years got out exactly three bundles of shingles. They planted a little corn, they had a little dairy herd, and up in the mountains above Zion Canyon they acquired a sawmill which was to furnish lumber for the building of the Millennial City. But the sawmill got so popular as a honeymoon resort for newlyweds that little lumber came back to Short Creek and none at all went out to Hurricane and other towns to be sold for cash.

Actually the wives got along a little better than the men. They co-operated with each other, took turns at entertaining the joint husband, consoled each other when he took a fresh bride up to the mill. They washed and cooked and had babies and quilted and canned and preserved. Occasionally they even had a little fun.

Fun was generally a dance, but here too schisms appeared. The young people wanted to fox trot, the elders wanted square dances. The young men staged a sit-out strike. If they wanted to drill, they said, they'd join the army. But that didn't bother the elders greatly. They had control; they knew more about how to win a woman and how to please her. If the boys wanted to sulk, that was just fine. It left more of the girls free, so that a man could bring a virgin or two to a dance along with his wives. Without apparently being aware of it, the polygamous elders of Short Creek were reproducing the youth problem that had caused trouble in the early days. Then, young men used to be sent out on missions until they passed the rebellious stage. On their return they could be given a wife or two and take their place in the priesthood, forgetting their first girls who had chosen to marry older men. Barlow and his brethren handled their youth problem in an even more direct fashion. They gave the stubborn young less food to eat and more work to do. That generally brought them around.

The City of Fair Colors, even during the years of its boom when Barlow and others were proselytizing through Utah and Nevada and California, was not a completely idyllic place. The Fish family, holding out on the United Order, became the center of a dissident group. It was not simply the outrage suggested when John Y. came to take over their furniture that bothered them, though that had bothered them enough. They had wedded one of their daughters to John Y. and the daughter had run away after the first night. That raised doubts too. And the proselytes who had a trade grumbled at being put to work hoeing weeds when they had come full of expectation of using their skills in the building of the city. Carl Jentsche and Lyman Jessup apostatized and went back to Salt Lake, and that cleared up some of the grumbling.

Other questions arose, however, questions intimately related to the conduct of the perfect society. The people from Los Angeles, used to the beaches, turned their kids loose in the road in sunsuits, so that Aunt Lizzie Colvin had to capture the squealing lot and slap them into decent ankle-length underwear, shirts, and overalls. Another Los Angeles neophyte, erroneously thinking that polygamy meant complete emancipation in sexual matters, started a home class in the facts of life for the young people. Aunt Susie Barlow polished off that heresy.

While Short Creek was enjoying its first slightly-bewildered ecstasy, rumors flew. Relief authorities, receiving blanks which listed one father as the head of three or four families, began to scratch their heads. And besides, it began to look as if John Y. Barlow's prophecy that five hundred families would move into Short Creek might come true. Five hundred polygamous Mormons, with their wives and voting children, could upset the voting balance of the whole county. Polygamy by itself wouldn't have warranted the trip from Kingman, but the voting balance of the county was another matter. So late in the summer of 1936

Sheriff Graham and County Attorney Bollinger beat their
way around through California and Nevada and Utah into
the Strip and began interviewing anti-polygamists and
Justice of the Peace Lauritzen. This nasty polygamy business, they said, must be stamped out.

They had trouble getting complaints. Nobody denied
that polygamy was all around, but some were reluctant to
bear witness and all of them lacked concrete evidence of
times, places, circumstances. Finally Jack Childers, a home-
steader, signed complaints based on "information and belief" against a number of families. Childers' belief may
have been sound, but his information was not. Some of
the families he complained against did not exist, some of
them were Does and Roes. Eventually the case came down
to charges against Price Johnson and Carling Spencer and
their respective second wives. The local Saints rallied to
the defense. Barlow said he would get a fancy lawyer from
Salt Lake who would tie the prosecution in knots, but the
lawyer never arrived. Instead came Joseph W. Musser,
who was no lawyer but who had, as Barlow said, "had a
lot to do with the law."

He knew enough about the law to demur immediately
when the trial opened on September 6. The complaints,
he said, being made only on information and belief, were
invalid. Justice Lauritzen, determined to maintain an im-
partial stand although the polygamists had been in his hair
for years, sustained him and threw out the case until valid
complaints were forthcoming. The County Attorney demanded that the prisoners be held until he could get some,
but the Justice said he couldn't hold anyone unless there
was a charge against him, and turned the prisoners loose.

By that afternoon Bollinger had what he thought were
valid complaints. But when court re-convened the prison-

ers had vanished. The sheriff and his deputy combed every house in Short Creek. No one had the least idea where the two men and their wives could be, though almost anyone in town could have found them on three hours' notice. All Bollinger could do was demand a new trial and hope he could catch somebody to bring to it as defendant.

Between trials, the sheriff and his deputy rode up and down the streets of town looking for Johnson and Spencer. The newspapers outside spread stories about posses combing the hills and canyons for the pious adulterers, about signal fires on the cliffs, a hostile village, and the grim sheriff sleeping with his boots on on the trail. All the time the four were within a few miles, camping in a perfectly accessible canyon and having their food brought to them quite openly by friends.

This is not to say that the inhabitants of the Strip, Mormon or Gentile, were contemptuous of the law. The Gentiles were amused, and they didn't give a damn. The spectacle of the sheriff making a great play for publicity when any ten-year-old could have caught the four cohabs made them laugh. Let the politicians make a big stir about polygamy if they wanted. Let them make their own reputations.

Eventually the four decided to stand trial of their own accord, and the town girded for the battle of the century. On September 28 Lauritzen's haystack was full of Paramount photographers and the town was jammed with the curious and the expectant. Tents were thick under the cottonwoods by the creek. They gathered for the trial in the schoolhouse, packed it, bulged it. Johnson and Spencer, a little scared, sat on the stand blinking in the glare of flash bulbs; the room was thick with man-smell and powder-smoke and excitement.

Bollinger, sure of his case this time, offered as evidence the relief blanks signed by Helen Hull, second wife of Price Johnson, and the birth certificate of one of her children, born in 1931. Immediately Attorney Hayek, for the defense, protested. The complaint charged that the offense was committed in 1935. All evidence about conditions prior to 1935 was irrelevant, immaterial, and incompetent. Bollinger asserted that he had a Supreme Court decision upholding the admission of such evidence, but when Justice Lauritzen asked him to produce it he threw up his hands. How, he said, could you get anywhere in a place like this? He would dismiss the complaints and have the sheriff arrest the prisoners over again and take them to Kingman for trial.

Attorney Hayek could have saved his clients right there, probably, if he had not been so dazed by a request for change of venue in the middle of the trial. He assented, and all the people who had jammed the schoolhouse a few minutes before, all the reporters and the newsreel photographers, all the sympathetic polygamists and the curious ranchers, got up out of the seats they had barely had time to get settled in. Short Creek's biggest excitement was over before it had properly begun. What might have been almost as much fun for the papers and the public as the Tennessee monkey trial fizzled out drably.

That was the end of national publicity for Short Creek. That was the passing of Short Creek as the Millennial City of Fair Colors. Price and Carling, later tried in Kingman, went to the penitentiary for two years apiece, the village began to disintegrate. Musser and the Salt Lake polygamists lost interest in it, and the threatened overturn of the voting balance of Mohave County was forestalled. Still, for a long time (probably there are some yet) there were men in town with odd relationships to various widows, aunts, and sisters. A few rods from the village, up across the Utah line, was a building where spare wives could be moved in case the Kingman politicians got troublesome again. But the fire was gone. The population dwindled. The dust is thicker in Short Creek than it ever was, and Lauritzen still owns the water, but a few families hang on to their belief in celestial marriage as revealed to Joseph Smith, and are positive of their reward in Heaven, no matter what the world may think of them.

The world scarcely knows they exist. The Church knows, and disapproves, but it is more politic to leave the few renegades alone than to stir up another scandal which would inevitably reflect on the Saints as a whole. Nobody much cares what goes on in Short Creek any more. The federal authorities prefer to leave bigamy prosecutions to the states, and the states are hampered by the strategic position of the town astride the state line. As long as there is no threat to local politics, the people of Short Creek can have as many wives as they please and nobody will disturb them. In other words, polygamy, which was once the "twin relic of barbarism," second as a national issue only to slavery, is a dead herring. It can be dragged back and forth across the Utah-Arizona line at will, and will confuse or bother no one, because no one any longer is following the trail. The Millennial City and the institutions it tried to revive are as dead as fossils, and have only a fossil's interest.

So sung, or would, or could, or should have sung, the modern Short Creeker, in tolerable prose and with a tone of gentle Gentile irony. So sings Jonreed Lauritzen, son of the Justice of the Peace, who was present during all of the town's brief dramatic period, and who generously furnished me with most of the details. Even the enemies of the neo-polygamy will admit that many of the United-Order-polygamists were perfectly sincere in their beliefs and practices. Isaac Carling, for instance, turned over everything he had and was an obedient follower of the leaders' orders. He had every reason to feel aggrieved at the way he was treated, but he never wavered or complained. Even when he needed fifty dollars for an operation to save his life, and the board wouldn't or couldn't give him back even that much out of what he had donated, he guessed to his wife that it would be a good chance to rest, and came back to Short Creek and died. Jonreed Lauritzen and two other non-polygamous townsmen dug his grave, and the Order sermonized over it and predicted what glories Isaac would enjoy in the highest Heaven. And Isaac would have agreed.

Short Creek's history is opera buffa. In another age, fifty or sixty years before, it might have been something a good deal more austere, a good deal more successful, and a good deal more tenacious. The same beliefs, the same peculiar social institutions, bred in the grandfathers of the people of Short Creek a fierce zealotry that would suffer any privation or danger to protect its own. The law of the land then found a worthier opponent. Look at the citizens of Cedar City who met together in 1857 in anguished prayer and then went out to cut the throats of a hundred and twenty-eight men, women, and children at Mountain Meadows.

Short Creek was made of softer stuff, but its faith was identical with that of the elders of 1857. The faith lingers after the driving force is gone. The United Order sleeps yet as a dream of the future in many a Mormon mind, and all over the Mormon Country there are little groups which secretly cling to plural marriage. Not all those groups are as inept or as open to ironic doubt as the Short Creek villagers. Joseph W. Musser is a shrewd leader, and one who is afraid neither of the Church nor the law. Mormon-haters say the Church cannot touch him because he knows too much about high members of the priesthood. I neither know nor care whether or not those charges are true. The Church has sufficient cause for letting Musser alone anyway; hauling him up to face criminal charges would be bad publicity for the Church. Most ordinary Mormons, as a matter of fact, will emphatically deny that polygamy exists any longer except among those families who were amnestied by the federal government in the nineties. Yet Musser openly publishes his newspaper *Truth,* and another of the sect, Mark Allred, published a half dozen years ago a book called *A Leaf in Review,* which is a passionate defense on theological and Biblical grounds of the peculiar institution. The Mormon Church finds it easier to deny the existence of these people in Salt Lake and in the suburb called East Mill Creek who live more or less openly with plural wives than to prosecute them.

Polygamy is dead, but its soul goes marching on. The belief lingers and even burns fiercely in a few breasts long after the institution and the economic justification of the institution have crumbled. It is evidence, if we needed evidence, that a faith crushed by law or force will merely go underground, that when outward resistance is impossible the inward resistance remains. Those two relics of barbarism, slavery and polygamy, have both been crushed, one by a bloody war and the other by economic and political pressure over a period of more than forty years, from 1849 to 1890. But there are still the unregenerate and the defiant, those who "won't be reconstructed and don't give a good God damn."

As long as Mormonism remains a religious force, and as long as the Confederacy is a green memory, there will always be the unreconstructed. Faith is a weed with a long taproot.

Looking Backward . . .

IN September, 1940, a large party of men and women on horseback went from Blanding, in southeastern Utah, to the Colorado River just above the point where the Escalante River comes in. They were met there by an automobile party which had come over the barely passable road to Hanksville and thence down past Boulder Mountain to the Colorado River cliffs. In that group which met at an unused crossing of the river there were state officials, Church officials, old men and women bent and withered and dried. On the Sunday morning following their arrival they held a sunrise service on the cliffs above the river, and after the service a kind of reunion picnic, with speeches and recollections.

What were they celebrating? What event led them into the desert? What were these old codgers and white-haired old ladies doing out in country where a Navajo has to look sharp if he wants to survive?

The answer is written in the cliffs on the west side of the river, in the place called the Hole-in-the-Rock. There is a kind of pinnacle which leans a little outward from the cliff as though a great piece had split off but not fallen, and between the pinnacle and the massive smooth cliff is a steep notch. If you look closely you can see a kind of ledge angling down from the mouth of the notch, starting about a thousand feet above the river and ending in a little clump of brush near the water's edge. That is, or was, a road. Look at it again. It comes down two thousand feet from the rim, directly through the notch, then swings along the cliff-face in a long incline. The average angle of descent is about fifty degrees. Through the upper part of the Hole the drop is one yard for every yard forward, and at two places along that trail there are sheer cliffs of fifty or sixty feet.

Eighty-two wagons came down over that trail in 1880, along with seventy families of Mormon settlers and hundreds of head of horses and cattle. Look at it again now. *Wagons* come through there? It's a hoax. You don't believe it.

Neither did an old Ute Indian the Mormons encountered some days after they had forded the river and started up their terrible route to the San Juan. His amazement was great enough at seeing them there at all; when he asked how they had got there and they told him they had come through the Hole-in-the-Rock, he quite flatly called them liars and rode away insulted. The Mormonee spoke with a forked tongue.

But they did come through that slot in the battlements. The half dozen old people with the party in 1940 are there to prove it. They came through with the wagons, and the almost-effaced scratch down the half-mile cliff starts them talking and shaking their heads and remembering.

Anyone who made that trip has plenty to remember. It was made after Brigham's death but it was made in the best Mormon manner. Cattlemen and settlers were coming in from the east, from Colorado. Unless the Saints settled the southeastern corner of the empire, others would get in there first. So President Taylor, Brigham's successor,

called selectees from central Utah, from Iron, Beaver, and
Millard Counties, to settle San Juan and "breed goodwill
among the Indians."

San Juan was then, and is now, the most barren frontier
in the United States. To reach it from Cedar City the Mormon pioneers had three choices: they could go far around
to the south, through Arizona; they could go far around to
the north, approximating Escalante's old route backward
across the Green River, crossing near the present town of
Jensen and then dropping far south again to their destination; or they could cut straight across the forbidding Escalante Desert. They chose the most direct way, though when
they started they were not even sure that a road could be
made through, and in traversing that desert and the even
worse desert on the other side of the Colorado they made
one of the most incredible wagon trips ever made anywhere.

Those old men and women who in 1940 began making
an annual pilgrimage to the Hole-in-the-Rock can remember many things. They can remember the camps at Forty-
Mile and Fifty-Mile Springs during the fall of 1879, when
the road back across the High Plateaus was blocked by
snow and the road ahead looked utterly impassable. There
was no forage on the bare rock desert, and the stock had
to be scattered out for miles in every direction. There was
so little wood or burnable material of any kind that the
whole camp had to get out and gather sagebrush or black
shadscale, a kind of bushy weed which burned like grass.
It took a bale of it to boil an egg. When the pioneers gathered in meeting at Forty-Mile and decided, with apprehen-
sion and misgiving, that there was no course but to go forward, the camp was split, half of it going on to stop at
Fifty-Mile, the road builders going on still farther to the
Hole. Silas Smith had already beaten his way back to Salt

Lake, got an appropriation from the legislature of twenty-five hundred dollars for dynamite and road-building equipment. With that equipment sixty men built a road where God certainly never intended a road to be.

They built it in midwinter, and a lot of it they built while hanging over the cliff on ropes. They drilled and blasted through the solid rock, and at night they danced on the smooth stone of their bluff camp to the fiddling of Samuel Cox. After two weeks of work they tried to get the horses down to the river, where forage was good. They lost nine of them over the cliff on the first attempt, so they postponed further attempts to take anything down. The dynamite was already used up, and the trail was still a long way above the river. They resorted to dugway where they could (a Mormon dugway was simply one slanting wagon-track cut so deep into the rock that a wheel couldn't get out of it. Put a wagon in it and pray), but when they came to a steep, smooth rock face they were stumped. It was too abrupt for a dugway, and they had no powder to blast a ledge. Ben Perkins found the answer. On his suggestion they put the blacksmith to work widening the drill points. Then they suspended drillers over the cliff and had them drill large deep holes on an even incline all the way to the bottom. Other men went out to the mountains and the river bottom and cut scrub oak stakes, and the stakes were pounded deep into the drilled rock. Across the stakes brush and driftwood were banked, and broken rock scattered on top of that. Give those Mormons credit. When they couldn't blast a road out of the cliff, they tacked one on as a carpenter might nail a staging under the eaves of a high house.

By January 26, about six weeks after they started blasting, a third of the wagons were down, lowered carefully on ropes down through the notch, grinding and heeling through the dugway. Down the steep rock-and-brush shelf they rocketed almost uncontrolled, but not a wagon or an animal was lost. On February 10 they were all down, but the road was practically gone. Every wagon weakened it, every successful descent took along a little avalanche.

Now for sure there was no going back. They couldn't have if they had wanted to. They were in the bottom of Glen Canyon, faced with a treacherous crossing of the river. The wagons they floated over without great trouble, but the stock got frightened in midstream, turned back, scattered, had to be rounded up and whipped into the current again. To get up the other side of the canyon took a week, every wagon going up behind four to seven span of horses or oxen. And then the plateau on the other side, which had looked level and easy from the cliffs, turned out to be so nearly suicidal that they almost lost heart. Their scouts, sent on ahead to find a passage across the badlands to Montezuma Creek, all but died of starvation and thirst en route, went ninety-six hours without food and with little water. Finally they located the little group of Saints who had come up through Arizona to settle Allen's Crossing the year before, got food and a few hours of rest, and went back to get the train.

From the Hole-in-the-Rock to the Montezuma it was about seventy-five miles as the crow flies. It was a hundred and fifty the way they had to go, through the Clay Hills, around the heads of bottomless narrow canyons, over the "Slick Rocks" where only an accidental encounter with a flock of mountain sheep had shown the scouts a way through. Every mile was enough to make anyone but an automaton weep. They fought over the waterless plateaus, skidded wildly down the slick rocks, the heavy wagons wheel-locked and coasting like otters on a mud slide. They filled arroyos, circumnavigated canyons, hewed their way through the scrub brush of Elk Ridge, built dugways, almost counted the revolutions of the wheels. The hundred and fifty miles from the river to the mouth of Cottonwood Wash took them just short of two months; altgether, from Cedar City to the new settlement, a distance by airline of about two hundred miles, and by their route of approximately twice that far, they were on the road six months. Their average—and they were not loafing along—was a little better than two miles a day. When they reached Cottonwood Wash there was not a person, an ox, or a horse in the train with the strength to go another foot. If the Wash had been starving ground, they would have had to sit there and starve. It wasn't quite starving ground: it was a sandy river bottom with crooked cottonwoods and a little pasture in it. They outspanned and camped.

The net result of that unbelievably toilsome trip was one pin on the map of empire; one settlement, Bluff, snatched from the encroaching Gentiles; one struggling, constantly-unsuccessful colony from which the colonists asked more than once to be released; one more bit of débris in the path of the San Juan floods, one little patch of fields for flash floods from Cottonwood Wash to cover with unprofitable sand. But they saved it from the Gentiles.

The Gentiles, as a matter of fact, wouldn't have had it as a gift. They came in, it is true, in 1892 and 1893 on the heels of a report that the bars and ledges of the San Juan were built of solid gold dust, but they went out again just as fast. Twelve hundred of them entered, and twelve hundred found the gold bars so thin they weren't worth working. There was not even that much excitement attending E. L. Goodrich's discovery of "coal oil springs" near Mexican Hat, and no oil companies got interested enough to drill until 1907, though Goodrich had found his oil seeps in 1882. Even the ultimate bringing in of a number of small producing wells has created nothing like an oil rush. Mexican Hat is just about the worst place on earth to have an oil well, considering the difficulties of transportation.

No, the Gentiles wouldn't have wanted it longer than to build a shack town or two during the gold excitement and then leave it to go ghost. But the Mormons have kept it, and even made it profitable after a fashion. Farming they discovered didn't pay, but stock raising did. The United States Army usually can pick up horses in that country, and in the canyons and bottoms and the Abajo and Elk Ridge Mountains there is good sheep and cattle range. And in early fall Bluff is a pleasant place to be— again because of the difficulties of transportation. The delicious winey grapes of the hot hillsides can be had for nothing, or at most for a cost of a cent a pound. Still, neither grapes nor gold nor oil can lure many people in over the difficult road from Blanding that is now the only way in or out. The people of Bluff, who numbered two hundred twenty-five in 1880 and seventy in 1930, are even yet, as they were when they came in through the Hole-in-the-Rock and over the terrible badlands east of the Colorado, dependent almost entirely on themselves. It is only in the fall of every year, when the old timers gather for the sentimental back-tracking into their own history, that the outside world even remembers that that lost village still hangs on under its massive cliffs, and that lombardy poplars go up in the sandy bottoms of the San Juan.

That sentimental back-tracking is important, because it is typical. Mormonism has always been interested in its own history; the Church Historian's office is a mine of material for any scholar who can gain access to it, and every little caravan of settlers had its official historian who kept in his journal all the details of travel and settlement. The Mormons were making history, and they knew it. When the Kingdom was built and the Saints could sit back and relax in felicity, it would be nice to be able to turn back to the records of the men and women who laid the first cornerstones.

People look back, all right. The Daughters of the Utah Pioneers are as militant an organization as the D.A.R. They publish pamphlets, set up markers and monuments (many of them historically inaccurate) to commemorate spots of antiquarian interest. They help promote Pioneer Day pageants in honor of the first settlers in the valley. They reverently gather up articles to be deposited in the Church Museum in Temple Square. They compete with the State Historical Society, they give their assistance to such elaborate shows as the sunrise services in Zion Park on July 24, the "Mormon Fourth of July." And there is something in all of that which, considering the attitude of the pioneers themselves, is a little sad.

Take it as a general rule all over the Mormon Country that the people who started out a hundred years ago to build the future have built instead a past: the State Historical Society, the Genealogical Society, the Daughters of the Utah Pioneers, the local celebrations, the fetes, the reunions, the pilgrimages to historic shrines, all look backward, all honor the accomplishments of a perfervid dynamism that believed exclusively in the future. The rock the fathers planted was the future; the crop the sons harvest is the past. The Mormon Country is not yet Heaven on Earth, and it no longer really expects to be. It is every year more and more like any other state in the union. Mammon has won most of the battles, the peculiar social organization of Mormonism has grown more like that of the world outside, and when it is revived in a town like Short Creek it looks as out of date as a dinosaur track. Maybe it is lucky that all of man's immortalities are either past or future, and never present.

PART II

THE MIGHT OF THE GENTILE

Buenaventura and the
Golden Shore . . .

T HE Mormons were not the first white men into the
country which they were to inherit under the New
Dispensation. Like other parts of the West, Zion had its
pathfinders before it had its pioneers, and other urges besides the desire for Heaven on Earth lured men from the
settled regions to the vast unknown stretching from the
Missouri to the Pacific. The first of those urges in time,
and one which contributed to all the others, was explorers'
itch, the desire to go where men had never gone before,
see what man never saw. Lewis and Clark, in 1806,
crossed the upper edge of the Mormon Country on their
way to the Pacific via the Columbia, and following their
trail came the trappers, motivated by a mixture of lusts:
action, adventure, knowledge, wealth. The unknown was
as full of possibilities for completely worldly men as it was
for men of the otherworldly Mormon breed. It had a fas-
cination for men of every caliber and every grade of intelligence. But it is notable that the first great man of that
country was almost as devout, almost as careless of the
chances for gain, almost as devoted to a purpose outside
the realm of profits, as the staunchest Mormon of the
period of settlement. The desire of Jed Smith to explore

and know the wilderness was as compelling a pull as if Heaven had waited at the end of the road.

Jedediah Strong Smith was a mountain man, one of the best of them, a trapper and beaver trader and hunter of lost lands. In 1823, as a member of General Ashley's fur brigade, he led a party overland across the present state of South Dakota and into the Black Hills, westward from there into the Powder River Valley, and on to a winter camp at the foot of the Wind River Mountains. Early in the spring of 1824 his party, which included William Sublette and Thomas Fitzpatrick, mountain men as famous as Jed himself, dropped further south to attempt a crossing of the Rockies. If the mountains were to be opened to the fur trade, a route overland had to be found, because the headwaters of the Missouri were difficult of navigation and the country was full of Aricaras and Blackfeet constantly on the warpath. From the Sweetwater Jed's party went up over a barren, rolling land, and about the middle of February made the first east-west crossing of South Pass, that famous gateway which in another generation was to see Oregon wagons, Mormon wagons, California wagons, rolling in an endless stream.

The party was through the pass before it knew the divide was crossed, so that there was no silent moment on a peak in Darien when the unknown world lay open before the trappers. But for the sake of poetic realization, let us imagine what that passage might have been like. It has already been imagined for us by John G. Neihardt, in "The Song of Jed Smith":

> *Empty skies*
> *Were straight ahead above a little rise*
> *Notched crooked like a hind-sight out of true.*
> *There wasn't any shoutingful to-do*

About it! But I galloped to the head
To have a look, and rode beside old Jed.
He didn't see me, didn't say a word
To anybody. Pretty soon he spurred
A ways ahead, reined suddenly, and stopped.
From where we sat and looked, the prairie dropped
Along the easy shoulder of a hill
Into a left-hand valley. Things got still
And kind of strange. The others, gathered round,
Quit talking, and there wasn't any sound
Except a bridle made it. Then it came—
That funny sort of feeling, just the same
I had out there a little while ago—
A feel of something you could never know,
But it was something big and still and dim
That wouldn't tell. It seemed to come from him
Just looking down the Sandy towards the Green
That had been waiting yonder to be seen
A million winters and a million springs
And summers! 'Twas the other side of things—
Another world!

It is psychologically accurate, whether it is historically correct or not, to attribute that sense of wonder to Jed Smith. Many of the trappers who opened up the Rocky Mountain country in the twenties and thirties were wild men, braggarts, tough, iron-throated, ribald brawlers, but Jed Smith was of another breed, a praying Methodist Yankee, a man of some education and great intellectual curiosity and an eye for far horizons. He was all man—he could thrash a blacksmith who got out of hand; he could lie calmly directing the surgery while James Clyman with a needle and thread sewed up his scalp, torn half from his

head by a grizzly bear in the Black Hills; he could endure
hunger and thirst and fatigue better than most of his wild
companions; he could be painfully kicked by a mule and
still go on the next day without even a complaint to his
journal. But he was more than the brute some of his followers were. He was an intelligence, and he was a string
on which the wind from beyond the world played an irresistible tune.

To General Ashley, Jim Bridger, Thomas Fitzpatrick,
Kit Carson, to a dozen echoing names, goes credit for the
exploration of much of the West between the headwaters
of the Missouri and the Colorado River, between the Missouri proper and the Sierra Nevada. But give to Jed Smith
the lion's share of the credit. Before the publicly acclaimed
explorers, before Bonneville or Frémont, Jed explored all
the way down to southern California, up the California
and Oregon coast, across the Great Basin deserts from the
Sierra to Bear Lake.

In 1826, just after he and Sublette and David Jackson
had bought out the Ashley interests, Jed took a party down
along the Wasatch, across the Sevier divide to the Virgin,
down that to the Colorado, across the lower Colorado desert to the San Gabriel Mission in California. He was definitely not welcomed by Spanish officials, but he played
diplomacy with them until he finally got permission at
least to go back the way he had come. Actually he went
only far enough inland to throw the Spaniards off, and
then cut northward along the Sierra to the Stanislaus
River, where he left most of his party. With two companions he crossed the high Sierra through the snow and came
straight across the entirely unknown deserts of Nevada and
Utah—a trail that twenty-two years later was to be paved
with the bones of oxen and mules. He survived by an eye-

lash the heat and lack of water, and rejoined the main body of trappers in rendezvous at Bear Lake. That journey, both going and returning, was pathfinding of the hardiest sort. For days on end the men lived on the meat of horses and mules which died on the trail, and water, in that country of few waterholes and springs, was a lucky accident much of the time.

But Jed Smith was not satisfied. The Buenaventura, that fabled river which ran westward from the Rockies and emptied into San Francisco Bay, had still eluded clear discovery. Jed had found the Virgin (which he called the Adams), and the Colorado, which he knew for what it was, but between that system and the Columbia-Snake system far to the north there should be another great river. In any event, there was unknown country in plenty, and unknown country was Smith's special province. A few weeks after his return across the desert, Jed took another party down the same way he had gone before, across the southwestern corner of the present Utah to the junction of the Virgin and Colorado. He crossed the Colorado on rafts, and in the middle of that operation, when his party was split, the Mojave Indians set upon the rearward half and massacred ten men. The rest escaped to San Gabriel, and ultimately rejoined the camp on the Stanislaus.

From the Stanislaus on it was wilderness again. No one knew anything accurate about the region either east or north except Jed Smith, and he knew that to the east lay a desert he did not want to cross again. So he struck north through the most rugged sort of country, laboriously inching his pack train over the spurs and ridges, having difficulty finding game and having some trouble with Indians. They passed through the redwood country, the only mention of which in the journals either of Jed or of Harrison

G. Rogers was a note that the cedars grew very large in that country. They had almost reached the Willamette Valley when they were again attacked by Indians, this time the Umpquas, and all but Smith and two companions killed. All the furs that had been collected by both parties on the long trek were lost, though they were later regained through the help of the Hudson's Bay factor, John B. Mc-Loughlin, of Fort Vancouver.

Jed wintered at Fort Vancouver, and in the spring made his way back to Pierre's Hole. That was in 1829. In the six years he had been in the country, Jed had crossed it, one direction or another, all the way from the Missouri to the Pacific Coast; he had been through the longitudinal axis from Pierre's Hole and the headwaters of the Yellowstone clear to the deserts of the lower Colorado River, and he had circumnavigated its whole area except along the eastern side. Several times he had escaped death by a miracle, and it was only luck or good management or exceptional skill that kept his hair from decorating the lodgepole of some Blackfoot or the hut of a Mojave or the shanty of an Umpqua. Less interested in trapping than in the fascinating job of exploring new country, Jed stayed with the fur trade only one more year before he and his partners sold out to Jim Bridger, Milton Sublette, Thomas Fitzpatrick, Henry Fraeb, and Baptiste Gervais.

In 1831, while he and Fitzpatrick were convoying a trading train to Santa Fe, they found all the water courses dry and were in peril of dying of thirst on the hot plains. They struggled on desperately toward the Cimarron, but the train was slow. Smith, going on ahead to hunt for water, succeeded in reaching the Cimarron and slaking his thirst. But when he rose up to start back for his companions he found himself face to face with a war party of Comanches.

On May 27, 1831, Jed Smith's explorations ceased. He was thirty-one years old.

Jed Smith might have been a great man if he had lived. He knew more about the West than any man alive, and more than any of his trapper companions he knew the value of his knowledge, had the education to do something with it. But he did not live to do it, and what he did do fattened the reputation of John C. Frémont, whose principal virtue as an explorer was that he had sense enough to take a whole band of mountain men along as guides and bodyguards. Frémont covered a good deal of ground, some of it new, but still the first Anglo-American tracks in a large part of the Mormon Country were the tracks of Jed Smith.

Jed's explorations did a number of things for geographical science and for the map makers who faced the unknown region below the route of Lewis and Clark. They pretty well established that the Buenaventura was a myth, that no large river ran from the Rockies into the Bay of San Francisco. Ashley, coming up from the Green in 1825, had thought the Weber might be the fabled waterway, but the Weber was soon discovered to run into Great Salt Lake, and Great Salt Lake was circumnavigated in skin boats and proved to be a distinct lake, and not an arm of the Pacific. There is little wonder that Ashley and Smith and all the early trappers were baffled by the drainage system, little wonder that they expected a river to be where the Buenaventura was obviously not, little wonder that they clung to the notion until Smith's journeys showed it to be false. The country around South Pass, which was beaver heaven and the main stamping grounds of the trapping parties, has an extremely complicated and confusing drainage system. It contains the headwaters of the Green, flowing into the Colorado and thence into the Gulf of California; the sources of Big Gray's and Salt River, tributaries of the Snake and ultimately of the Columbia; the headwaters of the Sweetwater, part of the Platte-Missouri system flowing into the Gulf of Mexico; and Bear River, which flows in a circuitous and inexplicable course northwest into Idaho and thence straight south into Great Salt Lake. To track down the destinations of all those streams which rise within a few miles of each other was the job of years.

By the time Smith had followed down the Santa Clara and Virgin and established them as tributaries of the Colorado, and had crossed the Sierra from the Stanislaus to undertake the immense dry sinks and ranges of Nevada, he had made it fairly clear that no great river flowed westward from the Rockies between the Snake and the Colorado. On his trip up along the California coast he kept a lookout for the mouth of the Buenaventura, and for a time suspected that the Carquinez Straits might be its mouth (thus confusing the Sacramento with the mythical stream), but that was about the last attempt to stay with the old maps. There was still the possibility of the Multnomah, another mythical stream supposed to join the Columbia near the sea, but the Multnomah turned out to be the Willamette. So there was no great river, there was no broad water highway to the Pacific. The drainage from the Rocky Mountains went south and north and east, but not west, except for those streams like the Weber and the Bear, which ran ineffectually into the Dead Sea, and the Humboldt, which died with an alkaline whimper in the Humboldt Sink. Though Frémont was the first to give a name to the Great Basin, it was Jed Smith's exploration that dissipated the legends and outlined that sunken area between Wasatch and Sierra.

By 1842 the fur trade was gone, and the general features of the intermountain country pretty well established. Of all the mountain men who had trapped and traded in the little-known valleys, only a few were left when the Mormons came in 1847. Kit Carson had settled down in New Mexico, Jim Bridger had a fort and trading post at Black's Fork, Miles Goodyear had built a cabin for his Indian wife and halfbreed children at the mouth of the Weber in Salt Lake Valley. That house, and the land around it for which Goodyear thought up an entirely fictitious Mexican grant, the Mormons bought outright with part of the pay of the Mormon Battalion, and cleared the valley of the last Gentile interloper. Jim Bridger they froze out—according to Jim's complaints, drove out—and the approaches to Zion were clear. The first generation of Gentile fortune-hunters had come and gone, as other generations of other kinds of fortune-hunters were to come and go.

There is an ironical quirk to the early history of the Mormon settlers. Fleeing the United States and the contaminating and persecuting society of the Gentiles, they yet found themselves constantly being overtaken and constantly even assisting the invaders. The Mormon Battalion members who participated in the gold strike at Sutter's Mill turned up the one lure calculated to bring the whole United States storming into the old Mexican territory. And the settlers in Salt Lake Valley, almost moneyless but with supplies of food and stocks of horses and cattle, had cause both to deplore and bless the streams of gold seekers who camped around Warm Springs and rested up for the dash across the desert by the Mormon Road. They didn't want the invaders around, but they found in them a useful market for produce, flour, hay, and draft animals. It was possible to take one good fat team down to the Gentile camps and get three or four worn-out teams in trade. Then the worn-out beasts could be fattened up and traded or sold to later wagon trains. With the Golden Shore in their eye, the Gentiles were easy to take advantage of in a trade.

They were stripping down for the last dash, and the Mormons profited. The Saints themselves, meanwhile, had been ordered by Brother Brigham to let the gold fields alone, to hoe their own gardens, and though a few ran off with the California trains, they were only a few. Brigham cursed them from the pulpit and let them go. If they didn't have sense enough to see that gold led only to sin and sorrow, let them go. The people who worked their fields in the valleys of the mountains would be both richer and happier than the ones who left.

Though the trains of emigrants were a nuisance, though they got drunk and disorderly and disrupted the pious quiet of Salt Lake City streets, they were not actually competing with the Saints for the ownership of land in the Great Basin. A few settled down to play storekeeper, but until General Patrick Connor came into Utah with his California Volunteers to police Utah after the withdrawal of the dragoons in 1861, the Saints had no competition in their chosen land. They built their agrarian state, spread the settlements, acquired all the water, and though they were technically squatters, no disposition having been made of the public lands in the territory acquired from Mexico, they did have possession, and by and large possession turned out to be nine points of the law. Connor made no attempt to fight the Mormons by importing farmers. He had no desire to and no need to. There was another field, deliberately ignored by the Church, where Gentiles could get a toehold. Mining, except for the half-successful coal and iron and lead mines that the Saints had worked, was wide open to exploitation from outside, and Connor made the most of the situation.

He was as anti-Mormon as he was energetic. He gave his soldiers leave so that they could prospect for minerals, sent out open letters inviting outside prospectors and outside capital to develop the mineral wealth that he was sure the mountains contained. Connor himself was a member of the first mining corporation in the territory, and helped draw up the laws for the West Mountain Mining District, the first in Utah. For more than a decade he was the mightiest champion of the "American Way" as opposed to the Mormon way, and from Fort Douglas, above the city, he defied the Saints to hinder his activities. It was under his tutelage that the anti-Mormon newspaper, the *Union Vedette*, was published, and when Mormon resistance to infiltration reached the point of boycotting Gentile enterprise, Connor and his fellows accepted the challenge and founded Corinne, on the Union Pacific, where they attempted to establish a rival city, populated and run by the Gentiles without Mormon interference. Connor built steamboats for the navigation of Great Salt Lake, devoted himself to the twin arts of transportation and mining which might give the Gentiles control of the territory.

There was no doubt in Brigham Young's mind that Connor and his activities were dangerous. The railroad had made it possible to ship cattle into the country in large herds, and the cattle business, largely Gentile, boomed. Ore could now get out cheaply to the centers of smelting and refining, and the mines opened up with a bang. Discovery of rich gold and silver mines in Idaho and Montana stimulated the need for produce and equipment, most of it handled by Gentiles. With transportation came eastern capital, too potent for the Church to combat, and the long struggle between the Mormon agrarian world and the Gentile world of commerce and industry was on. It is worth looking at that Gentile world to notice the differences between it and the Mormon economy of small farms and villages and handicrafts; here was one kind of society against another. The Gentiles imported ways of living, ways of thinking, institutions, methods, that were diametrically opposed to the Mormon ways. The lion had invaded the lamb's bed, and for a long time neither was quite willing to lie down.

The Burg on the Bear . . .

IN 1869 the Gentiles dreamed a dream. They had for years fought unsuccessfully against the stranglehold that the Church had on political and economic and social affairs. They were few compared with the Saints, and though they had friends in Washington, Washington was a long way off and federal edicts had a way of never coming to anything. Brigham Young, seated solidly in the Lion House, with the wires of the Deseret Telegraph at his finger tips and his whole empire within immediate call, calmly nullified all the strenuous efforts of outsiders to establish themselves or their ideas. He ruled the roost, and if the few Gentiles perched on it and squawking annoyed him, he shouldered them off. That was what brought about the Gentile dream, actually. The anti-Gentile boycott drove most of Salt Lake's unblessed merchants out of business, and as a last resort they gravitated to the railroad, just coming through from east and west. They induced the Union Pacific, for a consideration of every other house-lot, to survey a town on the main line, and they moved in en masse, determined to make a Gentile capital that would outshine Salt Lake City and be a haven for all the democratic ideas unpopular around the Lion House.

That town, Corinne, was on Bear River Bay at the north end of Great Salt Lake. Within two weeks of its location there were fifteen hundred people and three hundred buildings in the place. Lots sold for anything from three hundred to a thousand dollars. The boom was on, even before the Union Pacific and Central Pacific met at Promontory, a few miles west. When that historic junction took place, Corinne was the second largest city in the territory, and by all odds the busiest.

Transportation, the thing that the Mormons both welcomed and dreaded, because cheap freight rates and easy access were bound to be accompanied by a flood of unwelcome men, and because the fostered isolation of the region was sure to be broken down, was the backbone of Corinne's prosperity. By rail, by wagon, by boat, the Gentiles attempted to get control of all the hauling in the territory, and for a while they almost did. The rich mines of Idaho and Montana, cut off from the world, needed supplies, needed an outlet for their high-grade ores. Corinne took the situation in hand. One company alone, the Diamond R, had four hundred mules and eighty wagons constantly on the road, going and coming. Then, because refined ore was easier and cheaper to ship than raw ore, they built a smelter in Corinne. Slag piles mounted on the banks of the Bear, and bullion went eastward and westward by rail. The rutted streets were choked with wagons. Crews from "Hell's Half Acre," a construction camp up the line, flocked back to cavort in Corinne's twenty-nine saloons and two dance halls, or gamble their pay in the immense gambling tent that had followed the steel all the way from Omaha. Ladies came in to supply the feminine touch, and found so warm a welcome that John Hanson Beadle, the town's first editor, counted eighty soiled doves at one time in Corinne's sinful cote.

The Gentiles of Corinne were energetic people. Enter-

prise piled on enterprise. A slaughterhouse and meat packing plant, designed to provide beef for railroad camps and
the mines, rose like an exhalation. Warehouses groaned
with good Mormon produce going east or west along the
main line. When the silver mines of the Oquirrh range,
worked inadequately until transportation came, opened
into big production, the citizens of Corinne chipped in
four thousand dollars to build a boat for bringing the ores
to the new smelter. Here was none of the hand-whittled,
home-made industry of Mormondom. Engines from Chicago, redwood from California, were rushed in. The *City
of Corinne* was launched and for a time carried ore moun-
tain-high on her three decks. Other boats came out of the
local navy yard: the *Kate Connor,* the *Rosie Brown,* the
Pluribustah. Transport was going four ways from the Gentile stronghold, and the dreams blossomed. It became obvious that the Chicago of Utah Territory would have to
become the heart of a great political movement destined
to overthrow the priestly nabobs in Salt Lake.

They had their political caucus, organized the Liberal
Party on strictly anti-Mormon lines, Republican and Democrat uniting against the theocracy. They put up a candidate for Congress who got votes by tens where his Mormon
opponent of the "People's Party" got them by thousands,
but they were not dismayed. The future was bright. Preparing their town against that future, they drew up a set
of laws for Corinne as strict in its legal way as the regulations of a Mormon town were in their theological way.
Unfortunately, Corinne didn't have quite the same population as a Mormon town, and the laws had little effect on
the toughs and rowdies and *nymphs du pave.*

They went beyond politics, opened their arms and welcomed to the town's soiled but motherly breast all the

non-Mormon denominations they could lure in. The first
Methodist church, the first Presbyterian church, and the
first Episcopalian church in Utah were in the Burg on the
Bear. True, they did not have many communicants. Captain Codman, visiting the place in 1874, found one church
with two members, one with one, and the third with
eleven, and felt a twinge of pity for the lonely pastor he
discovered playing the organ to himself in his deserted
cathedral. The reminiscences of Alexander Toponce, a
salty old reprobate who made a good deal of money
freighting, staging, and furnishing beef all along the
Union Pacific right of way, mention one minister who,
for lack of anything better to do with his time, resorted to
prospecting and reducing the samples to powder with a
mortar and pestle. On one Sunday the minister and a
vestryman were the only attendants at worship. Dunn, the
minister, sat and talked prospects with his one customer
until it was clear that no one else was coming. "Well,
Brother Stein," he said, "what shall we do, preach or
pound quartz?" They decided to pound quartz, and a little
later, when Dunn in a rage ran a claim-jumper off Antelope Island with a shotgun, Bishop Tuttle gave him the
opportunity to resign. He wound up as a mining promoter
in Bonanza, Idaho.

Something similar happened to everything that Corinne
did. It started as one thing and wound up as something
else. In spite of its zeal and enterprise, the fortress of the
embattled Gentiles dwindled. Even so good a business, so
fool-proof a business, as that of Johnson and Underdunk
fell away and gave up. Johnson and Underdunk were law-
yers. Taking their part in the blaze of energy that dazzled
the town, they got up a scheme for granting mail order
divorces. For a price of two dollars and a half, they would

separate anyone from the bosom of his family. The petitioner didn't have to be present, and he could even get alimony if he wanted it. I have never been able to lay hands on one of those divorce decrees, but tradition says that they were completely official, ribbons and wax and the court seal and all. Either Johnson and Underdunk were skilled forgers, or they had a pipeline to the judge. Tradition also says that for ten years United States courts were unraveling the divorces that Johnson and Underdunk distributed with so lavish a hand. However that may be, it is rather charming to see all this going on practically next door to Brigham City, one of the strongest United Order towns in Mormondom, and jammed with polygamous wives. Johnson and Underdunk were in the main Corinne tradition: they helped along the faith that Corinne was destined to reverse everything that the Saints stood for.

But Corinne's road, after the first years, was down, and the Mormons delighted in contributing grease for the slide. Brigham Young built a railroad, the Utah and Northern, linking Salt Lake and the Idaho mines and virtually destroying the steamer traffic on the lake. Ogden, not Corinne, was finally established as the division point on the Union Pacific. The boats which had been launched with such exuberant ceremony went out of commission one after another. The *City of Corinne,* unable to dock at her home port because the river filled with bars, ended her days as an excursion boat off Black Rock, and finally burned with the Garfield Beach pavilion. Her hulk is supposed to lie somewhere in a swamp below the smelter town of Garfield. The *Kate Connor* sank with a full load of ore in the deep part of the river. The others are gone, no one knows where—*Rosie Brown, Pluribustah,* symbols of Corinne's enterprising dream, addresses unknown.

Transportation made Corinne, and transportation killed it. When the Utah and Northern was made standard gauge up to Silver Bow, Montana, the freighting business was gone. Ogden stole most of the railroad and shipping business, and other smelters closer to the mines reduced the flow of ores into the mouth of Bear River. The smelter closed down. Corinne couldn't have had worse luck if the Mormons' pious curses had been effective. For witness the outcome of the smelting business: Slag from the mountainous dumps had been piled behind the abutments of the Bear River Bridge and had been used to pave the streets, originally ankle-deep in dust or mud. In the waning days of the Burg on the Bear mining men came poking around, knocked off hunks of slag from the abandoned dumps, and ended by buying the works. The slag which Corinne's heedless citizenry had ground into the alkali with their heels, or dumped into Bear River, ran twenty dollars to the ton in gold when re-smelted.

The weak-spirited left early, but the die-hards clung. They even aspired to challenge the Mormons in their own field, agriculture. If Corinne's boom days as a transportation town were over, it could at least be a farming community. In 1890 the Bear Lake and River Water and Irrigation Company put in a dam and diversion canal in Bear River Canyon and opened ten thousand acres to irrigation. At first the land produced heavily; within a year or two the alkali and salts, leached to the surface by the irrigation water, turned the fields into worthless swamps.

But if it couldn't be a farming community, it might be a health center. Henry House, son of one of the founders, dreamed of a spa at the sulphur springs which bubbled from the base of the hills west of Corinne, and went so far as to evaporate the water and sell the resulting salts as a cure-all. Texas has no monopoly on fizz-powders and Alka-Seltzers. But House's plans for the health resort also died on the vine. The final blow came in 1903, when the Lucin Cutoff was built across forty miles of Great Salt Lake and Corinne was left stranded on a branch line.

The town was virtually ghost. The buildings were burned or torn down, the politicos were gone, the merchants had moved to Ogden, the warehouses were empty and falling apart, the railroad ran around the dead walls of the Gentile stronghold.

But now the metamorphosis, the ironic twist. Corinne is not dead as of 1942. It is not as big as it once was, and its twenty-nine saloons and two dancehalls and gambling tent and ladies of pleasure are gone, and the biggest of its saloons now languishes under the title of Dewdrop Inn. Two of the three Protestant churches are vanished and the other can scarcely be said to be in use. The Bear River has shrunk to half its former width, because of the canal which takes out the irrigation water, and everything that made Corinne a place of importance in the eighteen seventies is no longer there. But Corinne is no ghost. There is an L.D.S. Ward House in Corinne; there are two or three hundred farmers living in and around Corinne; the land which the first irrigation spoiled has been drained and reclaimed, and the Bear River Canal furnishes plenty of water. There are wells of marsh gas from which the farmers get heat and power. The alfalfa and beets raised in the valley have a ready market—and the bulk of the population is Mormon.

Quietly, without fuss, the Mormons waited until the Burg on the Bear burnt itself out. They disliked it, they did their best to boycott and ruin it, but they never made active war on it. But when the debacle came, when the quick money was no longer available and the hordes of the infidels had departed, the Saints moved quietly in and took over, transforming Corinne into a sleepy Mormon village.

And there, at least for the time and in that locality, Mormon society showed itself the more stable and lasting one. The might of the Gentile, unsmote by the sword, had melted like snow. The reason is plain enough. The thing the Gentiles were chasing was clearly no longer available in Corinne. But the thing the Mormons were after still was.

On other fronts the Gentiles did not succumb so easily.

Fabulous Mountain . . .

IT was a boom mining camp in 1864, part of that West
Mountain Mining District which was the first organized mining district in Utah. That should mean that it is
now ghost, but it doesn't. It will not, according to the
Mineral Yearbook, be ghost until 1990 at the present rate
of production. By that time, perhaps, some new miracle of
rejuvenation will restore the town that has been rejuve-
nated several times already.

Bingham, with its satellite towns of Copperton and
Upper Bingham and Highland Boy, lies in a canyon in the
Oquirrhs twenty-five miles west and south of Salt Lake
City. Along with Park City, whose mines have been persistently rich silver producers, it has inherited the mantle
of Corinne and Mercur and Alta and the other defunct
Gentile towns deserted now by their fickle makers. But
Bingham has not survived and grown by a continuance of
what might be called the frontier system. It has survived
by co-operation and the pooling of resources as surely as
any Mormon settlement survived by those means. The
only differences lie in the kind of co-operation, the kind
of pooling, and the ultimate motive.

Bingham began as a silver strike in 1863. General Connor, he of the Mormon-eating appetite, assisted in the
formation of the corporation and the district, and invited

all and sundry to come in and participate. But the quartz ledges of the gulch were hard to develop. Machinery was expensive, the canyon was so narrow that a decent road was next to impossible, and there was no transportation available at first for the ore. Bingham almost died in its infancy—would have if the miners attracted by Connor's open letter had not struck placer gold in the gravel bars. The three Clay brothers, at Clay's Bar, took out a hundred thousand dollars in dust and nuggets before they struck excessive water. Then they turned to and ran the tailings through the sluices, making wages of seven to fifteen dollars a day apiece, and finding among other things a single nugget worth one hundred and twenty-eight dollars.

This was interesting, and even profitable, but it was hardly big-time stuff. The two million in gold that came out of the gravel between 1864 and 1870 was distributed among a good many individual miners, and it made nobody really rich. The railroad in 1869 brought a second wave of fortune-hunters, however, jumping the population of the canyon to over a thousand and restoring the interest in the quartz ledges. Little by little, the big mines worked into profitable production. A smelter, a concentration plant, new strikes, made lead and silver ore profitable and kept them profitable until the depression of 1893 almost closed down the camp. That was when co-operation and pooling began in earnest.

One piece of co-operation arose out of the cyanide mill that Samuel Newhouse and Thomas Weir built in Carr Fork for freeing gold from oxidized ore. There was so much despised copper in the ore that the bill for cyanide almost broke the bank of the Highland Boy. So it merged with the Utah Consolidated, built a smelter west of Murray, on the railroad, and began to turn out copper. In

1899, when John D. Rockefeller came in for twelve million dollars' worth, a controlling interest, the pattern for all future developments had been established. If the Mormons knew how to manipulate men and make them work together, the Gentiles knew how to manipulate dollars.

There were other acts of co-operation going on. Colonel Wall had bought up a cluster of abandoned claims, had interested Joseph De Lamar of Mercur, and had brought in two engineers named Jackling and Gemmell to investigate the possibilities of making low-grade copper ores valuable. In the end they combined with Charles Mac-Neill and Spencer Penrose of the United States Reduction and Refining Company to form the Utah Copper. The original capitalization was a half million in 1903. When they reorganized under the laws of New Jersey (New Jersey was friendly to this kind of co-operation) they jumped it to four and a half million, and in 1906 they jumped it again, to six million. A year later a six thousand ton concentrator plant was built at Magna, and Jackling's pet idea of open steam-shovel mining went into effect. And in 1910 the Boston Consolidated (eastern and British capital) bought out the Utah Copper, mills and all. The delicately and skillfully graded ditch that runs from the Utah mines to banks and investment houses in Boston and New York had begun to carry its flow of dollars.

Now it was possible to do something. Now Bingham could move. Jackling and his associates were building an empire of dollars as surely as Brigham Young built an empire of men and towns. Railroads, smelters, concentration plants, flotation plants, all the apparatus of large-scale mining, went in, and the profits boomed. Co-operation continued. When Jackling formed the Utah Power and Light Company and sold the town of Bingham a contract for electric power that was to hold until 1970 he was using the same kind of tactics that Brigham had used, though for a different end.

There were, of course, occasional hitches. The Mormon farmers in the valley complained about the smoke from the smelters, even sued and closed the smelters down for a while until the companies found a way of purifying the smoke of its injurious sulphur. They had to pay out a half million dollars in damages for the crops they had ruined, but many dollars working together can afford the loss of a half million of their fellows. They can afford too to pay off a few perennial nuisances like the old guy who owned an abandoned mill in the gulch below a steep switchback in the railroad. Once or twice a year that gentleman could depend on an ore car's jumping the track and coming down through his roof. Then he could collect. It was a jumpy life, but economically secure.

There was only a little trouble with strikes. The Western Federation of Miners went out in 1912, Big Bill Haywood of the I.W.W.'s led another in 1916, and the C.I.O. United Mine Workers walked out in 1936. The first one the companies broke with scabs and armed deputies. The second petered out because Big Bill didn't have enough Wobbly support. The third lasted ten weeks and lost. Bingham is not a union town. There is no room in the philosophy of the mining corporations for that kind of ingratitude and apostasy.

But there is paternalism, widely advertised. There is the model town of Copperton, one hundred and twenty-six houses with a sliding scale of rent adjustable to wages and employment conditions. There is a tennis court, a baseball diamond, a community park, a club house where for a dollar a month miners can have most of the prerogatives of the idle rich. Coal and oil are sold to the townspeople at cost. Copperton is a spick-and-span and green and orderly community, even more spotless and orderly and regularized than the model towns of Mormonism which had their inspiration from above. Still, a lot of miners prefer to live in the crowded gulch of Bingham proper. Maybe they feel that a town that just growed is somehow healthier than one that was licked into shape before it was ever born.

And Bingham proper most certainly just growed. It never got any attention for its first forty years, but drifted of its own sweet will. From 1863 to 1904 there was no town government at all, no community services, no planning or control, though the camp had a population of several thousand. Like the Mormon Church, the mining corporations had their proselyting service to bring in labor, but once the proselytes were on the ground there was no one to take any responsibility about them. In the narrow gulch, barely wide enough at the bottom for a wretched, steep, impossible road rutted a foot deep by ore wagons, several thousand Englishmen, Americans, Finns, Swedes, Serbs, Austrians, Jugoslavs, Greeks, Italians, Armenians, Albanians, Chinese, Japanese, Koreans, and Mexicans crowded together. The houses went up steeply, overhanging the canyon bottom, piling on top of one another up the sides, and in them the miners lived as they pleased or as they could. Nobody bothered to devise a Deseret Alphabet to make their education in English easier. Nobody cared whether or not they learned English at all, and a lot of them didn't.

Nobody cared what they did. There was no town government, and hence no garbage disposal system. People chucked their refuse, rubbish, old iron, chamberpots, everything, into the creek. By the grace of God the creek, running over miles of copper ore, was a strong solution of

copper sulphide, and killed germs as fast as the Binghamites threw them in. Once or twice a year people got together from pure necessity and cleaned the creekbed out
so they could throw things in it for another six months.

From the beginning Bingham was a wide open town.
The state let it alone; Mormons felt no compulsion to put
pressure or impose order on the godless place. It was even
useful as a horrid example to contrast with their own sober
communities. So Bingham roared. The same Captain Codman who got around to Corinne in 1874 arrived in Bingham a little later and was treated to three murders in one
day. If he had stayed longer he would have got even a
fuller course. Strung along the canyon by 1900 were thirty
saloons. The red light district throve, gambling joints went
twenty-four hours a day. Though there was generally a
deputy sheriff or so hanging around, the deputies minded
their own business. Did Pete Sukanian shoot his wife six
times and not even kill her then? All right. It shows you
how tough these Bohunks are, even the women. Charge
him with wife-beating and fine him a few dollars and let
him go. If you can't find him to arrest him, let him go
anyway. It doesn't pay to monkey around too much. Is
Miguel Chavez found in the gulch with knife wounds all
over him? It won't do any good to look up his worst enemy
and question him. All he will do is shrug and say "No
savvy." They all pull that stuff. "Me no unnerstan'." If
you happen to run into the obvious murderer of Miguel
Chavez, take him down to the station and frisk him of his
revolver and knife (he's sure to be carrying them) and fine
him ten dollars for carrying concealed weapons and turn
him loose. None of these miners ever settle anything with
their fists. They always use deadly weapons. It ain't safe to
fuss around with them too much. Let 'em alone.

Let 'em alone. A dozen different nationalities, several thousand people, mainly men, of little education and only a rudimentary development of the bump of civilization. They don't speak English, or pretend not to, they herd with their own particular crowd, they are suspicious and husky and often murderous. Let 'em alone as long as they come to work.

That was the policy of the Gentile empire-builders. The houses went up anyhow and everyhow, clinging to the canyon walls. No Mormon colonizer would ever have founded a town in a gulch like that, even if there had been water and a little farm land. It was too obviously in the road of catastrophe, of fire and flood and avalanche and snowslide. As might have been expected, all those varieties of disaster have visited Bingham regularly. Fires went almost the length of the canyon time after time, in 1881, 1895, 1905, 1924, 1932. In at least the first three there was no fire-fighting equipment except a bucket brigade, and the flimsy frame shacks went up like kindling. Even in the 1932 fire, despite modern fire trucks, everything on both sides of the canyon for a third of a mile went up in smoke—very fragrant smoke, because this was during prohibition. Fire-men were menaced in almost every house by exploding stills. Moonshine ran in the gutters like water, and fire-men, bystanders, cats, dogs, children, birds, staggered happily in the drunken fumes.

Build a town in a kind of natural flue, and you must expect excitement. Fires were not the only kind. In 1926 the snow let loose at the top of Sap Gulch and came two miles down the main canyon, burying seventeen houses and a three-story boarding house. Thirty-nine people died in that one. Four years later a cloudburst turned the canyon into a river, washed cars down the steep street, poured

mud and water in cascading waterfalls into the upstairs
windows of houses and out the front doors. In the wake
of the cloudburst came the earth, slipping in a great avalanche that knocked down a hundred houses.

Take it all in all, Bingham has had an active life. But
it has stuck, and the reason why it has stuck is exactly the
reason Corinne failed, in reverse. The reason for Bingham's continued existence is reducible to dollar signs. The
value of the ores taken out of the West Mountain District
by 1934 totaled over a billion dollars. At the present time
the district produces something between thirty and forty
million dollars a year for its owners.

But even Bingham has felt the touch of civilization and
domestication. The curious fact seems to be that given
enough time, a camp as wild and rowdy as any in the West
will develop something like community spirit. Bingham
has. It has come so far that in 1930 the Copper King Pool
Hall could be stopped by the police from cleaning its spit-
toons in the gutter. It has a paved street, and movies and
beer halls have replaced the old saloons and gambling
joints. Of the "cultural life" of the old camp nothing remains. The Opera House that from 1907 on was a flourish-
ing institution, catching the overflow from the Salt Lake
Theater, which did not allow Sunday performances, has
gone the way of all mining camp opera houses. It has been
in turn a dance hall, a café, a roller rink, and a garage.
Bingham never had the chance that a place like Central
City, Colorado, had. It never became picturesque; no
wealthy people have bought up its shacks for summer
houses. No celebrities from the Met and from Hollywood
stroll up and down its steep street. Bingham will have to
wait until 1990 for that kind of posthumous ennoblement.

It still makes altogether too much money to be picturesque, though the enormous open pit of the Utah Copper
is a tourist attraction, and the new tunnel which connects
Bingham and Upper Bingham (the old canyon-bottom
road was too valuable as an ore body to be driven on any
more) creates a mild Moffat-Tunnel kind of excitement
in visitors.

The old days are very far off, however. The old catch-as-
catch-can society of the gulch has given place, over a period of thirty or forty years, to a community with a fanati-
cally-strong town spirit. Outcast, raucous, spit upon by the
Mormons and used politically by the Gentiles, the polyglot
population of Bingham has by now a strange solidarity of
its own. The town pride often takes the form of swaggering and fist fights, but it is undeniably pride. On the evening in 1926 when the snowslide out of Sap Gulch engulfed the town, I was in the stands of the Deseret Gym-
nasium in Salt Lake, watching the state high school basketball tournament. Bingham High School was playing, and
the entire west stands were solid with Binghamites, many
of them drunk, some of them quarrelsome, all of them
noisy and wildly loyal. There were a couple of fights in the
stands and one on the upper running track. It was the
gulch against the rest of Utah, and if the basketball team
couldn't do it the town could. In the middle of the game,
when news came of the avalanche, the west stands rose as
one man and left. You could hardly have asked for a more
unified reaction from Mormons.

There is an old yarn about a tract-passing sky pilot who
got in the road during a street brawl and was hit in the
chest by a bullet. He thought he was dead. So did everyone
else. But when he felt among his clothes for his wound he

found only a bundle of tracts, punctured to the last paste-board. His hide was intact, and the sky pilot, his piety rewarded and his faith given a miraculous proof, made a mighty impression and converted half the town. But the next night a cowpuncher in a poker game got suspicious, then sore, as he continued to lose, and finally he yanked out his equalizer and took a shot at the little gambler who was dealing. The gambler had no tracts in his pockets. But when he picked himself up off the floor and put his hand inside his coat he found the deck of marked cards in his vest pocket, and the result was the same. His hide too was intact.

Bingham is a little like the gambler. Crowded together in their gulch without bringing-up or ear-washing, the people of the camp have evolved into a community, though it took a long time and there were a lot of graves in the local Boot Hill before the transformation came about. Maybe the copper sulphide in the soil destroyed the germs of evil in those old rowdies as it destroyed the typhus germs in the garbage-laden creek. Or maybe the camp simply grew up. At any rate Bingham gets along better with the rest of the state now. It has local government and community institutions. The Mormons who for years left the place strictly alone have come in and mixed. In 1900 there were seventy-two Saints in camp; in 1930 there were twelve hundred. Mormon Ward House and Catholic parish church perch with equal precariousness on the sides of the fabulous gulch. It doesn't take geological time to bring changes in human affairs.

The Mexican in Minnie
Number Two . . .

LET us consider, as an exhibit of life in a mining camp, the strange case of Rafael Lopez, Mexican.

He drifted into Bingham with an imported lot of Mexican scabs when the Western Federation of Miners was fighting Utah Copper, Apex, and other mines for union recognition. The strike was soon beaten, but some of the Mexicans stayed on, Lopez among them. He went to work leasing in the Minnie tunnel of the Apex with a partner named Corelli. People liked him; he was quiet and good natured, did not get drunk, made no trouble. He neither looked nor talked like a Mexican, since his mother had been an Englishwoman and he had been born in Arizona and spoke English perfectly. Men who knew him well considered him a sober citizen with more than usual education and good manners. He sang at his work, he made jokes. If he carried a gun, why so did most others. The point was that he never showed any inclination to use it until the night in 1913 when he shot and killed Juan Valdez.

The reasons why he shot Valdez are obscure and tangled with gossip and legend. The only witness to the killing, another Mexican, testified that he and Lopez were walking down the canyon arguing about politics. They met Juan

Valdez. A little later, with the argument waxing hotter, Lopez suddenly drew his gun and waved it in the unnamed Mexican's face. Valdez, the third member of the party and an outsider to the argument, told Lopez he was a coward. Then, said the informant, Lopez transferred his anger to Valdez, told him a number of reasons why he was going to kill him, and did so. After that he cut back up the canyon to his house, picked up his rifle and some cartridges, and took off into the hills.

The motive back of that murder would make a good start for an Elizabethan revenge tragedy. According to the nameless Mexican who brought the tale to the law, Valdez and Lopez had apparently been acquainted since childhood. Valdez had been a close friend of Lopez' younger brother, and had gone with him down into old Mexico in search of adventure and work. There they had both fallen in love with the same girl. Young Lopez married her. A few months later bones found in a burned house were identified as his by remnants of his clothing and his wedding ring. Valdez had skipped. Rafael Lopez, said the informant, had sworn revenge, and had drifted around from camp to camp looking for Valdez, knowing that sooner or later he would meet him. He found him in Bingham, pretended to know nothing about the circumstances of his brother's death, and waited for a chance to get Valdez into a fight. The political argument and the rage were a put-up job. Lopez was not one to get heated about politics.

These were the things, the nameless Mexican said, that Lopez told Valdez just before he shot him. After the shooting there were other things that came out by grapevine. Grapevine said that Lopez was bitter at the law, and particularly at a deputy named Sorenson. Sorenson was a Swede, which in Bingham meant a Bohunk; he could not speak English without a heavy accent. One night in the summer before the shooting of Valdez two girls had run up to the Highland Boy mine to tell the deputy that a couple of Greek muckers had bothered them in the gulch, and that a Mexican had made them stop. Sorenson, going down to investigate, found the muckers out cold on the ground, and Lopez standing near. He had cracked them both over the head with his gun butt. Why Sorenson did what he did next is a puzzler. He waited for the Greeks to revive, took their names as witnesses, and jailed Lopez. Maybe his own difficulties with English made him impatient with Greasers who spoke better than he did. He apparently took a dislike to Lopez, and in the next few months jailed him again, abusing him whenever he got the chance, and riding him for things that anyone else in Bingham got away with and no questions asked.

Lopez was not, for all his quiet and good manners, a man to take what he felt to be insults. When he met Sorenson in the street after his third arrest he made a speech. He would, he said, kill Sorenson if Sorenson ever interfered with him again. He would kill anyone Sorenson brought along to help him. They would never again take Rafael Lopez into that jailhouse unless they took him feet first.

So when the frightened Mexican came panting in to say that Juan Valdez lay dead and that Lopez was just up the gulch a hundred yards, Deputy Sorenson played it safe. He telephoned for help, and he waited until help came.

When the posse assembled, there began probably the wildest man-hunt the state of Utah ever saw. They trailed Lopez up over Utah Copper hill. It was November, and his tracks were plain in the snow. By the middle of the next day they had followed the trail forty miles south, to a ranch owned by a man named Jones, near the north end of Utah Lake. They were spread out, searching the brush, when Lopez opened fire. Deputies Grant, Witbeck, and Jensen fell from their horses, dead or dying. Sorenson fell off his horse and was untouched. The enlarged posse which gathered later found the Mexican's ambush, and four ejected cartridges. The fourth had missed fire.

So now the score was four to nothing, and Lopez still at large. Sheriff Smith of Salt Lake County came down and took over, swore in deputies by the score, organized field-glass and horseback brigades to scour the country. The story of that hunt is told in "The True Story of the Hunt for Lopez," written by a Bingham miner who was one of the posse. Our Eyewitness waxes bitter and witty at the expense of the sheriff, who conducted the hunt from his automobile and then complained that working from a car hampered him in his search for the fugitive. "Of course," says Eyewitness, "he could have walked. Lopez was walking, and there were plenty of horses besides; but he wasn't used to riding, and besides, on horseback they might possibly overtake the fugitive, and that would be dangerous." So the sheriff stayed in his car with field glasses.

Groups of farmers, miners, deputies, went fearfully poking through the brush and among the hills. Their worst fear, apparently, was that they would be successful. "The party I was with," says Eyewitness, "had an awful scare and three of them disabled themselves seeking cover. They were hurt so bad they had to turn back, but by the speed they were traveling on the backtrack, one would suppose they had had a tonic or maybe a laxative. It happened this way. We were proceeding along a ridge somewhat scattered out, perhaps fifty feet apart, when a young fellow from Salt Lake City spied a jack rabbit. He threw up his gun in fun and took aim at the rabbit, not intending to shoot. Someone saw him aiming and gave the alarm. 'Lopez!' Several of the party gave a realistic exhibition of a man being shot. I saw one fall on his face and commence chewing out the ground, really trying to crowd into the earth; another in trying to get behind a rock went around it like an acrobat goes around the back of a chair; one fellow in backing away fell backwards over a rock and hit himself in the mouth with the butt of his gun, loosening several teeth." The rabbit shooter, meanwhile, was unaware of all the uproar he had caused. With his eye over the sights he said, "Shall I shoot him?" That broke up the posse completely. "What few had stood their ground at the first alarm hunted cover. Every man said afterward that he hollered to the Salt Lake boob to shoot, but they must have whispered, for no one heard a sound. One of the party pulled out for parts unknown, and I don't believe was ever seen at the hunt again. The Salt Laker finally took his eye off his sights and the rabbit and started to walk ahead, turned his head to either side to locate his companions and couldn't see anyone. There wasn't a soul in sight. Right away the joke worked both ways. He dropped down behind a bunch of brush, and commenced peering around in every direction, and finally in a quavering voice demanded of the surrounding country what the matter was."

Our Eyewitness should have taken up literature. His indignation at the ineptitude of the posse is beautiful to read. About ten o'clock on the second day of the hunt a party treed Lopez on a ledge in the mountains—or rather, he treed them. They exchanged a few shots with nobody hurt. Lopez called down asking them to send Sorenson up. He wanted to shake his hand. He was lonesome. The posse hugged the rocks and froze slowly, and at dusk they withdrew. When they came back the next morning and painstakingly surrounded the ledge where Lopez had been perched, he was unaccountably not there. They found ejected cartridges again—revolver cartridges this time, which not only indicated that he was short of rifle ammunition, but explained why he had not hit anyone the afternoon before. He had been out of range, and knew it.

Now there were tracks to follow again. There were, in fact, dozens of tracks. The posses followed them in every direction. They petered out at the edge of railroad grades, they merged with the jumble on main roads, they vanished in the maze left by a traveling sheep herd. Lopez was reported from southern Utah; he was killed by a band of Indians in Nevada; he had got on a train and got clean away.

All the time, Lopez was probably within hailing distance of one or another posse. Ten days after he had left Bingham, he came back in the night, his feet bloody and swollen, and slipped into the house of his friend Stefano, an Italian. Stefano was scared Lopez was going to kill him. He promised to help if he wouldn't be hurt. So the Mexican had him roll up a pair of quilts and all the provisions he had handy. He left his own rifle and took Stefano's, along with forty rounds of ammunition. He borrowed cloths to wrap his swollen feet, and a pair of rubbers to wear over the bandages. He had supper and gave Stefano specific instructions. Stefano was to go downtown in the morning and buy more rifle ammunition. He was to see Corelli, Lopez' partner, and tell him to bring money up to the Number Two tunnel of the Minnie. Sometime after midnight Lopez limped up the hill to the Minnie Number

Two, with Stefano lugging the quilts and provisions, and they parted.

If Lopez had been a Mormon lawbreaker coming back to his home town for help in escaping the law, he might have had better luck. If he had been John D. Lee, for example, wanted for his participation in the massacre at Mountain Meadows, he would have been hidden and protected and fed, shunted from house to house in the underground. His friends and neighbors would have stuck together, been poker-faced and ignorant under questioning, because as members of the cohesive Mormon society their first duty would have been to God and their second to a member of the group. But Lopez had to pay the penalty of living in a society that was completely individualist. He belonged to no group. There was no one among his friends who dared take the chance of protecting him, who even trusted him not to shoot his friends as well as his enemies. Stefano was scared. He went to Corelli, and Corelli was also scared. Corelli said that a quadruple murderer ought to be caught and hanged. So Stefano went to Tom Hoskins, the Apex foreman, and told him that Lopez was in Minnie Number Two.

Lopez must have known from the beginning that every man's hand was against him, that he couldn't trust either Corelli or Stefano. At any rate he took no chances. The moment when he and Stefano parted at the mouth of the tunnel was the last moment that anyone in Bingham ever clearly saw Lopez again, ever, alive or dead.

Not that they didn't try. Every tunnel opening was heavily guarded and groups of deputies were scattered through the mine. Within a few hours after Stefano came with his story they had Lopez effectively trapped. He couldn't possibly get out. But a mine is an uncomfortable place to hunt a man who will shoot on sight. It is very dark. The walls drip, the ceiling drips, the timbers creak as the mountain settles its weight on them. There are noises in the dark, and pebbles drop and roll down the inclines. In such a place a man does not dare go around with a light because then he is a perfect target for the killer who crouches in the blackness. The deputies couldn't possibly hunt Lopez down, because he could choose at any moment whether to shoot or hide—and there were approximately ten miles of underground workings in the Apex properties, all of them joined by shafts and inclines. In the black insides of the mountain Lopez could laugh at pursuit: he knew the Minnie and its adjoining workings better than anyone, even the owners, because he had worked and explored in them during his leasing job.

There were dozens of plans for getting him out. Excitement over the whole state was intense, and proposals came rolling in. Some were in favor of going right in after him in force. But, says Eyewitness, the people who got up that plan stayed a long way from the mine entrances. The deputies who lurked fearfully at tunnel mouths were in no hurry to go inside. They knew Lopez as a hip shot. He didn't need light on his sights. He could kill without aiming. They stalled.

Meantime Lopez held up two or three groups of miners in the dark without showing himself. The voice out of the black told them to give up their candles and lunches and git. They gave up and got. It was apparent that he could live in the mine indefinitely, stealing candles and food and tobacco from the shifts as they came in and out. By this time the press and public were almost hilarious. Bets were offered ten to one that Lopez would chase the sheriff

back to Salt Lake with his two hundred deputies, sur-
round and capture and kill the entire city and burn it to
the ground, unless the troops were called out.

The sheriff had to get the Mexican out of that mine or
lose face forever. He decided to smoke Lopez out. That
meant closing the mine, throwing two hundred miners
and mill hands out of work, and costing the company a
pile of money, but it was the only way. Some of the open-
ings were closed up, powerful lights were set at the open
tunnels, with doubled guards in the darkness behind them,
and hay and damp wood were brought in and fired. Even
then people cackled. It was dangerous, they said, to take
hay into the Minnie. Lopez already had the sheriff's goat,
and give him a little hay for feed he could live fat and
happy on goat's milk and cheese.

After a while the fires went out, and no Lopez had shown
up strangling at one of the entrances. They decided to
smoke him some more. Four men, only three of whom are
named in any of the news reports, went into the mine with
a bale of hay. Manderich, an Austrian, and a man named
Hulsey were ahead, dragging the bale up the Andy Incline
with a rope. Doc Ray and the fourth man were behind
pushing. Three red licks of flame spat out of the darkness
ahead and above them, and the tunnel roared. Manderich,
shot through the heart, rolled on down to the bottom of
the incline. Hulsey, with a bullet through his lungs and
another through his foot, rolled and floundered until he
was stopped by a post. There he lay groaning for a long
time. The guards could hear him from out in the cross
tunnel where they took refuge. While they were talking
about what to do, Lopez came down the incline and
opened fire again, chasing them back. The deputies were

trapped inside, unable to get out without running the gauntlet of Lopez' fire.

While they huddled, Sorenson came in from the tunnel mouth and shouted to them to shoot out the lights and creep past in the dark, and Lopez, recognizing the voice, invited him in. But Sorenson did not come in. None of the regular law officers came in. They were, says Eyewitness, outside toasting their shins by a blacksmith's fire, while specially deputized miners did the dirty work. In the end the imprisoned deputies shot the lights out and sneaked past without further losses, leaving Lopez still king of the mine and the score six to nothing.

Now the man hunters had to do their job thoroughly. They stopped off different levels of the mine by bulkheading, they forced smoke and gas into the entire upper levels and kept the fires going for five days and nights, sending out a terrible stink of sulphur and gunpowder. The fires ultimately went out for lack of oxygen, and when the bulkheads were removed heavy clouds of poisonous smoke poured out. No man could possibly have lived through it. They went in to locate Lopez' body.

They didn't find it. The second party found his quilts and his provisions, but no party ever found the Mexican, and for weeks thereafter the muckers sang and whistled coming in and out, for fear deputies would shoot them for Lopez or Lopez for deputies. The guards heard noises; there were rumors that Lopez was not dead. A woman jumped into the limelight by reporting that she had had a tryst with Lopez at the mine, but she later confessed that she just wanted to get her name in the papers. A Greek came out scared to death to say that he had been robbed of his pipe and candles and told to get out of the mine and stay out, but another Greek, coming along just behind him with another car of ore, saw and heard nothing and thought the first Greek was a liar. A guard reported hearing Lopez swearing in French and Spanish through a bulkhead, but he was not believed because Lopez seldom swore, and seldom used anything but English, even when talking with Mexicans. Sam Rogers, a mine shift boss, came out one day to say that Lopez had held him up and talked to him and told him blood-curdling tales of who-all he was going to kill next. So far as Rogers was concerned, Lopez could have the mine. Rogers left town, and some believed his story and some didn't. A good while after all the guards had been removed in the belief that Lopez was either dead or vanished, a whole shift of twenty-six miners came out of the upper workings to tell a story of being held up at the point of a gun and forced out of a drift and invited not to come back. Not one of the twenty-six would go back, but the replacement shift saw nothing, heard nothing, had no trouble.

Lopez has been reported from Los Angeles, from St. Louis, from Salt Lake. The safe chance is that none of these rumors has anything in it, because all concern fearsome-looking Mexicans, and Lopez looked neither fearsome nor like a Mexican.

He is faded into air, into thin air, this lone-wolf badman who kept a whole county at bay for upwards of a month, killed six men without being so much as seen more than once or twice, terrified the countryside, made the sheriff and his deputies look like silly and timorous boys, and then vanished. Among the legends of the rugged individualists, the anti-social wild men, put down Rafael Lopez, who, in the words of Ma Joad about Pretty Boy Floyd, wasn't a bad boy till they crowded him too hard. He was— or is—the apotheosis of the spirit of the mining camps, an animal with only a varnish of domestication over him. His career throws into strong light the differences between the camps and the Mormon villages in the valleys a few miles from Lopez' last hideout. He caps Bingham's lurid and brass-knuckled history, and demonstrates by contrast that the Mormon is above all else a domesticated animal. In a few miles, from Bingham to South Jordan, you can move into a different world.

The Wild Bunch . . .

SO there are three varieties of Gentiles—mountain men, railroad men, and miners—who have left their mark in one way or another on the Mormon Country. There have been other varieties, at least one of which came in, as mining did, with the railroad. That one is the cattle man, and along with the cattle man the inevitable concomitant, the rustler and outlaw.

The Mormon society that in the course of ninety-five years has made itself dominant from the Yellowstone to the Gila is the result of impact and adjustment and compromise. A dynamic, dedicated, regimented, group-conscious and Heaven-conscious people met a frontier as forbidding as any in the country. The institutions were pretty well set when the Mormons came into the valleys of the mountains, but they had to be adjusted. Sometimes, where the typical small-farm of Mormonism was not possible, the frontier even broke down the people who tried to subdue it. That happened most frequently on the edges of Mormondom, and the Gentile ways that were most successful in diluting the tight little village psychology of the Saints were the ways of the cattlemen.

Stock raising is a much more individualistic occupation than irrigation farming. It calls for wide stretches of unfenced and unoccupied range. It prohibits the typical clotting of population that kept Mormon practices strong. In the boom days of the cattle business, moreover, it lured in cowpunchers from Texas, Wyoming, New Mexico, Arizona, and those cowpunchers were not set apart from Mormons by their occupation as miners and railroad men were. On the cattle and sheep ranges of the Mormon Country Saint and Gentile worked side by side, doing the same jobs for the same pay, drinking out of the same tin can, rolling cigarettes from the same pack of Bull Durham, singing the same songs and swearing the same oaths. The Word of Wisdom suffered. There was no way for the Church to control cowpunchers as it controlled villagers. As a result, Mormonism was very early thinned and diluted at its edges.

Sometimes that dilution was not permanent. J. Golden Kimball and Jesse Knight, both ranchers, ignored the Church for some years and then came back in. Many did not. Many simply turned cowhand and adopted all the un-Mormon habits of the waddies from Texas and Wyoming. Generally speaking it was no reluctance to accept doctrine and counsel, no strong persuasiveness of the Gentiles, that broke young men away from the Church. It was the frontier, the lure of absolute freedom, the attractiveness of an unsocial and even anti-social way of life. They were not converted from one kind of society to another, but from a tight society to one that hardly existed as such.

It was fairly easy to be unsocial or anti-social in the Mormon Country as late as the twentieth century. Even yet the railroads tap only the comparatively settled regions, and towns that were founded in the eighteen-fifties may still be more than a hundred miles from the rails. And until the advent of federal aid highways and the National Park system the roads were merely wagon trails linking the settlements. Like the railroads and like the Mormons in their planned settlement, they followed the valleys and crossed the ranges at the easiest passes. The back country was left back country, the home of scattered ranches and long-riding punchers. The Church was not potent there, the law came hardly at all. And because it was so inaccessible, that country which weaned a good many Mormon boys away from their heritage offered them almost unlimited opportunities to turn rustler and prey on the society that had bred them.

There were—and are—perfect hideouts in the Mormon Country or along its borders. The old Outlaw Trail that ran from Montana to Mexico in the days of the cowboy outlaws ran along the eastern side of Mormondom, and of its three principal hideouts two were within the Mormon Country proper. The Hole-in-the-Wall, in the Powder River country of Wyoming, lay outside the boundaries of Mormon influence, though plenty of ex-Mormon badmen holed up there during the eighties and nineties. Brown's Hole, on the Green River, was just inside the eastern edge of Mormondom, and was exceptionally useful as a headquarters because it had excellent winter and summer range for stolen stock and was extremely difficult to get into. It lay, moreover, just in the corner of three states, where the Utah-Colorado line runs into the southern boundary of Wyoming. It took collaboration by officers of all three states to get any action in Brown's Hole, and in addition it took more courage than most sheriffs possessed, because every rancher for miles around was probably a rustler and perhaps a road agent as well. The third hideout, the one that has figured in Zane Grey's novels and that the horse operas of the movies frequently confuse with Hole-in-the-Wall, was Robbers' Roost, among the mesas and plateaus of the San Rafael Swell, in the dead desert heart of Mormondom. From Robbers' Roost the trail went on across the Colorado via Dandy Crossing, and thence on into Arizona and New Mexico and even across the international line into Sonora.

That trail was used, and its hideouts utilized, by some of the most spectacular bandits of the West. It was used by the McCarthy brothers, by Flat-Nosed George Curry and the Logan brothers, by the Ketchum gang, by such furious killers as Harry Tracy. And in particular it was used, and made famous, by a crowd of rustlers, bank robbers, train robbers, payroll robbers, known to history as the Wild Bunch, which was composed of about equal numbers of reckless cowpunchers and Mormon boys gone wrong, and led by another Mormon boy whose exploits have furnished material for the horse operas ever since.

More than any other western badman he approached the romantic and chivalric tradition of Robin Hood. Where Billy the Kid was a homicidal maniac, the leader of the Wild Bunch was a friendly, gay, reckless, and coolly daring young man whom everyone liked, even the sheriffs who chased him. He had so many friends through the Mormon Country and along the Outlaw Trail that he thumbed his nose at pursuing posses. By the evidence of a half dozen ranchers who employed him at one time or another, he was the best cowhand and the best shot they ever saw. He put the fear of God into law officers for hundreds of miles, took hundreds of thousands of dollars from express cars, banks, payrolls, yet he never, apparently, robbed an individual except as a prank, and he never, until his last twelve hours, killed a man.

His name was George LeRoy Parker, and he was the son of a pious English convert who settled at Circleville, Utah.

His brothers still live near Circleville, and his father died only a few years ago, a good Saint to the last. But it was not as George LeRoy Parker that the bandit made his reputation. When he drifted away from the unexciting stuffiness of his Mormon village and into the nomadic life of a cowhand and rustler and apprentice bank robber, he left not only his heritage behind, but his name as well. It was as Butch Cassidy that the West knew him.

It is hard to determine how many boys from the Mormon villages hit the Outlaw Trail. They did not keep diaries as their pious fathers did across the plains. They let genealogy alone. They changed their names and gave up both the future and the past for the exciting present. Almost any specific Mormon can be tracked through his family records or through the records of the Wards or Stakes, kept meticulously in the Church Historian's office. But the apostates cannot be traced. They are crossed off the books. If their antecedents have been looked up at all, the law has done it.

Still, there were enough known Mormons on the roll call of the Wild Bunch and other outlaw gangs to indicate a fairly frequent dissatisfaction among the young blades with the stodgy laboriousness of their homes. Charles Kelly, who probably knows more about the outlaws of the Mormon Country than anyone else, has checked the Mormon origin of a number. Dan Parker, Butch Cassidy's brother, tried his hand with his big brother's gang for a while, but was kicked out at the age of eighteen after getting himself grabbed in Wyoming for a stage holdup. Butch told him he was too damned easy to catch. Perhaps that was an advantage, because Dan Parker is still living near Milford. There is no real evidence that the McCarthy brothers were Mormons, though Tom McCarthy married the daughter of Bishop Christianson of Levan, and there was a complicated relationship by marriage with the Taylor family of Moab. Elza Lay, Butch's first lieutenant for several years, was probably a Mormon boy. So was Bob Meeks, who lost a leg jumping from a window in the Ogden jail and had to give up the outlaw business. Young George Law, killed in a bank holdup near Meeker, was a Mormon. So were Charlie Lee and his brother Rains, both sons of John D. Lee. So was a townsman of the Lees from Torrey, Pete Nielson. So, perhaps, was a four-flushing holdup man named Gunplay Maxwell, who married Pete Nielson's sister. So was Henry Lee (not related to Charlie and Rains) who still lives in Vernal and who spent several years in the penitentiary for operating around Fort Bridger with Bob Meeks. So were the Swazey boys, who ran an outlaw ranch in Millard County. So was Dave Lant, who was associated for a while with the killer Harry Tracy. So were the Ketchum brothers. So, finally, was the outlaw who next to Butch Cassidy himself was most feared along great stretches of the trail, the man who said he taught Butch all he knew about train robbing and sticking up banks. His name for posterity was Matt Warner, but he was born Willard Christianson, the son of the same Bishop Christianson of Levan whose daughter married Tom McCarthy. It is probably unimportant to note that he was the son of the good Bishop's fifth wife.

Until very recently it was possible to run across reformed members of that old outlaw tribe here and there in the Mormon Country. Matt Warner was for a number of years the marshal of Price, in Carbon County, and ran a little saloon and gambling joint on the side. He was a redoubtable old fire eater. When he was past seventy he collared a suspicious-looking Negro in an alley and took

him out to the arc light for inspection. The Negro, perhaps thinking that an old man would be easy to scare,
jerked out an automatic and started backing away. Before
he could fire Matt had produced a gun from somewhere
and shot the automatic out of his hand. It sounds like pure
Wild West hokum, and just possibly is, but I have been
assured by three or four people who attended the Negro's
trial that he blubbered on the stand and couldn't even say
where Matt's gun had come from.

Once, on a hurried trip to Price, I tried to call on Matt.
His saloon was open, in spite of the prohibition that still
pertained, but all I found was four white men and a
Chinaman playing poker under a green-shaded globe. The
Chinaman directed me to Red Jordan's place. "Got a but-
termilk sign out," he said. "He's an old friend of Matt's.
Matt might be there."

So I found the sign saying "Buttermilk" and went down
a dozen steps into a basement and found a little red-headed
man wiping off a short mahogany bar. He had a gambler's
face and suspicious eyes, and when I asked for a drink he
looked at me coldly and said, "Beer or buttermilk?" I
asked about something stronger. He wanted to know who
had sent me there. I told him. Eventually he pulled out a
bottle and poured.

"Have one with me?" I said.

He reached down two more glasses, poured one full of
whiskey and the other full of buttermilk. "Here's how,"
he said. I watched him pour about four ounces of whiskey
into himself in one gulp and immediately pour the buttermilk on top of it. "It's my guts," he said apologetically.
"Stomach's all shot." He sounded half ashamed of himself
for the buttermilk, and he looked frail and sick, but in the
course of the next two hours, while he was filling me full

of the tallest lies ever heard by man, he managed to pour four more whiskey-and-buttermilk compounds into his ailing insides. I decided then and there that if Red Jordan, who was a minor front man for the Wild Bunch, a gambler and smalltime bandit, could do that at a very advanced age and with his insides all shot, the Wild Bunch must have been all it was cracked up to be.

Probably it was. Matt Warner himself led a gang known as the "Invincible Three" in a wild series of holdups in Oregon and Washington, was in and out of jail two or three times under the pseudonym of Ras Lewis, jumped his horse into the swift current of the Columbia where the stream was a mile wide and swam across with twenty thousand dollars in gold and greenbacks in his saddlebags and a posse shooting at him all the way out of range. He had barely strength to thumb his nose from the other bank before he collapsed. He holed up one winter in Swan Valley, Wyoming, with Butch Cassidy and Tom McCarthy, gave away money by the handful, chastised and threatened a stingy storekeeper into extending the whole town credit, pasted a ten thousand dollar greenback on the wall behind his bar because he knew it was marked and couldn't be cashed. He married an impressionable Mormon girl from the village, roared and drank and talked loud in the hideout at Brown's Hole, and eventually was tried and convicted for the killing of two men and the wounding of another in a gunfight just south of Brown's Hole, in Dry Fork. Matt's own version of that fight differs in a good many respects from that of Charles Kelly and other investigators. According to Matt, he was ambushed by the three and his horse killed under him before he could make a move. As the horse fell he yanked the rifle from its scabbard, lit on his feet, and started shooting from the hip at the three men behind the log barricade, killing two and wounding the other in one burst of deadly fire. Kelly's version is much less heroic, but the fight was epochal, because it put Matt behind bars for several years and turned him into a halfway respectable citizen.

Matt Warner, except during the winter in Swan Valley when he was under the influence of Butch, was no Robin Hood. He had a raging temper, he was fairly often drunk and dangerous, and he treated his wife so roughly that she was afraid to open her mouth. And he was about as far as possible from attaining the prayerful serenity that might have been expected of the son of Bishop Christianson's fifth wife. He had been on the loose, on the edge of outlawry if not actually in it, since he was thirteen, when he got into a fight with Andrew Henrickson over who should carry Alice Sabey's books home from school. In the course of the fight he went berserk, seized a fence rail, and beat young Henrickson's head into a pulp. Thinking he had killed him, he lit for home, saddled a horse, and took out across the wild Uintah Indian Reservation in search of sanctuary. Eventually he found it with the McCarthy brothers, one of whom had married his sister, and from that time he was a long rider, dodging posses and vanishing into the impenetrable canyons along the Green. It was mere accident that he died in his bed. Most of his fellows died with their boots on.

As for Butch Cassidy, that gay caballero with the Robin Hood love of the little man and the lust for adventure and excitement, he was neither hot-tempered nor anti-social. He was pure adventurer, and years on the outlaw trail never made either a hard guy or a killer of him. He drank little, he stayed away from women, he planned his holdups coolly and carried them out with split-second timing. For weeks before a job he rehearsed the details. Before the Castle Gate payroll robbery he brought a blooded horse from the McCarthy string into Castle Gate, rode to meet all the trains, practiced the horse until it would stand quietly beside the very engine, trained it to stand while he came running up from behind and vaulted into the saddle over its rump (another thing he taught the horse operas) and then shoot off at full speed. He always had supplies and reinforcements and a change of horses arranged for the getaway. He built false trails and left posses gasping on their spent horses in his wake, and if he got in a tight spot almost any rancher in the country would help him out. He led a charmed life and almost a charming one. Other outlaws frequently stole horses if they got in a tight spot. When Butch stole them he left a half dozen double eagles behind in payment. If he came to a farmhouse hungry and shot the heads off some chickens he placated the frightened housewife with a handful of money that would have bought half the homestead. He paid his bills. He kept his word to the state of Wyoming, whose governor he had promised never to molest the state again if the governor would pardon him from the penitentiary. And he never killed a man until his last stand in San Vicente, Bolivia, where he and Harry Longabaugh held off a whole company of Bolivian cavalry armed with rifles, killed twenty Bolivians and wounded forty more with their revolvers, and ended their lives with their last two bullets.

Butch Cassidy was a bandit, but not a badman. His life had all the thrills and none of the brutality that outlaw life traditionally contains, and the country he was brought up in gave him the most romantic and efficient hideouts that any outlaw ever had. He could disappear into the ground, practically. In the Robbers' Roost country there were only a few waterholes, and nobody but the outlaws knew them. A sheriff had to contend with the country as well as the road agents if he ventured in. And every time the officers did get active and shoot somebody in a bank holdup or an express car robbery, they were sure it was Butch, if only because they wanted him so badly. Once he rode through a town in a covered wagon in order to view his own body laid out on display. He was an exciting fact in the Mormon Country in the eighties and nineties, and he was an even more exciting fact in South America, where until 1909 he kept up his exploits. And he was also a legend. Like most legendary figures, people will not let him die.

Some years ago Doctor R. G. Frazier of Bingham (he later accompanied Commander Byrd to the South Pole) was making a boat trip down the Green, and in one of the lost canyons ran upon an old Negro outlaw, Speck Williams, the "Speckled Nigger" of the old Brown's Hole gang. Within a week or two there were rumors around Salt Lake that Butch Cassidy was still holed up on the Green, that he hadn't been killed in 1909 in Bolivia at all. Last year a grand-niece of his assured me that he had come back to Circleville for his mother's funeral, long after he was supposed to be dead. There are old timers who swear profanely that it wasn't Butch who died in the inn yard at San Vicente with Harry Longabaugh, but a minor outlaw named John Dilley. Butch has been reported from Mexico, where a former friend saw him dealing faro in a gambling house. He was reported to have saved the life of a Mormon caught by Villa's raiders in 1912. Old timers have run across him in Lander, in Spokane, in Idaho. Some say he died a natural death on an island off the coast of Lower California in 1932.

There is something peculiar about the Mormon Country. It breeds legends. A loved or feared individual has a hard time dying. Anyone out of the ordinary who disappears from view is granted immortality. Lopez vanishes in Minnie Number Two, with not a chance to get out, with guards at all the entrances and poisonous smoke filling all the drifts and tunnels. But he lives. Butch Cassidy quietly leaves the Southwest and transfers his attentions to South America, is reliably reported killed by Bolivian cavalry, is identified by pictures. But he lives. He lives at the age of his prime; if he were really alive now he would be seventy-five years old, but whenever he is seen he is likely to be what he was forty years ago. Legends do not get gray and acquire rheumatism. Broken-down operators of buttermilk bars may, but legends do not.

The Terrible River...

UNLIKE the majority of the American frontiers, the Mormon Country did not owe its settlement to the rivers. All through the East and Middle West, and as far west as the Missouri, the rivers were the first highways, but in the Mormon Country there were no rivers that could be used as highways. The Snake, bursting through its canyon in the Antelope Hills, cutting through the lava fields, turning northwestward into the mountains again, was no highway except for salmon. The only other major river, the Green-Colorado, was a barrier rather than a highway; it was so effective a barrier that it was not even explored until 1869, except for a short exploratory journey made by General Ashley in 1825. Major John Wesley Powell, conducting the first scientific expedition down the terrible river in 1869, did not even know about Ashley. When he came upon the inscription, "Ashley, 1825" scratched on the canyon wall, he misread the date and assumed that Ashley had been wrecked at Ashley Falls and had made his way overland to Salt Lake, where he got a job working on the temple. But Powell can hardly be blamed for not knowing Ashley's Journal; scholars dug it up a good many years later. The important thing is that except for a few trappers and an occasional prospector who tried going down the Green and soon discovered that it was wise to get out again, nobody attempted the river between 1825 and 1869, and since 1869 there have not been so many expeditions that one couldn't count them on his fingers.

To Powell belongs the credit for first exploring the fiercest river in America. He was one of the big men of the West, one of its foremost explorers, and in addition the father of half the scientific government bureaus. He fathered the Geological Survey and for years was its director; he founded the Bureau of Ethnology which gave us our soundest studies of the western Indians; and he was an instigator of the Reclamation Service, to which thousands of western farmers owe their living. Those three government departments have had an incalculable influence in shaping the intermountain West, and through his sponsorship of them, Powell affected more people's lives than all but our greatest presidents have.

Put together a man whose qualities were a kind of cross between those of Brigham Young and those of Butch Cassidy and you have something like Powell. He was a bright and polished intelligence, a hotbed of ideas, an organizer, a martinet, a man of cool courage and the ability to plan. He had only one arm (the other he lost at Shiloh) when he came out to Green River Crossing in 1869 to start down the unknown river. But he had brains and courage to make up for his handicap, and he was no reckless plunger into danger. His boats, built in Chicago, were made for rough use, were practically unsinkable, and were furnished with supplies and scientific instruments against any eventuality. The river before them was, so far as Powell knew, completely unknown. It might at any moment plunge over falls as high as Niagara. There were even rumors that for long distances it ran underground. There might be, and probably were, sucks, whirlpools, cascades, cataracts, rapids. Whatever was there, Powell wanted to find out. On May 24 his four boats pushed off from the landing at Green River.

Even with all his careful preparations, Powell was almost beaten. The Green wrecked a boat for the party at Disaster Falls in the Canyon of Lodore, and although that was the only boat of the four which was actually lost, the trip itself grew grimmer and grimmer. Their oars were broken, their flour soaked, their instruments lost overboard in the frequent upsets. The river whirled them through rapids, lashed them with twenty-foot waves, shot them through narrow canyons at heart-stopping speed. One man quit in the Wonsits Valley and made his way out to the Uintah Reservation. Three more, the Howland brothers and William H. Dunn, decided in the depths of the Grand Canyon that they had had enough, and attempted to make their way over the cliffs to the Mormon settlements to the north. All three were ambushed and killed by the Shivwits Indians about the same time that Powell and his remaining two boats were running triumphantly out of the granite canyons and into the easy water at the mouth of Grand Wash. They were whipped, cold, starved, exhausted; the total supply of food left them was ten pounds of flour, about fifteen of dried apples, and seventy of coffee. But they had run through a thousand unknown miles of the most hair-raising canyons, and had made a highway out of a river that was about as clearly designed to be a highway as a tornado is designed for transportation.

What they knew, after their history-making journey, was that the Green, a pleasant little stream at Green River, with a belt of cottonwoods and a gentle current, was tame only about as far as the Wyoming-Utah line, and that from

there to the site of the present Boulder Dam it was as wild
as any river could be. The channel turned out to be an
almost endless series of canyons. For miles on end a man
in the canyon cannot get out, a man on the rim cannot get
down for a drink if his life depends on it. When the walls
open out into a little park, or "hole," they close in again
almost immediately, and the solid rock goes up for a vertical half mile. Below Green River are Flaming Gorge,
Horseshoe Canyon, Kingfisher Canyon. Then comes a little
park, then Red Canyon, then Little Brown's Hole and
Brown's Hole, rendezvous for trappers and hideout for
badmen. At the bottom of Brown's Hole the river dives
directly into the Uintah Mountains, which run east and
west across its course, through Swallow Canyon and the
terrible Canyon of Lodore, where Powell's boat was
wrecked and where he found the scattered wreckage of a
prospector's outfit and thought it part of Ashley's leavings.
Below Lodore the canyon opens briefly, for about a mile,
in Echo Park, walled with monolithic and echoing sandstone, where the Yampa River comes in. It closes again for
the chute through Whirlpool Canyon, widens for Island
Park and a few meanders, gathers itself and bores directly
through Split Mountain, literally cutting a tremendous
peak in two.

At the bottom of Split Mountain Canyon it leaves the
mountains for one of its two stretches of open country in
the whole thousand miles from Green River to Grand
Wash. Through the Wonsits Valley it winds for eighty-
seven miles past the Dinosaur National Monument and
the Uintah Reservation. In Wonsits it is swelled by Ashley
Fork, the Uintah, and White River, and at the bottom of
the valley it dives again through the Canyon of Desolation
and Gray Canyon, to break out into its second large open-

ing, the Gunnison Valley, where the Denver and Rio Grande and the main highway between southern Utah and Colorado find a way across. There is quite literally no other place where road or railroad could get across that barrier river between Green River and Lee's Ferry except the Wonsits and Gunnison Valleys. In almost eight hundred miles of river only two spots where frontier pathfinding and modern engineering have been able to effect a crossing. And from Lee's Ferry on there is no practicable trail until Grand Wash, another two hundred and sixty miles by river. Along the whole eastern and southern sides of the Mormon Country the Green and the Colorado are a Chinese wall, and in all its thousand miles there are only three gates.

And after those eight hundred miles to Gunnison Crossing, after traveling in the cold depths of sunless canyons for days on end, soaked to the hide, laboring like madmen to prevent catastrophe, Powell and his men still had the worst part of the river to run. From Gunnison to the junction of the Green and Grand was easy water, though deep in the rock. Labyrinth Canyon, Stillwater Canyon, were almost a picnic. But now the Grand comes in, almost as big as the Green, and the united waters rush headlong through Cataract Canyon and Narrow Canyon. Below those is quiet water again most of the way through Glen Canyon, the walls broken by the chasms of other streams, the Escalante, the San Juan, the Paria, until the crossing at Lee's Ferry.

And now Marble Canyon, the walls rising higher and higher, the river steepening, and the Little Colorado coming in through a cataclysmic gorge, and from here on is the Grand Canyon. The river runs deep in the black granite in a narrow chute which in flood time carries water over a hundred feet deep, with waves at every rapid and cataract big enough to toss a small boat like a chip. There is no time to watch the miraculous walls above, lifting more than a mile in cliff and talus and again cliff, banded with shades of red and gray and yellow. For two hundred and seventeen miles the muddy water goes at a velocity that sometimes reaches twenty miles an hour or more; from the head of Marble Canyon to the foot of the Grand Canyon, a distance of under three hundred miles, the vertical fall is well over two thousand feet, and the river which in open country spreads out to a width of fifteen hundred feet is bottled in a channel sometimes only fifty or sixty feet wide. It is no wonder the Howlands and Dunn, after running through that for endless days, lowering boats down on lines, laboring a whole day sometimes to make a mile or two of bad water, decided that even the unknown dangers of the cliffs and the Indian country were preferable.

There have been boat trips down the Green and Colorado since Powell's, a number of them. But give Powell the credit. He ran the river when it was entirely unknown, and he not only ran it but he did what he could about measuring and exploring it. The walls were difficult for a one-armed man to climb, but he climbed them at every opportunity to take elevations and get a look at the surrounding country. At least twice he got stuck on cliffs where he could get neither forward nor back, up nor down, and had to be rescued by his men—once with the help of a suit of long underwear.

What he saw of the country back from the river must have appalled him—and interested him—almost as much as the gorge itself. The depth and verticality of the canyons is enough, God knows, to keep interlopers out, but whoever arranged that part of the Mormon Country went

further. The back country, except for the Wonsits and
Gunnison Valleys, is high, arid, forbidding, inaccessible
mountains and barren plateaus and waterless desert. Every
little rain channel is a gulch hundreds of feet deep, and
in the rock plateau country only a few yards wide. Start
across the country in southeastern Utah almost anywhere
and you are confronted by a chasm too steep and too deep
to climb down through, and just too wide to jump. It will
take you ten miles upcountry before you head it, and after
a half mile you will probably meet another just like it. It
is a country that calls for wings. In some places there is not
even sand to blow, and the rock is so bare it is actually
polished. It is no wonder that although white men first saw
the country along the Colorado in 1540, less than a half
century after Columbus found landfall in the Indies, it
was more than three hundred years before any white men
made an effort to settle it, and still another generation
before the Green and the Grand and their tributaries
could be called explored.

Much of the first scientific study of that back country
was also Powell's work. As head of the Geological Survey
he kept men in the Plateau Province for years, mapping
and triangulating and sketching, studying the rocks and
the faulting and the volcanic extravasations. Almost to a
man, the people he selected to do that work were of exceptional caliber. Their names are more than a roll of honor
of early American geology, because they were more than
geologists. The lure of the unknown that had pulled Jed
Smith into the wilderness pulled on Powell and his assist-
ants too, but in a different way. Theirs was a lust for
knowledge, their frontiers the frontiers of science. Because
they existed before the age of specialization and brute fact,
they felt obliged to try to see the whole instead of merely

the part. It seems rather curious now to read geological reports that are as charming as much of the literature of the time, to come upon geological sketches of rock strata that exhibit a sensitive appreciation of form and texture and a more-than-draughtsmanly skill.

W. H. Holmes, for example, whose drawings appear in a number of Geological Survey monographs, is by almost any standard the best artist who ever attempted the monumental job of reproducing the canyon and plateau country. In Dutton's *Tertiary History of the Grand Canyon District* his drawings are side by side with several by Thomas Moran, ordinarily spoken of as probably the best Western artist of the period. It is not Holmes that suffers by the comparison.

Or Captain Dutton, Powell's particular protege, who worked in the high plateaus and in the Grand Canyon region. He found, as everyone who ever attempted to write about that country has found, that word pictures are about as inadequate as painted ones. The country is too big. The eye simply cannot take in, the imagination cannot compass, a thing like the Grand Canyon, a hole in the ground big enough to accept into its maw the whole White Mountain range and not have a single peak, even Washington, sticking above the rim. Buttes that in the canyon are mere details, even minor details, are likely to have a mass greater than any mountain east of the Rockies; the whole immense mountain-range-in-a-ditch is calculated to render words, paints, and camera all inadequate. Add to the enormous size the delicate shadings of color, changing at every hour of the day, with every passing cloud, and the peculiarly architectural, almost symmetrical forms that erosion has filled the canyon with, and the job becomes almost impossible. For all that, Dutton not only tried to describe it, but did. His monographs are at least half nature writing, as far from stiff geology as they can well be, and there is no one who ever tried the Grand Canyon as a literary subject who approaches him in accuracy, strength, and sensitiveness. From that lost and forgotten geologist whose works collect dust on library shelves Charles Dudley Warner on occasion stole whole paragraphs. Both John Muir and John Burroughs read him before they dared take off on the Grand Canyon, and both borrowed more than they put quotation marks around.

They were monumental men in a monumental country doing a monumental job. No one knows the plateau and canyon country if he does not know the work of Powell and Dutton and Holmes and Hayden and Gilbert. There has seldom been a group of similar stature gathered together on one project. They added something to that country by their presence there. As surely as Brigham Young and the Mormon settlers, they were pioneers, and they built broadly and well.

Notes on a Life Spent Pecking at a Sandstone Cliff...

THE August sun was hot in the gulch as he climbed. Heat blazed from the bare rock faces. Light pouring over detritus and boulders was broken into a pattern of glare and shadow blinding to the eyes. From time to time the man in the prospector's boots bent to examine the exposed edges of the strata, tipping back his hat as he stooped. The heat left a red line around his forehead. At last, following the outcrop of the beds, he left the gulch and climbed to the top of the ridge.

From the naked comb of sandstone he looked down across the flats to the Green River, swinging in a slow bend to the west and south past the lone cottonwood where Powell had camped in 1869, past the shallows where Escalante was supposed to have crossed in 1775, and on in a meandering line smudged with dark green, through the scorched sage and sand desert to a turreted gateway miles and miles southward. The comb on which he stood ran east and west, a sharply tipped escarpment of sedimentary strata, ragged and toothed and flanked by dune-like foothills, leaning northward toward the broad dark uplift of the Uintahs. Northeastward was the magnificent red door of Split Mountain Canyon.

A half mile below, at a point where three narrow rain gullies debouched on the plain, he could see the wagon, with the horses eating from the box. Up the middle of the three gullies Dad Goodrich was climbing, hunting as he climbed, searching the rocks for the bones that had eluded them for more than a month. Since early in July they had been exploring every geological horizon of fossil-bearing interest. Now it was the nineteenth of August, and unless something turned up along this ridge he would have to go back to Pittsburgh and admit that his hunch had been false.

Under a juniper he sat and mopped his brow. But that hunch wasn't false! Bones—there were bones all over this country, fossils of dinosaurs of a dozen different kinds, weathered out and scattered below the ridges. Like the one he had found last fall, the thighbone of a diplodocus, so large that two of them couldn't get it back to camp on their saddle horses. That one had been gone when he returned this summer of 1909. Another collector had taken it, not too ethically, for Earl Douglass had left it earmarked.

Oh, yes, plenty of bones, but in fragments. No sign of their source, no spot that would warrant concentrated excavation. Apparently nothing in this gulch either. But it must be somewhere along here, somewhere in the Jurassic beds exposed all along the frontal line of this ridge. . . .

The flies were bad under the juniper, and he sought other shade. Beyond the crest the ridge sank into a saddle, then rose again at a sixty-degree angle along the smooth upper surface of the strata. Something in that slope caught his geologist's eye. It was the same soft gray shaly sandstone that cropped out near where the diplodocus thighbone had been found.

Forgetting the shade he had been hunting for, he went plowing down the soft talus, kicking up clouds of hovering dust. Down through the saddle, up the steep smooth slope. . . . Almost before he reached the slope he saw it.

Taking the gun from his pocket, he fired twice in the air to signal Goodrich that something had been found. By the time his rancher-helper came puffing over the ridge a half hour later, Earl Douglass was sure. Here was what the Carnegie Museum had sent him to find—what he had boasted he *could* find.

Marginal sand, that wall. Shallow water deposits, probably the mouth of an ancient river, buried and then lifted and then exposed by weathering. And in the exposed wall, which disappeared at his feet under the top edge of an overlapping layer, were seven immense vertebrae etched out in high relief. But what to his mind was the clinching sign of success was the fact that those vertebrae were in line, separated only by the space taken up by normal cartilage. This might be, possibly was, the almost-articulated skeleton of a brontosaurus.

The more he looked, the more Douglass was sure that here was a veritable dinosaur graveyard, a bone quarry. If it was, it was the greatest paleontological find in years. Bones enough for all the museums on earth, bones enough —and big enough—to satisfy Andrew Carnegie's desire to attract people to education with something as big as a barn.

The job of excavation was clear. Douglass pointed it out to his helper. Pull off this covering layer, expose the fossil stratum all along this wall, follow the stratum and chisel out the bones by hand. When Goodrich objected that that meant moving hundreds of tons of rock, Douglass simply snapped his fingers. It would take time, yes. And money.

Andrew Carnegie had the money, and Douglass had the time.

On the edge of the foothill ridges of the Uintahs, between the mountains and the Wonsits Valley, Earl Douglass spent the next fifteen years of his life in two things: pioneering in the field of paleontology, and building a home on the arid sand flats of the Green.

Douglass was not a Mormon. He had come into this country, the last land-rush area in the United States (it had been sliced off the Uintah Reservation and thrown open for settlement in 1906) on no command of the priesthood and with no obligation to build up Zion. But he was as enthusiastic a pioneer and as dedicated a spirit as any Saint in the sandrock country.

His schooling had been up and down, broken by long field trips, interrupted by various jobs: peddling the *Practical Home Physician,* accompanying the botanist C. G. Pringle on a collecting trip into Mexico, cataloguing specimens for the Missouri Botanical Gardens. He had taught school and dug fossils in Montana, had discovered the duckbill dinosaur, had found mammalian remains in the Fort Union deposits and established the age of a whole geological horizon. By the time he landed at the Carnegie Museum in Pittsburgh he was a distinguished field geologist and one of the first authorities in the world on Tertiary mammals. He had added several new genuses and many new species to the obscure chain of mammalian development.

But Pittsburgh was too civilized. He itched for the badlands and the out-country. In 1908 he went fossil-hunting in the White River country east of the Uintah Basin, and on a short exploratory trip into Utah near Vernal he heard stories of colossal bones scattered over the Green River sand. He saw some that sheepherders had collected. He ran across the diplodocus thighbone that he couldn't carry out.

Somewhere near here, he thought, is the place where all these bones came from. Somewhere not far off—maybe the ridge west of Split Mountain. It might be all weathered out, but there's a chance that there's a regular dinosaur quarry around here somewhere.

He took his speculations back to Pittsburgh with him, and his colleagues kidded him. But Andrew Carnegie, inspecting the new wing of the museum that was to become the great Hall of Vertebrate Paleontology, stood in the middle of that vast space and wondered what he would fill it with. Something big. It had to be big to catch people's attention. Something big as a barn.

Then, remembering the enthusiastic yarns of one of his field men, he turned on an attendant. "Where's that mon Douglass?" he said. "Send Douglass in here. I've got a job for him."

So here was Douglass, in the autumn of 1909, writing excitedly back to Pittsburgh, arranging for funds to excavate his find, looking over sites for a winter camp, writing long patient argumentative letters to his wife explaining why she couldn't come out and stay the winter with him. It was a barren spot, sage and sand and rock. Winters were bleak, and there would be no house, only a tent or sheepwagon. The baby was only a year and a half old; it would be dangerous to bring him out to a place six miles from the nearest mail delivery and twenty-two from the nearest source of supplies. It would be a cold and hard and lonely life. He himself didn't mind, but for her and the baby it was impossible.

But Pearl Douglass was as enthusiastic as he was, and a little more persistent. In September she came, and brought the baby with her.

Douglass, in a rented buggy, was waiting on the bank of the Green when her stage was ferried across, and he drove her out along the rocky, washed-out trail that he and his men had scraped in the side of the ridge along the river. He was full of plans, full of the future. As the buggy lurched northward toward the quarry he talked about the opportunities for nature study, planned to send for his microscope, wished he had a camera to record the endless and intimate details of the flora and fauna. He pointed out the location of springs, wished he could stay here longer, even make his home here. The flats below the springs could be irrigated, and the soil was fair. And what a place to live in!

At last, turning left into the next-to-last gully, he clucked the horses up the wash and pulled up on a level sagebrush flat a few acres in extent, where a sheepwagon slept by a squawbush and a horse grazed on the withered grass. "Here we are," he said.

Their first home in the gulch was a frame of two-by-fours covered with "factory" cloth. In that they cooked and ate. They slept in another tent and stored their supplies in a third. The three workmen slept in the sheepwagon.

It comes to us strangely, that first winter in the wilderness, like something out of an octogenarian's memories, exaggerated and not quite believable. Yet it was only thirty-three years ago. The frontier is that recent.

The winter was severe, thirty below at times, with bitter

winds, and more than a foot of ice sheeting the Green. Sometimes they were unable for weeks to get into Vernal for supplies; they put themselves on rations and went ahead. Pearl Douglass cooked for the crew, propping the baby on the table by the stove to keep him warm. Her husband and the three men spent eight hours a day at the quarry, blasting away the sheath of rock to lay bare the fossil stratum, but in the evenings he and his wife would sit close to the little red-hot iron box in the flicker of a kerosene lamp, reading aloud the works of Gilbert and Powell and Dutton and the other pioneer geologists.

Visitors were infrequent. The country was thinly populated. Weather and roads were bad. In those first months every stray caller was cause for an entry in Douglass' journals, though later he got sick enough of squiring curious visitors through the quarry at all hours of the day or night. For all their isolation, they were not lonely. Pearl Douglass still remembers those days as the happiest of her life. They didn't have time to be lonely. There was too much to be done. Douglass was in a constant blaze of excitement; his energy was amazing. Haunted by the short time he thought he could spend in the wilderness, he drove himself to rise at four or five in the morning to write in his record books and journals; then climbed the slippery gulch for an eight-hour shift at the diggings; then returned to organize his notes and plan the work for days to come. From the beginning, he realized that his situation was unique. Before him was what promised to be the biggest dinosaur graveyard on earth. Its excavation would be a colossal job, and he hadn't too much time. He wanted to get in under the surface and see. Yet oddly enough the dinosaurs were not the most interesting thing about the place to Douglass. As a fossil hunter he preferred mammal remains, on which he was a recognized authority. But beyond that preference he had interests and enthusiasms that kept his life at a constant racing tempo. He wanted to study every bird that inhabited the region, note what it ate, where it nested, where and when it migrated. He wanted to collect every plant in the gulch and classify his collections. He wanted to trace the geological history of the area completely and in detail. He wanted to get a camera and microscope and record the minutest details of the animal and plant life. And—the pioneer farm boy in him emerging—he wanted to irrigate, to compel growth and productivity from the Green River sand, to build a home in the wilderness.

All these things, to a greater or less degree, he did. He bought a Graflex and shot everything in sight, leaping out of bed on Sundays and holidays in the bleakest depth of winter to tramp through the gulch on exciting hunts. He must have been an absurd and somehow heroic figure. His journals show him going out, wrapped in woolen underwear, flannel shirt, vest, sweater, hunting coat and sheepskin, with a pair of carpenter's overalls pulled over his trousers, his feet swathed in wool socks, fleece-lined shoes, and overshoes, to tramp around through powdery snow in sub-zero weather snapping pictures of the tracks of mice and weasels and wildcats, or stalking a humped and freezing chickadee in a juniper. Pearl Douglass still has in her possession a filing cabinet five feet high and two feet across jammed with negatives and prints of indescribable variety. Tracks, exotic rock formations, trees, grasses, flowers (sometimes with insects in them), the progress of work at the quarry—everything the man saw was worth recording.

Later in the year he got his old microscope from Minnesota and with it studied the microflora and microfauna of the springs and river. Of all these studies he kept elaborate notes. Sometime, a long time from now, when he had finished the excavation and had completed in his own mind the skeletal outline of life on earth, he would write them up, write many things, among them a history of the earth based on his knowledge of geology, botany, paleontology, paleobotany. And if he never found time to write up what he found out, he would at least have satisfied the itch to know.

It is plain enough what Douglass was; he was a Heaven-hunter, of a different breed from the Mormon but just as surely seeking the absolute and the final. That itch to know was really his driving power. He collected—Heaven only knows what he didn't collect. Fungi, plants, petrified wood, fossil shells, fossil flowers, fossil mammals, fossil raindrops, fossil cacti, fossil dinosaurs, insects. The tents were crammed with his boxes.

And he kept journals. Besides the careful records of the work at the quarry and the expenditure of Carnegie funds, he observed every detail of his physical and mental life. Piled next to the filing case of photographs in his Salt Lake City home there used to be no less than seventy-five journals of all sizes and shapes, from formal daybooks to children's pads, pregnant with the scrawling accounts of excursions, discoveries, hopes, wants, observations. Haunted by Time, he scribbled in an increasingly illegible hand, sometimes mixed with shorthand. Those journals alone are half the work of a lifetime. The photographs are another half. But they were both incidentals, hobbies indulged in in addition to the solid work of digging out dinosaurs. There were other hobbies. In that same collection he left behind him is a thick folder of poetry. Not even his wife knows when he found time to write that. Add to that the children's stories, scientific articles, popularized science papers. Add to that the job of damming springs, irrigating, gardening, house-building, all the thousand and one tasks of pioneer farming. It is no wonder that Douglass' journals contain frequent complaints about the shortness of the days.

To many people, that first winter in the desert would have been unbearable. Douglass and his wife apparently never even noticed that they didn't have comforts. There was drama in their life. On the one hand they were breaking a desert as other pioneers had done, and they gloried in it. When, a year or two later, Douglass' vegetables won prizes at the county fair, they celebrated like children. On the other hand, Douglass was exploring a scientific frontier, making discoveries and adding to the knowledge of man, filling in tiny link after tiny link in the chain of the world's history. And that was exciting.

Layer by layer, chip by chip, the covering came off the dinosaur beds. The seven great vertebrae were approached from both ends, and at both ends the diggers found bone. Douglass was jumpy and nervous. So far, so good. But if digging didn't uncover more and more and still more, his hunch would be proved false and the quarry would be nothing but an expensive hole in the ground. The work was exasperatingly slow as they worked inward, but after weeks of careful chiseling a workman struck bones, larger ones. They took off their hats and cheered. Here was the pelvis, in its proper place. Then limbs, the immense hind legs. The hunch was working out. Back along the tail they chipped patiently, until the whole tail was exposed in relief, more than thirty feet of it. Back to the pelvis again, working forward toward the shoulders. The shoulders and front limbs were there.

Douglass, standing back to get a perspective on the skeleton exposed now for three-quarters of its length, was excited. Perhaps they would find the skull, and no one had ever unearthed a complete brontosaur skull. What a specimen this would be if the head were there! A complete brontosaur, even to the tiny finger bones, and almost a hundred feet long. Even without measuring he knew it was the largest complete dinosaur ever dug up.

Then disappointment. The diggers' tools found no bone after the shoulders. Head and neck were missing. The workmen, who had been digging with mounting enthusiasm for weeks, went back that night sour and let down, but Douglass stayed behind and with no particular purpose pecked away at the rock behind the shoulders. Bone again! For an hour he chipped carefully. Small bones, dozens of them, lay behind the shoulder in an intricate network. Until they were uncovered he couldn't tell, but maybe . . . the head and neck might be twisted back. . . .

In two weeks that hunch too proved correct, or partly so. Doubled back along the body was the neck, complete, but the skull was missing. Probably it had broken away and floated downstream. The loss was disappointing, but not too much so. Even without the head, this was the most complete skeleton in existence.

And imagine, if you please, the job of packing and crating and shipping those bones in their blocks of sandstone. Plaster of paris was needed. Bought through the drugstore in Vernal it would have cost a fortune. So Douglass took a coffee grinder, ground up a piece of gypsum previously burned in the cookstove, and tried the powder to see if it would set. It did. He hunted up a farmer who had a kiln, and contracted with him for wagon loads of crude plaster made from the gypsiferous shales. Then every block of bones had to be packed in plaster, crated in heavy planks, hauled out along eighteen miles of rocky, crooked, wretched road, ferried across the Green, and shipped east. The block containing the pelvis alone weighed six thousand pounds, with the other blocks in proportion. Four men with horses got that shipment out, but it almost sank the ferry.

After the excitement of the first skeleton, discoveries at the quarry were taken more equably. Douglass had been completely right in his hunches. The whole wall in which he had seen the seven vertebrae was criss-crossed and interlaid and packed with bones in a bewildering network. Great finds were so common that only a skull could excite them now. A skull always called for a thanksgiving dinner of turkey and cranberry sauce and three kinds of pie. Both in Mrs. Douglass' accounts and in her husband's journals there is a pathetic attention to the details of the menu that tells how fine these celebrations must have seemed, what a thrill of social life they added to the routine. Eventually they found the brontosaur skull they wanted, though it was not the one belonging to the great skeleton. And there were others, among them a diplodocus head complete even to the sclerotic coating of the eye—by all odds the most perfect dinosaur skull ever discovered. They took a whole day off for that one.

The first year passed, and Douglass found to his delight that he could stay another. He built a house of logs at the mouth of the middle gulch, and they moved into the opulence of solid floors, carpets, glass windows, a coal range. Hundreds of dollars painfully earned went into the damming of the rain gully. Here was the first snag. Gardens flourished in the seepage from the higher springs, but on the flats below the loose soil sucked up water as fast as it came down. By midsummer the expensive reservoir by the house was ankle-deep in dust. But Douglass persevered, filed a homestead claim and water claims on three springs. To protect the quarry from souvenir-hunters he tried to take it out as a mining property, but found that fossil bones were not classified among the minerals. Eventually, in 1915, with the help of the director of the museum, he succeeded in having it set aside as the Dinosaur National Monument.

By now he was something of a scholarly adviser to the community. Here was one kind of Gentile the Mormons not only tolerated but admired. People met regularly to hear him talk; he organized a discussion group to study science and nature lore. For the papers of Vernal and other towns he wrote dozens of articles, free. But the attempt to compel his homestead into productivity kept him drained of money; the house of squared stone that he was building on the bank of the river was another expense. Then, in 1924, the Carnegie Museum decided it had enough bones (it had received almost 600,000 pounds in the years Douglass had worked the quarry), and rather than leave the desert he loved, Douglass elected to sever his connection with the institution which had sent him there. The land had ties on him now. His sister and his father, brought out to live with him, were buried under the dune-like hills. His son had grown almost to manhood on this spot.

Douglass was not made for the world. As soon as he retired from the Carnegie staff, representatives of the University of Utah came asking him to dig them some bones.

After some discussion, Douglass agreed, apparently on the assumption that he would be retained to mount and describe the new specimens, one of which was a species of allosaurus new to science. He needed the money; a position at a university near his own home was just what suited his inclinations best.

One nearly complete allosaurus and parts of two other dinosaurs were excavated, packed and crated. They were hauled to Salt Lake City by wagon train in what a Salt Lake newspaperman called "the greatest funeral procession of all times." It was a picturesque procession. All along the route crowds turned out to watch the heavy wagons, driven by skinners in ten-gallon hats who cracked their bullwhips and scared the kids with their yelling. They pounded on the crates with the butts of the whips and roared at the quiescent dinosaurs until the kids hopped with curiosity.

"What's in the crates?" they asked.

The skinners looked fearsome and pounded some more. "DINOSAURS! Down, Bronto, down! Down, damn your eyes, before I knock your horns off!"

It was a spectacular caravan, and it made headlines. It attracted, in fact, national publicity, which means more in Utah than elsewhere. Pictures of the wagon train, of the president of the University of Utah, of the head skinner, of the university geologist, adorned papers and magazines. But Earl Douglass' picture did not appear, not once. His name was mentioned only once or twice, and then only as that of a kind of menial assistant, a pick-and-shovel man. The glory-grabbers had begun to function. It is written that many a desert prospector has had his nuggets stolen by pack rats.

For two years Douglass, who was retiring enough to desire the obscurity into which he was pushed, worked with two helpers in the university museum preparing the bones for mounting. When he had completed the difficult preliminary work, work which only a skilled paleontologist could do, he was quietly shouldered out, his extension classes "postponed," and his name blotted so completely from the university's memory that I could be told some years later, when I was writing publicity for the university and was after a story, that Douglass had had no connection with the school.

"See the head of the geology department," the president told me. "If there was any connection he would remember."

But I had already seen the head of the geology department. He had managed, with prodding, to remember Douglass, faintly.

So now Douglass, having let his taxes slide on his homestead, was in Salt Lake eking out a precarious living as a consulting geologist. All his holds on the gulch where he had spent fifteen of his best years were gone. The water rights on his springs reverted. On the banks of the Green his house of squared stone remained unfinished, and a quarter-mile away the log house that in 1910 had been such a palace stood deserted. Sand sifted around its door, and lizards sunned themselves on the sills. Windows and doors were long since gone, carried away by needy neighbors.

From one point of view, the fifteen years of labor that had gone into the homestead and the quarry were wasted years. Many of his discoveries he had seen written up by other men, because he himself was too busy to get at them immediately. There was not a good paleontological museum in the world that was not richer for his labors: Jensen, Utah, is almost a trademark of excellence for dinosaur bones. But all Douglass got out of it was wages, plus a five thousand dollar honorarium and a curt line from Andrew Carnegie: "Another Scotchman makes good!" In his hope for a responsible position at the University of Utah he had been betrayed for a reason that probably never entered his head. The professorship of geology at Utah is a chair, its incumbent subject to Church approval. That system kept certain sciences dangerous to fundamentalist belief under the thumb of the priesthood. Earl Douglass simply ran into one of the survivals of early Mormonism. He was too good a scientist, and he was too stiff competition for the Church's geologist.

Still, Douglass did not himself feel the failure of his life. He did not waste time thinking how abused he was, did not complain any more than Mormon settlers in an unfriendly location complained. He dove into whatever work he could find, and to relax after days of writing articles for everybody under the sun, from newspapers to mining reviews, he took his wife and son into the Wasatch Mountains east of the city and had a wonderful day collecting more fossils. He died on January 13, 1931, in comparative poverty.

It is one of the penalties of pioneering that the consummation of the work is almost always left to later and perhaps lesser men. That Douglass escaped the bitterness which might have come from seeing his scientific discoveries brighten the reputations of others was due to the enthusiasm for living and knowing that never left him. His life proves one thing: that it takes zeal, it takes dedication, it takes some drive or urge, to break any frontier, physical or intellectual. The Mormons had the Kingdom of God;

Douglass had the prospect of reconstructing the long and obscure history of life on the earth. That prospect kept him pecking at a sandstone cliff for fifteen years. Vision sustained both Mormon dirt-farmer and Gentile scientist, and to both of them the vision was in the end the best reward.

Artist in Residence . . .

YOUR old men shall dream dreams, your young men shall see visions.

From the time when the Negro Estevanico hurried on ahead of Fray Marcos in 1539, steaming through the Pima villages like a calliope ahead of the circus parade, hugging to himself his pose as conquistador and wearing in his black skin the sign of his slavery, the plateau country has been invaded by the dreamers. Estevan's dream was a dream of escape and freedom, although he had no intention, probably, of staying permanently ahead of the laboring priest. He took out his desire for emancipation in simple and direct ways: he liked women, and until he made passes at the Zuñi women he had his most sultry desire. The Zuñi, being part of the country, living as the country lives, being, as the country is, relatively contemptuous of dreams and hostile to them, resented Estevan's amorous and arrogant airs and killed him. But the Zuñi were themselves a vision; they were part of the Seven Cities of Cibola which drew Coronado in the next year up through the desolation to the north. They did not know it and they did not will it, but they and the country they inhabited had become part of the New World myth—and the New World myth has been a potent lure from the time of Leif Ericson and Madoc. The Seven Cities of Cibola, the

New Jerusalem, the fat land over the next range of hills, the gold one can scoop up in the hand, are one with the vision of Columbus and the golden lands of Mexico and Peru: marsh lights and will-o'-wisps, irresistible and cheating. The witch in medieval romance is a beautiful woman, but strip her and she is a wrinkled hag. She whispers enchanting promises, she sings like a Lorelei, but she is the bane of all good knights. Circe, the sirens, Morgain le Fay, la belle dame sans merci—she trades on strangeness and beauty and her kiss is death.

The story is as old and new as the world, and it takes strange forms. The valleys in the mountains brought the Latter-day Saints, according to one rather cynical view, from the Golden Plates to the Utah-Idaho Sugar Company, from revelation and prophecy and the hope of the Kingdom to the statue of Brigham Young in Temple Square, "with his fanny to the temple and his hand to the bank." The lure of brown women and the sweets of swaggering importance brought Estevan to his death, the Golden Cities of Cibola turned into mud huts before the disappointed eyes of Coronado's men, the gold rush emigrants left their bones scattered from the Missouri to the coast, or died disappointed on the Golden Shore. And in Park City, Utah, in 1893, two old timers exploring an abandoned tunnel came across a skeleton with its heavy boots still on its feet, and by it a sheet of paper: "Dear God, I am dying. I have found wealth at the cost of my life. The samples in the bucket are from a ledge on . . . my hand trembles, my eyes grow dim . . . I am . . ." Maybe that note was planted, but phony or not, it comes close to expressing the whole American Dream.

Put it any way you like, the contented ones are the ones whose visions are so unattainable in this life that disappointment and failure are temporary or unimportant. The average Mormon, still with his eye on Heaven, is not perturbed by the number of directorships that the President of his Church holds in industrial enterprises. Earl Douglass, pecking away at his cliff, lived on the excitement of his dream of knowledge, as attractive in its way as millennium. There are also the spiritual and artistic athletes who die young. Everett Ruess was one of those, a callow romantic, an adolescent esthete, an atavistic wanderer of the wastelands, but one of the few who died—if he died— with the dream intact.

What Everett Ruess was after was beauty, and he conceived beauty in pretty romantic terms. We might be inclined to laugh at the extravagance of his beauty-worship if there were not something almost magnificent in his single-minded dedication to it. Esthetics as a parlor affectation is ludicrous and sometimes a little obscene; as a way of life it sometimes attains dignity. If we laugh at Everett Ruess we shall have to laugh at John Muir, because there was little difference between them except age.

Call him adventurous boy. At eighteen, in a dream, he saw himself plodding through jungles, chinning up the ledges of cliffs, wandering through the romantic waste places of the world. No man with any of the juices of boyhood in him has forgotten those dreams. The peculiar thing about Everett Ruess was that he went out and did the things he dreamed about, not simply for a two-weeks' vacation in the civilized and trimmed wonderlands, but for months and years in the very midst of wonder.

He had no business in the Navajo country or the rock deserts of Utah and Arizona except to see, to write, and to paint. He was not a good writer and he was only a mediocre painter, but give him credit, he knew it, and he was learning. It didn't matter greatly that he was not in command of his tools. He was only eighteen when he started traveling by horse and burro and on foot through the canyons and plateaus. He was only twenty when he finished, but in three years from 1931 to 1934 he came to know intimately a wide stretch of country that few people ever see. He lived among cowboys and Indians, danced the Antelope Dance with the Hopi, learned Navajo, made friends with traders over a thousand miles of trails, sang and rode and fooled around with the Mormon kids in the little isolated towns. When he needed money he took a job or sold a few water colors. He stopped where he pleased, left undone no "strange or delightful thing" that he wanted to do.

Deliberately he punished his body, strained his endurance, tested his capacity for strenuousness. He took out deliberately over trails that Indians and old timers warned him against. He tackled cliffs that more than once left him dangling halfway between talus and rim. With his burros he disappeared into the wild canyons and emerged weeks later, hundreds of miles away, with a new pack of sketches and paintings and a new section in his journal and a new batch of poems. From his camps by the water pockets or the canyons or high on the timbered ridges of Navajo Mountain he wrote long, lush, enthusiastic letters to his family and friends, damning the stereotypes of civilization, chanting his barbaric adolescent yawp into the teeth of the world. He stood on windy rims and shouted poems to himself, he climbed to almost inaccessible cliff dwellings and poked reverently among the undisturbed remains of centuries. Once he worked for several weeks helping an archaeological expedition excavate in a high cave, and scared the archaeologist half to death with his habit of leaning casually over a thousand-foot cliff, or running like an ape up the sheer worn handholds of the ancients.

On November 11, 1934, young Ruess left Escalante, Utah, with two burros and a good stock of supplies, to go out in search of painting and writing subjects among the unexplored cliff dwellings of the Escalante Desert. He had made a long loop from Kayenta to Gallup to Grand Canyon to Zion to Bryce. The trip from Escalante was to be the last and wildest leg. It would bring him out, he told people rather vaguely, probably at Wilson's Mesa, near Navajo Mountain. He might go on down toward Marble Canyon, or he might come back through Boulder. He expected to be out of touch with civilization for two months.

Eight days later a sheep man, Clayton Porter, saw him near the confluence of the Escalante and the Colorado, almost the wildest and most desolate section of North America. After that no one ever saw him again.

At first no one thought anything of his absence. His parents, knowing his irritation at being worried about, waited dutifully for two months before they made inquiries. They wrote to the post-mistress at Escalante, to park rangers, to sheriffs, to traders. All answered that there was probably no cause for alarm. Everett was trail-wise, experienced, well equipped, knew the country. He had planned to be gone a long time, and had said so to the Mormon family with which he had stayed in Tropic, and to people in Escalante as well. During his short stops in those two towns, riding the range with the Mormon boys, filling up on apples at an orchard picnic, going to the Ward House, having fun at a "sing" with a band of traveling Navajo, he had managed to convince everybody of his complete ability to look after himself. He was not officially reported

missing until February 14, 1935, more than three months
after he started into the desert.

At the end of February Captain Neal Johnson, a placer
miner from Hanksville, passed by Ruess' Los Angeles
home and offered to take three Navajo out on a search
party. Nothing came of that hunt. In early March a crowd
of Escalante Mormons under H. J. Allen went out again,
concentrating on the country around the mouth of the
Escalante River, where Everett had last been seen. After
three days of searching they found his burros, their halters
gone and their packs missing, corraled in a little natural
park in the bottom of Davis Canyon. The burros had been
there a long time, for they had eaten all the herbage in
their corral down to the dust, and were half starved. There
was no sign of young Ruess. Still, there were optimistic
reports from Captain Johnson, who quoted the Navajo to
the effect that the boy could not simply disappear. Tracks,
especially tracks in the canyons where the overhanging
cliffs protected them, would last for years in that arid
country. A good Navajo trailer could follow a track sometimes two years old. And there was no trail out of Davis
Canyon, only the track of Everett's number nine boots up
under a cave, and the forlorn burros in the bottom.

By that time southern Utah was aroused. People could
not disappear and leave no trace in their country. For all
its wildness, it had become since the disappearance of the
Wild Bunch a law-abiding region, and the Indians were
not only peaceable but were many of them personal
friends of young Ruess. Fifteen civic clubs (notice the in-
trusion of secular institutions into the Mormon village!)
from different towns organized a party under the command of Captain P. M. Shurtz. For ten days they combed
the country both north and south of the Colorado, bring-

ing in expert trackers, some of them Navajo. But not a trace, not a sign, except one: In a cave near Davis Canyon they found what they thought to be Everett's last campfire, and on the smooth walls the scrawled legend, "Nemo, 1934." A mile away they found the same inscription on the doorstep of a Moqui house.

No one in the party knew what Nemo meant. Was it an Indian word? The Navajo didn't recognize it. Did it have some cryptic significance? Was it a message of some kind? They put through a long distance telephone call to Los Angeles to see what Everett's parents thought about it. The explanation that it meant "no one" was both useless and tantalizing. Trust a boy with his head full of poetry and his eye full of cyclopean scenery to carve that word on the sandstone. But did he carve it just because the cave he was in reminded him of the Cyclops episode in the Odyssey, or had he been reading *Twenty Thousand Leagues under the Sea* until he fancied himself the same sort of lone-wolf pioneer as Captain Nemo, or was this scrawl a cryptic notice to the world that he intended to disappear, to cast off his identity? The fourth possibility, that the inscription meant that Everett was going to head for No Man's Mesa, near Navajo Mountain, nobody apparently thought of, but presumably that would have helped not at all, because No Man's Mesa was across the Colorado, and all the Navajo insisted that if the white boy had come across the river the Indians would know of it. The search party scratched their heads and tried again to find a trail out of the canyon. Nothing. They hunted for Everett's body along the bases of all the cliffs for miles, down in the depths of the canyons. Nothing. The cliff wall behind them as they gathered to go back still said enigmatically, "Nemo."

By now the search was handicapped by the spread of rumors. Captain Johnson, in spite of the Navajo, insisted that Everett must have crossed the river and must now be living somewhere in that vast, almost roadless wilderness. There was a report that Everett was living in disguise in Blanding, but an investigation proved the report false. A skeleton was found in the New Mexico desert, but a dental examination demonstrated that it was not Ruess.

In August, nine months after the boy disappeared, Captain Johnson was still so certain that he could be found somewhere in the Navajo reservation that the Salt Lake *Tribune* sent down its star reporter, John U. Terrel, to accompany Johnson on an eleven-day tour of the Indian country. They followed Everett's summer route from Kayenta to Navajo Mountain, stopping on the way to visit a medicine man and his wife. The medicine man held a sing, the wife ran sand through her hands, built a cone of it, drew quick wriggly lines. The cone was Navajo Mountain, the lines the Colorado and San Juan Rivers. "Go to the fork of the rivers," said Natani, the medicine man.

The white men pressed him. Was Ruess there?

He had been there. They would find a camp, a dead fire.

Had Natani seen him?

The boy, said Natani, had gone away from there.

Was he dead?

He had gone away and did not intend to come back.

Sometimes the metaphor of an Indian is ambiguous. Were the searchers to interpret Natani's words to mean that Ruess was dead, or was there the possibility of deliberate disappearance? Natani would say no more. They were back facing the enigmatic scratches on the wall. Nemo.

But Johnson and Terrel went on anyway, because every trader said that no one who knew the Navajo would neglect a medicine man's words. Medicine was silly, sure, but if you stayed around you saw some funny things that medicine did. At Navajo Mountain the two picked up a half-Ute, half-Navajo guide named Dougeye who had seen Everett in Escalante a little while before his disappearance, and who was called the best tracker in the country. Dougeye agreed to go along, but only on condition that the camera was left behind. He wanted no part of the winking-eye box. At that he was more intrepid than most of the Indians gathered at the post. When the word got around that Johnson and Terrel were searching for a man who might be dead, a good many of them quietly disappeared. They would not help search for a dead man. What if they should find him?

Dougeye led them over the twenty-five miles of spectacular country between the mountain and the river, swam them across the San Juan and searched the peninsula. There was no sign of a camp or a dead fire. Natani's words, then, must have applied to the camp further north, in Davis Canyon where the trail had petered out. Dougeye went over the ground carefully. Everett could not have built a raft and floated down the river. There were only a few places where a raft could have been built, and Ruess had been to none of them. Besides, the river at Lee's Ferry was watched closely. He would have been seen. Even an empty raft and floating packs would have been seen.

That narrowed the possibilities still more. There were many places north of the river where a man might die, but few where a man might camp. Dougeye counted them on his fingers. Navajo horse hunters had been to all of them within the past few months, and all the Navajo knew about the white-boy-who-was-lost. If he had been at any of those camps his sign would not have escaped them.

So the three swam the Colorado and went on up to Davis Canyon. They found no more than the previous parties had, though Dougeye spent two days circling like a baffled hound. His verdict was succinct. "White boy went in, not come out."

Did that mean that he had been killed and buried somewhere?

"No grave," Dougeye said. "Could find."

So he was dead, but there was no body. Or he had disappeared, and there was no trail, though he couldn't have disappeared without leaving one. And getting out of the gulch without his burros would have been a virtual impossibility anyway. He might have trailed down the north side of the Colorado to Lee's Ferry (but the Navajo said he hadn't, and to Lee's Ferry it was a hundred terrible miles). He could have crossed the Colorado and gone over into the country through which Terrel and Johnson had just come. (But the Navajo would have known it if he had, and no Navajo could keep a secret.) He could have gone back to Escalante (but that again was a hundred mile trip with few waterholes, and besides he would have been recognized by the villagers). Or he could have got supplies from wandering sheep or cattle men and dug deeper into the canyons. (But all the sheep and cattle men in the country knew of his disappearance, and most of them had been enlisted in the search.)

There was only one conclusion for Terrel to come to, and even that had its unknowns. Everett Ruess was murdered, presumably for his valuable pack outfit and supplies, and his body hidden somewhere in or near Davis Canyon.

Only who murdered him? The fact that none of his personal articles or bits of his pack had turned up among the Indians meant almost certainly that Indians were not the murderers. A tracker as good as Dougeye, and a large and expert search party, had found no tracks of anyone but Everett around the Davis Canyon camps. The problem of the disposal of the body was—and is—still unsolved. It is just about as difficult to see how Everett Ruess could have been murdered as it is to see how he could have got out of the Escalante Desert.

And there is always the word Nemo on the cliff face and on the doorstep of the Moqui house, and the letter which Everett wrote to his brother just before he disappeared: "As to when I shall return to civilization, it will not be soon, I think. I have not tired of the wilderness. . . ."

So there we leave it. Many people in that country believe Everett Ruess to be still alive. A woman who had met him once ran into a boy she was sure was Everett, hitchhiking in Mexico. The Mormon boys with whom he hunted horses and went to the Ward House in Tropic and Escalante have a sneaking suspicion that he lives, wandering in a gorgeous errant way around the world, painting and writing poetry. Except for the painting and the poems, they can conceive that life, because it is close to their own adventurous dreams. Because they will never themselves go, they would much rather not have Everett Ruess dead. It is a nice thing to think about, that maybe tonight he is sitting under the shadow of some cliff watching the light race upward on the mountain slope facing him, trying to get it into water colors before the light leaves him entirely.

It is just possible that the loss of identity is the price of immortality.

Because Everett Ruess is immortal, as all romantic and adventurous dreams are immortal. He is, and will be for a long time, Artist in Residence in the San Juan country.

The Home of Truth . . .

The big bugs have little bugs
On their backs to bite 'em,
And the little bugs have smaller bugs
And so on, ad infinitum.

O N Highway 160, about forty miles south of the Colorado River town of Moab and fifteen miles short of
Monticello, a trail turns off to the right through the rusty
sand. At the corner is a plain weathered board bearing the
words "Home of Truth."

A trail like that, and a sign like that, stop you short.
Because this is San Juan, the largest county in Utah, a
great triangular wedge of abysmally eroded and weathered
sandstone bounded on the east by the Colorado line, on
the south by the Arizona line, and all along its hypotenuse
by the Colorado River. Its southern end is Navajo reservation; its southeastern corner is the meeting place of four
states. Here, in an area just smaller than the state of Massachusetts, live about three thousand people, a quarter
of them Navajo. Of the thirteen white settlements, only
Blanding and Monticello deserve the name of town, and
one, Bluff, is one hundred thirty-five miles from the
nearest available railroad. Within the county are spaces
as large as Rhode Island which the maps leave com-

pletely blank; they have never been surveyed and can scarcely be said to have been explored. In all this region there is exactly forty miles of paved road, all on one stretch between Moab and Monticello, and about fifty-five miles more of surfaced highway. Otherwise the county is road-less except for trails—and at least six of those are dead-ends. Some can be navigated, painfully, by car. Others would break down anything but a burro.

For just that reason, any side road in San Juan is inter-esting: the moment you break off that one surfaced high-way that leads down across the corner of Utah to Mesa Verde and Santa Fe, anything can happen. And here is a trail labeled "Home of Truth." What is Truth, and where? Well, here, in the middle of the most primitive and un-known country in the United States, is its home. You turn in.

A mile or so of driving across the sparsely-grassed plain, typical desert grazing country, brings you to a group of buildings. They are of board-and-batt construction, stained light brown, and are newer and in better repair than average desert ranch buildings. One, up on a little rise, is quite large; it looks like a dormitory or boarding house, with a quilt hanging out one open window.

A decent housewifely little woman opens the door of the nearest building and looks out inquiringly. You ask if this is the Home of Truth. No, she says, this is only the Outer-most Point. Only the Community House and the Men's Dormitory are here. Most of the buildings are in the middle cluster, a mile on, called the Middle Portal; and the real Home of Truth, the Inner Portal, is on another mile.

Truth, apparently, is hard to come at. You are reminded of the symbolic labyrinth that Father Rapp constructed around his temple in Harmony. What's at the Outer Portal, you ask. You are told that that is where Marie lives.

The sun is intense and dazzling in the bare yard. There are no gardens, no trees, no shrubs. A discouraged little clump of petunias wilts in the shaded court on the north side. May you come in, you ask? She holds the door wide. Her name is Daisy Naden; she has a rather sweet and peering face, the skin worn sallow, the eyes bright blue.

"You don't know about us?" she says. "You don't know about the Kingdom That Is Being Built?"

You know nothing except that you saw a sign, "Home of Truth," and came seeking.

"Well," she says, "you set right down, if you'd like me to tell you about it." You set, and are told.

You are, it appears, on the very axis of the earth—or would be if you went two miles on to the Inner Portal where Marie lives. It is a good place to be, because in the great and terrible last days, which are coming upon us now according to prophecy and revelation, only those on the axis will not be shaken down. Marie, you discover, is Mrs. Marie Ogden, the founder of the colony. She controls and directs the community with the aid of messages from the spirit world and from Jesus Christ. The messages come to her upon a hill near her house, and she takes them down on her typewriter.

You ask how many colonists there are, and a film clouds the bright eyes of Daisy Naden. Not everyone is fitted for the great work. Many have come and gone, because the sacrifices demanded are great, and too many put materialistic and selfish desires above the sanctification of their lives and persons. This sanctification consists in giving up all worldly ambition and worldly goods, abstaining from liquor and tobacco (you slip back into your pocket the pack of cigarettes you have been tentatively fingering), and laboring for the common good.

Laboring how? How does the colony support itself?

They used to raise chickens, Daisy says, but they have stopped eating any flesh but fish. They have stopped planting gardens too.

But how does the group get food then?

The Lord, says Daisy Naden, provides.

When you look skeptical she smiles at you. Her voice, the voice of a farm wife starved for talk, goes on. You don't believe, she says, but I can show you. This spring, for example, we were almost out of food. Everything that people had brought in was gone. But the Christ-teaching tells us that if we are worthy we shall be supplied, and we were. Just when we didn't know where the next meal was coming from, some men from down the valley came over wanting the men to help them in their fields, and their wages provided for us all.

Although this seems a strange method of divine provision which prohibits the growing of gardens but allows day labor for wages, you refrain from comment, because Daisy Naden's triumph over your unbelief is too plain. You hear her voice over the drone of the flies in the big bare clean kitchen, talking of the Spiritual Plane, and about two lamas that she converses with on that level, and how not long ago they stopped off to visit and instruct the Queen of Siam, who at first scorned them and later repented and sent for them to return. One of them was still there with the Queen. Daisy had talked with him day before yesterday.

Out the window the plain lies bare and hot, with ledges of red sandstone cropping out above the shallow soil. The heat, the baked, discharged look of the bare earth, the scrubbed neatness of the kitchen, the decent worn look of the guardian of the Outermost Point, are very real, but what she is saying is not real. You blink your eyes and shake your head, but her voice still goes on talking about astral forms and the Aquarian Gospel. In a pause, you rise, wondering if you could see the establishment.

You are shown two unfinished bedrooms sheathed inside with tarpaper, a dining room, a club room with a round-bellied stove and a little case of books. In the shelf, bold and red among the volumes on Horoscope Analysis and The Age of Faith and The Promise of Life, is Earl Browder's *What Is Communism?*

Oh, that, Daisy Naden says, when you hold it up questioningly. A young man and his sister came to us from Maine, very good worthy young people. He had several of Mr. Browder's books along. I read them, and I was surprised. I always thought of Communism as, you know, dangerous, but you read in there where it says Communism seeks the same thing we seek, the brotherhood of men and the destruction of selfishness and greed.

Were the young man and his sister still there?

No, said Daisy Naden, they had gone back for their property. They had left their books behind, and would be returning soon.

You have taken a good deal of Daisy Naden's time, and you put Earl Browder down beside Stoddard's *Lectures* and prepare to depart. Before you go she steps down into the cellar hole and brings up a pitcher of cool water, and you have a drink together. You like her, but she is still not real, and as you drive on though the Middle Portal and out to the Inner Portal you wonder how, and why, a Communist organizer should light in this desert. You wonder if perhaps this whole three miles of road is a mirage, or the result of the icy beer you had in Moab.

At the Inner Portal there is nothing to detain you but the view, a good one out across the broken plains to the Abajo Mountains—the view and the realization that you now stand on the one spot where you would be safe if the last days should come suddenly. It is very quiet; you can smell the scorched ground. In a hurry you get back in the car and drive out again, past Daisy Naden's lonely Community House, to the sanity of Federal-Aid Highway.

In Monticello you stop for a cold drink, and from the Mormon kid in the café you begin to pick up information on the Home of Truth. It is a mad enough story, but somehow natural. The Home of Truth is close enough to the Mormon experience, its theology and its record is so recognizably a descendant of the religious upheavals that produced Joseph Smith, that the theosophist colony in the middle of the Mormon desert is appropriate, is right.

The wilderness has always had a double attraction to the founders of religious cults: it is closer to God, and farther from man. The history of cults in America is full of instances of sites divinely appointed for the establishment of the Kingdom. The Great Basin was Heaven-dictated sanctuary for the Mormons; the axis of the earth in Dry Valley, San Juan County, was pointed out to Mrs. Marie Ogden by divine manipulation of her typewriter.

She came in 1933, with a little band of followers recruited mainly from around Boise, Idaho, where she had been lecturing on occult subjects, but the origins of Marie's occultism go further back than Boise, go back to 1929, when her husband died and she began devoting herself to spiritual studies. For a time she was associated with other seeking groups in Newark, N. J., and at one time had a kind of alliance with none other than William Dudley Pelley, then just formulating the ideas that were to lead to the Silver Shirts. Pelley was more spiritual and less political in those days, but he was already developing dangerous symptoms, and Marie removed her School of Truth from the contamination of his touch. She established reading societies, study groups, spiritual soul-fights. She toured the country lecturing. The messages which came to her typewriter told her eventually to seek out the spot where the Kingdom should be built, and she arrived with all her impedimenta in Dry Valley, leading a colony pledged to complete renunciation of personal goods, to semi-vegetarianism and soul-searching, to obedience and diligence and acceptance of the Word scattered broadcast, many times a day, from Marie's prolific machine.

The Mormons among whom she settled took her calmly enough. There was, after all, a Mexican Holy Roller colony a few miles from Monticello, and the Mormon background was similar. The communism of the group didn't scare them; they, or their fathers, had lived United Order for years. Direct revelation, and Marie's astonishing intimacy with Jesus Christ, didn't startle them either. They were of a people whose every act had been guided direct from the throne of Heaven. The only possible innovation was the typewriter: Joseph, and all the major and minor prophets after him, had used a secretary. (Morris, the heretical schismatic whose party had been broken up in a little civil war below Weber Canyon in 1862, had kept three secretaries busy, in two or three languages.) There was nothing in the Home of Truth that was strange or remarkable to the Mormon settlers of Moab and Monticello. Obedience, communistic living, direct revelation, personal abstemiousness and intense religious conviction, flight from the world and sanctuary in the desert, were an old story.

Still, they were curious. They stood around speculating on the mysterious Mr. Jackson of Denver, who appeared shortly, announced himself a millionaire, and started negotiations for large undertakings in the name of the Home of Truth. He tried to buy out a big stock-raising company, he dickered for leases on gold-bearing creeks. Eventually he disappeared, unexplained, and life went on much the same as before except that by this time Mrs. Ogden had bought the *San Juan Record,* the only newspaper in the county, and established herself as the Press. She negotiated leases and sub-leases and set her community to work, but there was little profit in the slim gold deposits on Doosit Creek. The Mormons, knowing there never had been anything in that wildcat prospect, stood around and watched what the community would do next, and listened to Mrs. Ogden's exhortations to the business men of the county to bring in more settlers and more business by co-operative effort. If they cynically observed the discrepancy between these commercial worries and the avowed anti-commercial spirit of the colony, they did not rub it in. They were settled, and they were tolerant, and a little break in the monotony was a pleasure.

They watched the colony move out of its tents and into houses, they watched the laying out of the foundations of a chapel calculated to seat a thousand persons, they read Marie's messages in the *San Juan Record.* They might have gone on just watching and being edified if Marie had not stepped over the bounds of their own background and their own credulity, and attempted to deny death.

Among Marie's colonists was a woman, Mrs. Edith Peshak, afflicted with cancer. She had joined the cult in hope of a miraculous cure; her husband had sold his property, turned the proceeds over to Marie, and come along. Marie worked hard on her spiritual therapeutics, but on February 11, 1935, Edith Peshak died. This alone would never have caused talk. Mormonism from its beginning has been suspicious of the medical profession, and the annals of the church until very recent years are full of cures effected by the laying on of hands and other miraculous means. The annals are also full of cases where the patient did not respond, generally because his faith was too weak. It was all easily explained, but Marie Ogden did not undertake to explain. She undertook to test her beliefs with the ultimate test. She asserted that Edith Peshak was not dead, but in an interregnum state, being purified, and that she would return to life. At that point she broke with the conventions of her neighbors by enunciating a "peculiar" doctrine, just as the Mormons had broken with established convention in the establishment of various peculiar institutions, notably polygamy. And like the Mormons, Marie got into trouble.

Actually there was no great difference in doctrine involved. The strict Mormon believes in death only as a transition; in the last days the dead are raised up, not symbolically or in the spirit, but in the flesh, and live everlastingly in the flesh in a state consonant with their careers on earth. It would be no great step to affirm reincarnation on this earth, as a good many cults have done. But the Mormon is normally as materialistic as his belief in material resurrection, and to deny that a corpse is dead, when clearly the last days are not at hand, offends his sense of values. It also scares him a little to hear about astral planes and spiritual forms and Love-Energy and the denial of the importance of the flesh. So when Marie started raising the dead and giving herself the Lazarus-test, the Mormons of San Juan began to talk.

Rumor leaked all over the county. Cult members said they detected signs of life; Mrs. Ogden was constantly distributing messages from the "dead" woman; the body remained miraculously free of disintegration and corruption, and Marie's sixth sense detected "vibrations" in it. Three times a day Mary Cameron, her chief helper, washed the corpse in a salt solution and introduced food into it.

The more rumor leaked, the wilder the stories circulating around the country became. There were tales of weird dawn rites, obscene ceremonies. People began to cross the streets of Monticello when a Home of Truth member approached. Still, San Juan is not a country where things happen fast. It was June, four months after Edith Peshak's death, before Sheriff Palmer got around to investigating. He was refused admittance. When he ordered a forcible investigation on sanitary grounds, the newspapers broke the story in Salt Lake and Frank Peshak, the dead woman's son, read of it. He came down from Boise and accompanied the county nurse and the traveling FERA nurse when they demanded and got admittance to view the body.

It could hardly have been a pleasant moment for young Frank Peshak. He saw his mother's body, blue-black, mummified, shrunken, and shouted hysterically that he would take it and bury it immediately. For some reason he did not, perhaps because his father was still a cult member, still clinging to the hope that his wife would be restored, and perhaps because the nurses' report had to say in truth that the mummy was not a menace to health. The body remained in Marie Ogden's possession, and the rumors ballooned.

There was little but rumor, actually, for two years. The

Home of Truth shut down on visitors; a good many of the original thirty colonists had apostatized and vanished; only a dozen or so grimly held the fort. Some people said that the body had been secretly buried, some that it had been removed to a secret place and that the obscene rites went on. Then in February, 1937, Mrs. Ogden was indiscreet again. She announced publicly that Mrs. Peshak (on the spiritual plane Jessica-Edith) would soon return to life. The vibrations were stronger, the messages thicker, the conversations in soul language more frequent.

With this reminder of the unchastened defiance of state regulations, the authorities revived the case. By April they had got around to writing and demanding that a death certificate be signed for the Bureau of Vital Statistics. Mrs. Ogden declined, on the grounds that Edith Peshak was not dead. The state insisted. Mrs. Ogden defied it. The Salt Lake papers had another field day, interviewed Mrs. Ogden, corralled all the apostate Home of Truth people they could locate. Just at the moment when Mrs. Ogden was forced to yield to the persecution of the state officers, an enterprising *Telegram* reporter dug up one Tommy Robertson. No trace had been found by the officers of the body of Edith Peshak. Tommy Robertson could explain that. He put the final macabre touch on the story, in a sworn affidavit for the Salt Lake *Telegram.*

He testified that in August, 1935, two months after the original investigation, he had received orders from Marie to wrap the mummy in two sheets and a thin mattress, bring a gallon of oil, and follow her. He put the wrapped mummy on his back, got the oil, followed her to a dry wash about a quarter mile southwest of the Peshak cabin. There he built a pyre of cedar, piñon and juniper four feet high, seven feet long, and four feet wide, laid Jessica-Edith on it, covered her with the mattress, soaked the whole thing with oil, and set it afire. Mrs. Ogden stood on a high place and watched until everything was consumed, and then revealed a message to the effect that Tommy should gather up all bits of bone and bury them in the exact spot where she had stood to watch the cremation.

Tommy did as she told him to—but he had been before her in one detail. He told the *Telegram* that he was interested in the mummy. It was a curiosity, sort of. He had sniffed carefully while it burned, to see if there was any stink, but there was no odor at all—only the sweet smell of burning juniper.

And one other thing, Tommy said. He had wanted a souvenir of some kind, just to remind him of Edith. So before he followed Marie down to the wash he took his jack knife and dug out a couple of vertebrae, just for keepsakes, sort of.

"My God!" the reporter said. "Have you got them now?"

Tommy Robertson shook his head. His voice was regretful. "A damn sheep dog snitched them from me," he said.

That was the end of Mrs. Ogden's experiments in resurrection. It was also, to a great extent, the end of her colony. After the debacle there were only seven members left. There are about that many now, tolerated by the community, eking out a bare living from day labor and the paper. Contributions are scarce now, few colonists come in. Even the nice young man and his sister from Maine have probably not returned. The Kingdom That Is Being Built is a lonely place. The foundations of the grandiose chapel stand just where they stood seven or eight years ago, no higher.

The dynamism that produced Mormonism produced

the Home of Truth, but into Mormonism went something that the Home of Truth lacks. With the same kind of divine guidance, the same basic institutions, the Home of Truth must be called a manifestation of the lunatic fringe. Mormonism, because it has maintained itself, must be reckoned with. Unorthodox as much of its theological and social experimentation has been, it never lost its hold on the things of this earth. In the midst of the most incredible theological labyrinths, it has always been at bottom, among the people, a practical religion, dedicated to the affairs of the world as a preparation for the material resurrection into the millennium. It has been a creed that, for better or for worse, men have stuck to through far worse debacles than the episode of Jessica-Edith, and through far worse poverty than the Home of Truth experiences now. The Mormons of San Juan will be there a long time from now. The Home of Truth, I have no doubt, will not.

The Last of the Sticks . . .

O F all the regions of the United States the Mormon Country is the least known outside. Even the football writers have a blind spot when they look over the muscle map of the country. Ivy League, Southeast, Big Ten, Big Six or Missouri Valley, Southwest, Pacific Coast —those are all conferences with national broadcasts and intersectional Roman holidays. But who ever heard of the Rocky Mountain Conference, except on the infrequent occasions when it produces a Dutch Clark or a Whizzer White, so good that he can't be overlooked?

And football obscurity, though it may sound a little silly, is symptomatic. Tell an easterner that you come from Arizona, and he has a label for you. He or friends of his have spent a marvelous month on a dude ranch or have flown out to Phoenix for a midwinter sunburn. A native of Arizona has stature outside, wears a kind of halo. Probably in his youth he rode the desert ranges with a rattlesnake-skin hatband and Navajo conchs in his belt. Arizona, in other words, has color.

The same goes for New Mexico. Ah, Santa Fe, Taos, Acoma, Coronado and the Seven Cities! Ah, D. H. Lawrence and Mabel Dodge Luhan! Ah, Death Comes for the Archbishop! Billy the Kid and the ornate ricos, and Spanish vaqueros riding the streets of Santa Fe singing songs fit to break your heart.

But tell the same easterner that you come from that part of the world which is most centrally and typically Mormon Country. Tell him you come from the Great Basin, from Utah or Idaho or Nevada, and he feels a little sorry for you. Except for the bell-like note of polygamy, which raises the echoes—and the questions—in everybody, Utah is a blank. Nevada conjures pictures of dusty ghost towns and endless sagebrush deserts, and is likely to be confused, without apology, with Nebraska. Idaho is the home of Sun Valley and Senator Borah, no more, and is sometimes subject to confusion with Iowa, again without apology.

The Mormon Country has never caught the national imagination, has never acquired glamor. Its tourist business, though in recent years it has been a large and increasing business, has not been of the kind calculated to put the country on the map, because most of the tourists run a perfectly regular loop through the southern Utah parks and the Grand Canyon and go on again. No one is likely to announce that he is going out to southern Utah or southeastern Nevada for the winter, though the climate of that part of the Mormon Country should, other things being equal, have made St. George a winter capital, and the scenery along that sheer edge of the High Plateaus can hardly be matched anywhere.

Given the American tendency to hunt out the warm spots for winter vacations, there is something odd about the ignorance people display about Utah's Dixie. With magnificent country all around it, with a climate that grows figs, grapes, peaches, apricots, walnuts, almonds, cotton, Dixie sleeps peacefully all winter with hardly a Gentile intruder except the transients going up or down on

Highway 91. Except for Charlie Plumb, the Ella Cinders cartoonist, who has a picturesque ranch on Cave Lakes up from Kanab, I know of no outsiders who have come in to make summer or winter homes. The reason is simply that there is no place for them to come. Mormon farmers long ago owned all the suitable land and home sites, as well as all the water, and Mormon farmers are of a breed that does not sell out. With a limited arable acreage and a tradition of large families, the Mormon Country has been exporting manpower for a generation. Brigham's dream of settling up the empire so solidly that a Gentile couldn't get in with a shoehorn has come completely to pass, and though there are plenty of roadside cottage camps and overnight accommodations, there are none of the inns, hotels, and dude ranches on which other parts of the Southwest live half the year. The Mormon is grateful enough for the money that comes in from tourists, just as he is grateful for the river that runs past his land, but he makes the same use of the tourists that he makes of the river. He does not want to live in the river, or have it rise and come over his doorstep, but he will fish in it or let it water his fields.

The result of that attitude is that the thousands of travelers who before the war visited Utah almost invariably went through it on their way to somewhere else. They flowed down a highway strategically designed to link the great scenic attractions and at the same time be on the road to the coast or to the Southwest or to Yellowstone. For all the Chambers of Commerce which toot the scenic wonders of the red rock plateaus and the mountain lakes, the Mormon Country remains comparatively untouched by the tourist traffic; the society which is actually more interesting than the country in which it was planted keeps to

itself, aloof and as self-sufficient as Brigham could ever
have hoped it to be. It is not bothered that it is the last
of the sticks, the outlands. It does not worry because its
institutions and its occupations are not fascinating to city
people and easterners.

The Mormons are not, as Mormons, a colorful people.
For all its persecutions and its struggles, their history has
not been the kind of history which titillated the adventurous blood. The colorful episodes of Mormon history
are likely to have been furnished by the apostates, by the
Gentiles, by the cowpunchers and all the floating and reckless elements on the fringes of the region. A Mormon's
whole training incapacitates him for recklessness; adventurous as the pioneers were, bold as they were, indomita-
ble as they were, they were adventurous and bold and in-
domitable in pack, on orders, and their story has not been,
until recently, very well remembered. In the past few years
the vogue of the historical novel, plus the interest in sociological themes, has brought the Mormons into fiction
again after a long absence. The first novels in which they
figured can be found on almost any library shelf: they deal
with impressionable virgins caught in the net of polygamy
and agonizing worse than any soap-opera heroine through
endless difficulties. The recent outburst of Mormon novels
is of a considerably higher type, but even these recent ones
suffer from one disability. It is almost impossible to write
fiction about the Mormons, for the reason that Mormon
institutions and Mormon society are so peculiar that they
call for constant explanation. The result is local color, an
almost unavoidable leaning toward the picturesque qualities of a unique social order, and the Mormons as people
get lost behind the institutional barriers that set them
apart. Still, it is the sticks which furnish the best material

for historical best sellers, and the Mormon Country will be the sticks for a good while to come.

There are compensations to living in the sticks. It is well to have the Great Salt Desert flanking the western gate. It is well to have the gorges of the Green and Colorado swinging around the eastern and southern bastions. It is well to have the San Rafael Swell and Robbers' Roost and the Escalante Desert, it is well to have the bare and forbidding San Juan country. There is sanity as well as protection in mountains and deserts. But if the tourists ever discover in numbers the back country that lies behind the loop of national parks and monuments, if they ever by any chance get up on Thousand Lake Mountain or the Aquarius Plateau, if they ever make their way into the Colob up from Zion, if they discover the permanent wilderness in the Grand-daddy Lakes Basin in the Uintahs, if the promoters ever succeed in exploiting to the full the skiing at Alta, that old sinful ghost town in Little Cottonwood Canyon where the United States Army trained paraski troops during the winter of 1941, the valleys of the mountains are no longer going to provide sanctuary. The Gentile world, this time as tourists instead of miners or railroad men or cowpunchers or scientific explorers, is going to dilute Mormondom again, and from that dilution the separate and eccentric Mormon society may never emerge. Because the Mormons have never been an imaginative people; they never noticed much about the land they settled except that the sagebrush growth was sturdy or thin. In all that country you seldom find a house built to take advantage of the view, though the view is likely to be something tremendous.

There are few products which can emerge in their finished state from the Mormon Country. Like much of the

West, it is a colonial possession, useful for the production of raw materials. But in the one matter of scenery the country has the finished product, and one that sooner or later it is going to make valuable. When it does, even the little settlements off the railroads and the main highways will be in the world again, and the process by which the Mormon Country has slowly been assimilated into the United States will have gone another step.

Another age, with different values from the age in which the Mormon Country was first settled, is likely to find in that country much more than the Mormons found, certainly more than the Gentiles who went through it like a high wind. It is a good country to look at, and with the initial hardships out of the way a good country to live in. There is even glamor of a kind. As it offered an opportunity for the Mormons to escape the United States, as it gave Marie Ogden a place in which to build her spiritual kingdom, as it offered the wide vision of an unknown world to mountain men and explorers and scientists, and the vision of fabulous wealth to miners and promoters, as it offered impregnable sanctuary to outlaws from the Hole-in-the-Wall to the Blue Mountains and raised up a fantasy of unutterable loveliness for Everett Ruess, so it has offered a refuge to the floating myths and the undying legends. That desert has in very truth been sanctuary to outlaw and zealot and artist and scientist and White Indian and Nephite. For all its homey domesticity and its tradition of laborious piety, it is a country that breeds the Impossibles.

Index

VERMONT COLLEGE
MONTPELIER, VERMONT.